"*Archetypes for Writers* by Jennifer Van Bergen is a book for the creatively Jung at heart. The Swiss founder of analytic psychology, Carl Jung, also believed we carry around archetypes that impact our goals, dreams, motivations and 'neuroses' all our lives. Van Bergen has used the archetypal paradigm as a way to help writers understand and identify their characters and story archetypes with exercises that can help them discover these. While not overly academic, the book is meant to be used as a tool for delving into the subconscious to unearth the archetypes which define character and story. A great resource for novice and seasoned creators who suspect or are already hip to the fact that what lurks beneath the sub-cortex (along with the common slug) have a lot more to offer writers than most literary agents."
— **Jeffrey M. Freedman**, writer and consulting producer (*Vivaldi*)

"Much more than merely a book on writing, it is an in-depth guide to the inner realm where all stories reside — and the keys to unlock it! This book not only gives writers tools for greater creativity, but principles for more powerful living. Read it. Contemplate it. And take your writing to the next level!"
— **Derek Rydall**, author of *I Could've Written A Better Movie Than That!* and *There's No Business Like Soul Business*

"This book is like taking a series of college courses in the subconscious, mythology, and the hidden archetypes that drive our behavior. Yet it is also a fantastic resource for writers who want to dive into the shadowy realms of what truly makes us, and our characters, tick. Van Bergen writes with mastery — she really knows her stuff, providing tools and exercises that can move your writing from the surface of basic storytelling to a much deeper level, where universal principals can help you connect with your readers in profound and powerful ways."
— **Marie Jones**, *AbsoluteWrite.com* book reviewer

"This book goes beyond the nuts and bolts of standard books on screen-writing to a deeper, subconscious level. Allowing the writer to truly explore the world they are creating."
— **Matthew Terry**, *hollywoodlitsales.com*

"Inventive and unique, the subject matter is sure to appeal to anyone seeking alternative approaches to writing, art, or any creative pursuit. Thinking at the 'archetypal level' will certainly be a helpful guide to those who want to convey their personal inner journeys through creative expression."
— **William Indick**, PhD, author of *Psychology for Screenwriters*

"Jennifer Van Bergen dares to create a new language that changes our perception of archetypes. I especially appreciate the way her exercises evoke questions since true creativity comes from questioning and not hurrying for an answer."
— **Sande Shurin**, author of *Transformational Acting* and director of Sande Shurin Acting Studio, New York

"When I signed up for Jennifer Van Bergen's characterization class at the New School I had no idea what it would be like. I have been in fiction classes where the teacher stands at the blackboard and we go around the room, everyone contributing an attribute. 'Who wants to choose his occupation?' I thought characterization was an exercise of one's imagination. This work is something very different. There are many parts to it — the observing, the taking apart and putting back together. More than anything, it has taught me to identify the core components of what makes someone who they are. And once I can see that, everything else — everything they do, their whole story — follows from that."
> — **Rachel Steuermann**, Global Head of IT Communications, UBS Inc.

"Intriguing and very well thought out; a 'recipe' for detailed exploration — something that is sorely needed and I say that from being in the trenches."
> — **John de Lancie**, actor/writer/director (*Star Trek: The Next Generation, The Hand That Rocks the Cradle, The Fisher King, Bad Influence* and many other film and TV roles)

"Read Jennifer Van Bergen's book, *Archetypes for Writers*, and wash away your writer's block forever! Comprehensive and accessible, Ms. Van Bergen's book is an urgency for all writers."
> — **Jeffrey Alan Haas**, playwright, actor, singer, director, The Artists' Shakespeare Festival, Minneapolis

"This extraordinary book is a testament to a remarkable life's work and the discipline and artistry of the one who lived it. It is also a gift of insight and skill and those of us who accept it are fortunate, indeed."
> — **Jeanmarie Simpson**, founding artistic director of the Nevada Shakespeare

"Jennifer Van Bergen offers a writer's guidebook that includes description of the world where archetypes are formed, the means of accessing that world, how to glean the wisdoms of that realm, and how to utilize archetypes. Rich with psychological and literary references, this book will please those writers who really want to understand the writing process so that they can confidently repeat it at will and not be at the mercy of a whimsical muse who sometimes brings writer's block as well as inspiration."
> — **Pamela Jaye Smith**, author of *Inner Drives* and founder of Mythworks (*www.mythworks.net*)

ARCHETYPES
FOR WRITERS

USING THE POWER OF YOUR SUBCONSCIOUS

JENNIFER VAN BERGEN

Published by Michael Wiese Productions
3940 Laurel Canyon Blvd. # 1111
Studio City, CA 91604
tel. 818.379.8799
fax 818.986.3408
mw@mwp.com
www.mwp.com

Cover Design: MWP
Book Layout: Gina Mansfield Design
Editor: Paul Norlen

Printed by McNaughton & Gunn, Inc., Saline, Michigan
Manufactured in the United States of America

© 2007 Jennifer Van Bergen

The copyright holders have generously given permission to quote from
the following works:

The Prisoner of Second Avenue © 1972 by Neil Simon, copyright renewed
2000 by Neil Simon. Inquiries for stock and amateur performances
should be addressed to Samuel French, Inc., 45 West 25th Street, New York,
NY 10010. All other inquiries should be addressed to Gary N. DaSilva,
111 N. Sepulveda Blvd., Suite 250, Manhattan Beach, CA 90266-6850.

Oh Dad, Poor Dad, Mamma's Hung You in the Closet and I'm Feelin' So Bad
by Arthur L. Kopit. Reprinted by permission of William Morris Agency.

Hecuba by Sophocles (translated by William Arrowsmith) from University
of Chicago Press.

Library of Congress Cataloging-in-Publication Data

Van Bergen, Jennifer, 1955-
  Archetypes for writers : using the power of your subconscious /
Jennifer Van Bergen.
       p. cm.
  Includes bibliographical references.
  ISBN 10 1932907254
  ISBN 13 9781932907254
  1. Characters and characteristics in literature. 2. Archetype (Psychology)
in literature. 3. Archetypes in literature. 4. Authorship--Psychological
aspects. I. Title.
  PN218V36 2007
  808.3'97--dc22
                                        2006032908

TABLE OF CONTENTS

ACKNOWLEDGMENTS

This book would not have come into being without the comments, critiques, and suggestions of Rachel Steuermann. Rachel went through the New School course in 2001 and has continued as an advanced and private student since that time. While I, alone, am responsible for the content of this book, Rachel's understanding of the archetypes approach, her insights, and her organizational skills contributed much to the final product. Her friendship, patience, and kindness throughout have marked her as not only a true practitioner — an arkhelogist — and proponent, but a true friend. Thank you, Rachel.

I would also like to thank all the students who worked with me over the years, who had patience with my refusal to engage in theoretical discussion, and who threw themselves into the relative unknown to learn this approach. Most of all, I would like to thank those students whose work is quoted herein and those who participated in private advanced classes with me when the New School decided not to offer it. All did wonderful work that contributed to the development of the approach and this book.

This book would also not have happened but for the work of Bettina Olivier, a great scientist and mentor to me. Her work on mind structure helped me to figure out many parts of this method and is woven into the fabric of my own work.

My early acting teacher, Toni Donley at the Bennett Conservatory in Croton-on-Hudson, NY, was instrumental in my discovery of these things early in my life. I started training with Toni at age nine and continued through high school. I would never have been able to stay the course to development of this method or completion of this book without that early love and faith in me, nor without the special discipline of acting, that Toni gave me through her acting classes and that is so much a part of this work.

Attorneys Myron Beldock and Henry Gluckstern both have repeatedly shown their faith in, if not always their understanding of, me and my pursuits and stood by and for me when I could not alone. This book also owes them thanks.

And to my two grown daughters, Sarah and Giselle, who have put up with me for all these years and of both of whom I am so proud.

FOREWORD

Isaac Stern once said, "Discipline frees the artist."

Jennifer Van Bergen, a trained Shakespearean actor, a political writer and teacher with a law degree, is no stranger to discipline or art. Well known for her reports and commentaries on Findlaw, Raw Story, CounterPunch, Truthout, and other progressive Internet news and opinion sites, her writing has a vivid muscularity that cuts to the "quick o' the ulcer," turning over the ground of the subject and quickly exposing the honest underbelly.

The book you now hold in your hands is a call to excellence and a magic breadcrumb trail that leads you there. Early in the narrative, Van Bergen lays bare her revolutionary agenda:

> This approach has little to do with how to "create" characters or plot stories. Rather, it is more about how to *find* your character and story archetypes, or even how to have them find you. Underlying this approach is the premise that each person carries within them a given set of character and story archetypes.

Not a New Age technique that asks one to "channel" or "visualize" one's characters, *Archetypes for Writers* contains a deeply organized set of exercises that puts one on a track to unimagined potential.

In the throes of a new script myself, Van Bergen's work came to my attention when I needed it badly. Feeling frustrated with my characters, mired down in the quicksand of my own unwieldy dramatic structure, I was given respite by the opportunity to read the book and by the radical notions contained therein.

Although following an instructional pattern appropriate for a how-to book, Van Bergen's passion for social activism and the connection between personal creativity and mindful existence as a citizen of the world becomes clear.

One reads the book with new eyes. To the writer who approaches the blank page with trepidation and humility, at once elated and dreading the task, it is a godsend. Within the pages of *Archetypes for Writers* are ancient terms and concepts as old as human thought. What is world shattering is the extraordinary way that Van Bergen frames the information. One feels that one is having a conversation with a great teacher who is also someone with whom one might want to go out and have a beer — and who hasn't had some of his or her most creative moments in such a setting? However, hanging around drinking beer does not get the story made, the play written, the work composed. The discipline of the writer is the discipline of the human being — to delve and pry and wrench the pieces of the puzzle from the depths of our subliminal selves is not for sissies — to live while awake, with mindful attention to the details is the fodder that gives great writing its edge. *Archetypes for Writers* guides us to the knowledge of what we didn't know that we knew. Van Bergen's own lucid and vibrant writing style has created a treasure that one values as much for the beauty of the language as for the groundbreaking information it carries.

Jennifer Van Bergen has demonstrated her own incredible discipline level by writing *Archetypes for Writers*, a book that synthesizes four decades of her life as an alert, alive artist, journalist and instructor. This book is much more than a self-help book for writers. It's a self-help book for humanity and the reader receives the potent impression that no one is pulling harder for the writer's success than the author, who generously says:

> In order for you to write your own writing, there must be at least one other person who recognizes expressions of your own writing and wants you to do it. That's my role and this book carries it to you.

This extraordinary book is a testament to a remarkable life's work and the discipline and artistry of the one who lived it. It is also a gift of insight and skill and those of us who accept it are fortunate, indeed.

Jeanmarie Simpson
May 2006

Jeanmarie Simpson is founding artistic director of the Nevada Shakespeare Company and the author of many performance works including "A Single Woman," based on the life of Jeannette Rankin and the forthcoming new play, On Track, *about Vietnam veteran and peace activist, S. Brian Willson.*

SECTION ONE

Arkhelogy:
Archetypes for Writers

Chapter One

ARCHETYPES FOR WRITERS: METHOD TO THE MADNESS

Creation is only the projection into form of that which already exists.
— Shrimad Bhagavatam

ARCHETYPES & ARKHELOGY: WHAT ARE THEY?

This book is about how to find and use archetypes to create characters and stories.

What is an archetype? *An archetype* is an *imprint of a pattern of human behavior.*

The traditional concept of an archetype calls for a name, such as the Villain, the Hero, the Gatekeeper, the Shape-Shifter, the Black Widow. Even names such as Stage Mother, Dissident, Tyrant, Back-Stabber, Muckraker, and so on, although not viewed as archetypes in the most fundamental Jungian sense, have attained such wide recognition as types that they may be considered archetypal patterns.

However, in the archetypes approach there is no place for the use of pre-conceived archetype names. Rather, this approach requires the use of a certain set of skills that, when mastered and used together, enable one to *do archetypes*. In this approach, we call "doing archetypes" *arkhelogy*. Arkhelogy focuses on the discovery and delineation of an *imprint* that is *embodied or carried in a person we observe*. This imprint is the archetype.

In this book you will learn how to find your own character archetypes. *Character archetypes* contain the *action-principles* of particular human behavior. Each character archetype contains different principle sets, each embodying unique life courses and destinies. The work of finding character archetypes does not begin with identifying or naming archetypes, but rather with the *application of a set of skills and activities*, that is, the skill of arkhelogy.

Arkhelogy is a highly advanced human skill that has existed in humankind since the beginning of time. But it has largely been forgotten, buried, and lost in today's world — perhaps as a result of the split between science and religion that occurred during the scientific revolution of the sixteenth to eighteenth centuries, or possibly as a consequence of the suppression of nature-based spiritual beliefs during the rise of Christianity. It is not a skill taught in any school, college, or university.

Arkhelogy is not a scientific pursuit or a matter of relative belief. It is a genuine skill that draws on innate human resources and abilities. It is a skill shared by all human beings and it is a crucial skill for humankind, requiring the use of highly evolved mental/emotional mechanisms that lead to higher levels of human understanding and communication and assisting in the development of the highest levels of personal writing.

It is a *global skill* that is made up of a handful of *component skills*. All the component skills must be mastered separately before they can be woven together and used as a single global skill. This may be another reason why the skill was lost. It takes time and effort to learn each component skill and to integrate them. The leap into the practice and mastery of the entire set as one global skill is a great task. Until now, complete mastery of the skill of arkhelogy belonged only to a rare few.

This book teaches the component skills that underlie the overarching global skill of arkhelogy and explains the leap from the component skills into arkhelogy itself. While arkhelogy is a discrete skill of its own, it emerges through the practice and integration of the component skills.

ARKHELOGY: DOING ARCHETYPES[1]

While humans have engaged haphazardly throughout history in arkhelogy, the skill has not been acknowledged, named, developed, or taught. And because it is a global skill, comprised of numerous component skills, none of which have been isolated or named before this, arkhelogy has remained largely unseen and unused, until now.

Through history, people who practiced the art and skill of arkhelogy — arkhelogists — have been viewed as seers, prophets, medicine men and women, wizards, and shamans (and increasingly as pariahs or Cassandras), but the skill eluded most folk. People who were able to engage in arkhelogy did not know how they acquired the skill. They just knew how to work their magic. Sometimes such people guarded their specialty by keeping it a mystery and even promoting the idea that the skill was magical. Once in a while, such a person was generous enough to apprentice someone with promise and teach him or her by example. But generally arkhelogists were not teachers and arkhelogy was considered an innate gift or one bestowed from above.

Again, arkheloging includes the use in simultaneous combination of all the component parts of archetype work, but that skill — the skill of juggling and even beyond that, of resolving the separate movements into a wholly new use and purpose — is also a discrete, unique, separate skill of its own.

HOW A GLOBAL SKILL WORKS

While this global skill is an innate universal human ability, the process by which the skill is acquired and ultimately becomes natural is challenging. Betty Edwards described the process of acquiring a global skill in her book, *Drawing on the Right Side of the Brain*:

[G]lobal or whole skills, such as reading, in time become automatic. Basic component skills become completely integrated into the smooth flow of the global skill. But in acquiring any new global skill, the initial learning is often a struggle, first with each component skill, then with the smooth integration of components.

Edwards notes that while none of the component skills in drawing can be omitted, the final global skill, the *gestalt*, "is neither taught nor learned but instead seems to emerge as a result of acquiring the [component] skills."

This is also true of arkhelogy. The skill of "doing archetypes" is acquired through the combined use of all the component skills together. Yet, it is also a separate skill itself, a separate brain function of its own, which will emerge as a result of acquiring the component skills and which ultimately you will be able to use smoothly and directly.

ARCHETYPES FOR WRITERS

Archetypes for writers is an approach to writing that enables writers to discover and use their own, intrinsic character and story archetypes. It teaches the component skills and the overarching global skill of arkhelogy: "doing archetypes" or "working at the archetypal level." Developing these skills will lead you to the deepest places in your being and to the greatest reaches of your writing abilities.

The archetypes approach was developed over a forty-year span, twenty of which was spent teaching it, haphazardly at first and with increasing focus and accuracy as time went on. Hundreds, if not thousands, of writers have found this approach helpful to their goal of realizing their characters and stories in their writing.

This approach has little to do with how to "create" characters or plot stories. Rather, it is more about how to *find* your character and story archetypes, or even how to have them find you. Underlying this approach is the premise that each person carries within them a given set of character and story archetypes.

This approach changes the way you think about people and things, and the way you use your own mind. As such, it is powerful, revolutionary. But, like any true discipline, the archetype approach takes time (hours, days, weeks, months, years) to learn — and years to master. Saying "I already learned it!" or "I already did it!" is not adequate. One must adopt it as a life-practice for its full power to be acquired.

Since the archetypes approach teaches the component skills that make up the global skill of arkhelogy, the approach is based on the obvious premise that these are skills that can be learned.

The component skills must be learned separately before they are integrated. There is no necessary sequence to learning them or using them. However, each component skill is as important as the next and all ultimately merge into one global skill. The whole functions something like a nuclear reactor, breaking down molecules into atoms, stripping atoms of their electrons and re-combining them into something different than the mere sum of parts, something more pure and powerful.

WHERE DID THE ARCHETYPES APPROACH COME FROM? THE *LAW* OF ARCHETYPES

People ask me how I found this approach, did I make it up, invent it? No, I didn't make it up. I didn't invent it. I found it (or it found me), I learned to use it, over many years I gradually figured out what it was and separated out its parts, organized them, and developed the way to teach it all to others.

In this sense, it is mine. But in another sense, it doesn't belong to me, since it exists completely independent of me. In other words, the thing exists outside of me in some kind of objective reality. Because the components and principles apply to and work for everyone who uses them, whether the person aspires to writing or not, the approach has the significance of a scientific law — a law about human beings, about a fundamental way in which our brains and beings work when we are doing our *own writing*. (I distinguish "one's own writing" from writing that is done for another purpose. The purpose of one's own writing is the expression and realization of oneself. We discuss this more later.)

This does not mean that the approach I have developed is the only way of applying the law that underlies it. It is simply the best and easiest way that I have found to teach the discipline to others.

The archetypes approach thus embodies a law about the inner Self of every human being.

A relatively small percentage of people today know how to find or access the inner Self. This fact has tremendous consequences to the world, to the continued viability of humankind. It affects each of us in our professional and personal relationships, and also affects the state of the world, the quality of international interrelationships, the effectiveness of diplomacy, the extent of peace (or war), of human rights, the operations of government, and so on. Support for the conclusion that our culture has lost touch with a core human ingredient, and that this loss is doing terrible damage to humankind, can be found in many places, but I will save that discussion for another time, as it is not the focus of the book. YOU, the writer, and the quality and meaning of *your* life, are the focus here.

GET SET, GET READY, GO!

I intend to keep this book as short and simple as possible. In fact, the approach is short and simple, but that does not mean it is not challenging. Learning the mechanics of the approach is the easiest part. Putting it into practice is hard. Using it well is hardest.

During the early work of learning the component skills, you may not yet understand how they work together or what each has to do with the other or with the whole, with doing archetypes. I will do my best to ease the frustration inherent in the task of learning and mastering these skills, to provide a roadmap and then guide you through the arkhelogy forest, but you will also have to do your part. This work is not for the timid or lazy. It requires continual practice and concentration. It is hard mental work even without the emotional content that always arises as part of it. Emotional responses may be triggered by various phases of the work as well, especially as you start to apply the skills to your own life and deeper issues.

Thus, in this book, students will first become acquainted with and learn to use the techniques which develop the skills. You are asked to draw material from your own life but because the techniques are discrete and somewhat mechanical, you have the opportunity to develop some level of mastery before you begin to apply the skills to more emotionally triggering material.

I recommend approaching emotional triggering material only after one has begun to grasp and master the full global arkhelogy skill. This requires, at minimum, being able to juggle all the component skills while engaging fully and competently in the arkhelogy work itself — the work set forth in detail in the Arkhelogy chapter.

Chapter Two

SKILLS & EXERCISES: OVERVIEW

Let's jump right to the exercises. This chapter will introduce you to the exercises used in the archetypes approach, describe how they are each done, and what each is for. I also spend a little time describing how they ultimately work together as a whole. This is an overview. Don't worry about remembering it all. Just relax, read, and let it sink in.

INTRODUCTION TO EXERCISES

For each skill, I engage students in an exercise. Each exercise is done in writing, but I specifically ask students *not* to try to create a piece of finished writing, a product to satisfy their ideas of form, structure, style, or any other preconceived idea. I ask everyone to try to satisfy only the requirements of the exercise itself, nothing more.

In class I usually ask students to be prepared to do each exercise at least twice, since hands-on working through the material is essential. Each time a student submits a completed exercise, I comment, focusing on what they did or did not do that the exercise required. If in the exercise, for example, they were supposed to avoid adjectives, I point out any adjectives they used and direct them to try to find another way to say what they observed.

If you are not in one of my classes as you read this book, I recommend you find a partner or group to work with. Each of you should pledge to each other that you will pay close attention to the requirements of each exercise and that your comments and critiques of each other's work will focus only upon whether you have fulfilled the task of that exercise.

If you cannot find a partner or group to work with, I suggest you do each exercise, set it aside, then come back to it a few days later. When you return to the work, first review the requirements of the exercise and reread the examples I provide, then reread your work and ask yourself only whether you have fulfilled the exercise.

There is absolutely no limit to how many times you can do each exercise or redo any particular one. In fact, as you begin to integrate the work, you will begin to do the exercises all the time in your daily life.

Now, onward to what these exercises are. The exercises are divided here into two major sections: separating-out work and integrative work.

SEPARATING-OUT WORK

Character Facts (Nos-anthro)

Although there is no required order to learning these skills, I usually begin with *character facts* ("CFs"). *Character facts are simply facts that relate to anything about a person.*

The main rule for this exercise is: no adjectives and no personal opinions, just observable facts (usually actions).

The task here is to learn to suspend your judgment about people and see what is visibly discernible about them. Note that this approach is different than traditional wisdom on characterization, which teaches that adjectives, description, and (psycho)analysis are primary, if not essential.

The character facts exercise demands a kind of stripping away of the various coatings we superimpose on what we see. Doing character facts sounds easy, but don't be surprised if you find it challenging.

The practice of stripping away one's own judgments is an essential part of doing archetypes. You cannot learn to discern archetypes, in fact, without learning how to undo your own biases and restrictions in seeing.

There will be plenty of examples of character facts in the chapter on that topic, but let's take a quick look at one here. Say you write: "She's beautiful and men swarm around her." How do you avoid the adjective here? Consider saying that men swarm around her because of the way they think she looks. See how different this is? See how it makes you dig into the cause of your foregone conclusion?

Adjectives can isolate a person within his own views, creating a tautology, a self-fulfilling loop that is hard to see beyond or break out of. Such writers are limited in what they can understand outside of themselves and therefore their works tend to be one-sided and shallow. This exercise breaks you out of that self-limitation.

It takes some courage to let go of one's pre-conceived notions to do this exercise.

I have named the skill *nosanthro*, from the Greek *nos* (to know) and *anthro* (humans), meaning "knowing people." When you are doing character facts work, you are *nosanthro-ing*.*

Universal Drives (Nos-amianthy)

Next is *universal drives* ("UDs"). *Universal drives are the basic drives that every human being possesses.*

Learning to discern universal drives as they become manifest is another fundamental component of archetype work and is another kind of stripping away task. As you consider what drives a particular person in a particular situation, you entertain and discard different ideas, working backwards to a bottom line. You find that there really are very few drives: the drive to survive, the drive to be loved and to love, and a few others. All others appear to fall under these few. The drive for recognition may break down to the drive to be loved, for example.

It is usually necessary to observe a person in a context and in action to separate out his goals and drives. Drives are not the same as goals. Goals are specific and context-based. Drives are broader and deeper. A goal might be to acquire money but the drive could be to be loved or to survive. What is essential here is the act of finding the bottom line, that which this human being shares with others and how he acts upon it.

---

*The reason I have constructed new names for these skills is to reinforce the fact that they are new and different from anything else, but also it is nice to have an alternative to saying "I'm using the skill of doing character facts." While at first the new names may seem strange and cumbersome, I have found that in the long run, they become invaluable short-hands. There is no requirement to use them, however, and in this book, I continue to use the full phrases for the skills (e.g. "doing character facts," "doing discrepancies," etc.)

Although doing universal drives is a kind of stripping away like character facts, it is different from character facts in another way: character facts are about external actions; *universal drives are about finding a person's internal direction.*

Universal drives work is similar to analogue work, discussed below, because both require you to think about things from the point of view of a person other than yourself.

The way I teach the universal drives exercise is by asking students to pick two monologues: one from Ginger Friedman's book *The Perfect Monologue*, and the other from Stefan Rudnicki's book *The Actor's Book of Classical Monologues*. I ask the student to identify (in writing) the goals of the character in the monologue and then try to discern the underlying drive.

I use these two books exclusively for two reasons: (1) Friedman teaches her readers how to condense a scene into a monologue by using universal drives. She does not call them universal drives but that is what she does. She also provides a page or two of discussion on each monologue. Although her tone is declamatory, which is not important to our work on universal drives, her ability to zero in on the character's basic drives is superb.

(2) I use Rudnicki's excellent rendition of the classics because the monologues are exceptionally pure and powerful, in terms of universal drives, as well as in the purity and beauty of the language. Rudnicki makes no comments like Friedman's after each monologue but he does provide a short synopsis of each play or set of plays and the history or myths they are written about, as well as a sentence or two about each character.

With the Friedman exercise, I ask that students not read her comments until after they select a monologue and make their own observations. With Rudnicki, I ask students to read his comments first and then elaborate.

I have named the skill of finding universal drives: *nos-amianthy*, which means "to know the indestructible thing." Here we use it to mean "the skill of identifying universal drives." When you are identifying UDs, you are *nos-amianthing*.

Discrepancies (Parably)

Discrepancies ("discs") set up the framework for working with ectypes and isotypes (which we discuss below).

Discrepancies are *differences*. For our purposes, *discrepancies are differences between two things within a person, manifested by their actions and/or words.* You could call these *character discrepancies*. Thus, for example: the difference between what someone says and what he does, or what he says to one person and what he says to another.

Discrepancies are framed in a two-part sentence. Thus a simple discrepancy sentence might be: He insists he likes women with long hair but every woman he dates has short hair. (This is not necessarily a particularly revealing discrepancy. We start simple.)

The importance of working with discrepancies is that they provide bookends that frame a particular behavior. Human behaviors are so vast and complex, it would be nearly impossible to separate out something discrete enough for us to construct the archetype if we didn't have a way to isolate them.

While other kinds of juxtapositions of behaviors are useful in doing archetypes, discrepancies are the fastest and clearest way. Other kinds of juxtapositions belong with advanced work, which is discussed in the final section of this book.

I call the skill of finding and isolating discrepancies *parably*, which means literally "to put next to." Here we use it to mean "the ability to discern discrepancies, to see one thing in contrast to another." This is distinguished from the simple ability to discern facts from opinions that is used in character facts. When you are doing discrepancies work, you are *parabling*.

Analogues (Homopathy)

Analogues ("anlgs") are another type of two-part work — you'll find a lot of arkhelogy work is in two parts — but while discrepancies focus on differences within a person, *analogues focus on similarities between two different circumstances and two different persons*.

An analogue is where you find yourself saying "I've been through something similar to what that person went through. I think I know what it feels like." You may have been through something completely different, factually, but you can "relate."

Analogues are a form of analogy, but I use the term "analogue" rather than "analogy" to distinguish this exercise from other forms of analogy.

The analogue exercise requires you to find an example of something that happened (an "incident") to another person that you feel you can relate to. Write out the incident and what you feel that person experienced and then write out your incident and how what you experienced was similar to what you think the person in the other incident experienced.

Obviously, in this exercise, in contrast to character facts, you must rely on your opinions and feelings, but in a quite different way than in other arenas generally. Here, you are relying on your sense of how *another person feels* in a certain context. In order to do this, you must distill the relevant facts and you must find a way to relate to the person you are focused on.

An example of an analogue: A friend of mine had to move out of her apartment because of water damage due to a hurricane. She felt that everything she had worked for was falling apart. I would probably not have felt as she did if I were in the same circumstance, but I could relate to how she felt because other things that have happened to me, which might have seemed inconsequential to another person, made me feel that all my work was for nothing.

The intention of experiencing what others might have experienced, feeling what others might feel, thinking what they may think, is crucial to archetype work. In everyday life, we are more often required to stand up for ourselves than to feel for others. The simple, primal act of *relating* to others is often overlooked and forgotten, even in artistic professions. Clearly, however, if we are to write books that many others can, themselves, relate to, we ourselves need to be able to relate to others. Interestingly, despite the fact that we live in a culture dominated by selfishness, most people find this exercise a breeze.

I have named the skill *homopathy*, which means "having similar feelings." You feel or identify with what another person feels. When you are doing analogue work, you are *homopathing* or *homopathizing*.

Being in the Moment (Kronobo)

Most people have a good idea of what *being in the moment* means generally, but this exercise tends to be one of the most challenging for students. Being in the moment ("BIM") is like character facts in that it requires you to suspend some consequence. With character facts, you suspend your opinions. **With being in the moment, you suspend time**. Of course, you don't actually suspend the movement of time. You just focus your attention on a slice of it. This prepares you in several ways for archetype work, which I will discuss in a moment.

I usually ask students to do the exercise in three parts: first, just write out a moment; second, slow it down and replay it; third, whittle away at it, remove everything beyond one single, bare instant, anything beyond the first split second of experience.

This sequence also requires you to remove what you think about the moment and to remove all subsequent moments.

People generally go very quickly from one instant to the next in their writing, since they feel it needs to get somewhere. Writing is linear. It moves from left to right, top to bottom. It fills pages. It leads from start to finish. But being-in-the-moment work requires suspending this progression. This is hard to put into words. It may end up being a "word salad."

Often it is good to start with bodily sensations. "I sit and hear my breathing." But being-in-the-moment work is not merely sensorial. It is not just "I am here now. I feel the sensation of the warm coffee cup in my hands." It is also "I am. I am aware. I am aware of my breathing, my thinking, my seeing…" It is ontological. It is about what the moment *is*. It is a sense of yourself and outside yourself as part of everything else, at the same time.

The acting technique called "method acting" became renowned for its practice of developing "sensory awareness." Actors would spend hours trying to "recreate" the sensory awareness of, say, a warm coffee cup in their hands.

This technique apparently came from a description by Marcel Proust in his great multi-volume novel, *Remembrance of Things Past*, in which he describes a memory that was called up by a warm drink.

Proust did understand *being in the moment*, I think, but the sensory awareness technique is not, in my opinion, the whole thing. Indeed, I think it is misleading. Proust understood that a moment in time became something outside of time when it was juxtaposed with a memory of a past moment. The memory could be sensory in the tactile sense, but it could also be visual, auditory (sounds), or specifically verbal (i.e. words), etc. It could be circumstantial, kind of like *déjà vu*, in which an entire sequence triggers a sense of having been there before.

Proust describes losing his step on an uneven cobblestone. The incident instantly calls up a memory that flashs before his eyes and he stands there on the street, to the amusement of passers-by, trying to recapture that flashing image by stepping back and forth over the cobblestone. This type of "hovering" in the instant is what this exercise is about. *It is the practice of hovering in the moment that you are trying to achieve in this exercise, and that is all, nothing more.*

Many people have asked me to provide examples of being in the moment, but the trouble is that what is being in the moment to me may read like pure word salad to you. What I try to discern in working with students on this exercise is whether they are *experiencing the moment*, whether they are truly in it and not immediately beyond it, or just doing free association (which is just rambling thinking). Nonetheless, I do provide some examples of being-in-the-moment work in that chapter.

Truth be told, it is almost impossible to attain the complete *being-in-the-moment* state of its own accord. It is more easily accessed when trying to imagine what it is like to be another person. You can "go into the moment" in your imagination of what it is like to be someone else: walk through that person's life for a moment, feel what it is like to be him or her.

Being in the moment is similar to the analogue exercise, in one respect: analogues require you to imagine what it is like to be someone else and find a way you can feel what they felt. That requires going into a moment, but does not (necessarily) require the suspension of time, or hovering.

In terms of how *being-in-the-moment* work prepares you for arkhelogy, it helps you to develop what Marcel Proust described as the "extra-temporal being," which is akin to what I call the Author Self, which I will discuss later. As Proust puts it, this is the part of yourself that

14

enables you to discern that which is "common both to the past and to the present" and is thus "much more essential than either of them."[2]

You cannot, however, create or forcefully recall past moments and juxtapose them with a present moment to create or elicit this "extra-temporal being" in yourself. It is something that must be developed through arkhelogy work overall, not by mere mechanical steps. You can ready yourself by learning how to stop yourself long enough for past moments to arise in your mind (or for other juxtapositions, such as present and imagined future moments). You can learn how to *be*, how to *hover* in the moment, experience yourself and accept what is there, without forcing cogitation or linear movement forward. It is, in other words, a form of meditation.

Robert Lawlor defines being in the moment as "poise of mind" — "a consciousness which is capable of temporarily arresting both conceptually and perceptually, segments of the universal continuum."[3] This part of yourself is able to perceive "the moment... of transformation, from one state to another, from one quality of being to another, from one form or level of consciousness to another [which] is always a leap, a jump, an incomprehensible velocity, as it were, outside of time, as when one cell divides into two."[4]

I have named the skill of being in the moment: *kronobo*, which means "time song." When you are doing BIMs, you are *kronobo-ing* (or *krono-boing*, which sounds more fun).

Universes of Discourse (no skill name)

This exercise teaches about the way in which the conscious and subconscious minds work and interact. It does not require the application of any component skill. It simply provides information to students about the workings of the dual mind. When you are doing universe of discourse work, you are "doing UoDs."

Using films from a select list, you identify the two *universes of discourse* (UoDs) in each film. Each of the selected films contains two primary universes or worlds that interact in a particular way. This way of interaction is, interestingly, nearly identical in all genuine UoD films, no matter what the genre or who wrote or directed it.

After you identify the two worlds, the next step is to identify the *laws* or *rules* of each of the two worlds, and the *points of contact* between them.

The movies are ones I specifically chose for their accurate rendering of the two parts of the human mind (conscious/subconscious) — which I sometimes call "the dual mind." The films are mostly from the following categories: ghost movies, spy movies, alien (abduction) movies, movies about split personalities, and movies about time travel or parallel universes.

All the movies on my list are UoD films, but not all movies from these categories generally are UoD films, nor are many other movies that have two realms or worlds necessarily UoD films. So, please always work from my list. (The list accompanies the UoD chapter.)

Unlike the other exercises, this one cannot be used in tandem with the others. In other words, you can do character fact work, analogues, discrepancies, universal drives, and being in the moment with any subject on which you want to do archetype work, but you cannot do the UoD exercise in any situation other than with the UoD movies. It does *not* apply to persons.

When you watch a UoD film, your task is not to look for screenplay, story, script, plot, or character elements. Your *only* task is to find the two UoDs, the rules of each, and the points of contact.

Doing UoD work requires you to look at these movies in a very different way than when you view to observe screenwriting or story techniques, or for that matter, just for entertainment. The two approaches should not be mixed.

Generally I recommend that students work with the UoD films before learning more about the dual mind and my views on it. Nothing can replace direct experience, but if you feel the need to learn more first, see Chapter 18 on UoDs (page 229).

Emotional Access Work (Anthropathy)

All work on one's writing is about gaining emotional access ("Emotional Access Work" or "EAW"), but there are three specific activities that the archetypes approach focuses on:

(1) **Empathetic or sympathetic feeling:** Bringing the circumstances of other people to your attention and trying to feel what it would feel like to be in that circumstance.

(2) **Self-observant feeling:** Also can be called "self-feeling." Looking at your own life and situation and seeing what it means and feeling it. Feeling and owning your own feelings.

(3) **Outward-observant feeling:** Also can be called "impersonal or humanitarian feeling." Seeing, understanding, and feeling the consequences and destinies that result from people's actions. Understanding the internal logic of what people do and why, but also what it means about their lives.

The skill is called *anthropathy*. When you are doing emotional access work of any kind, you are *anthropathing*.

Number (1) is similar to but not quite the same as analogues. In analogues, you try to find a situation in your own life which enables you to feel what some other person feels. Here, you simply try to feel what another person might be feeling, try to put yourself in his or her shoes. It is simply an exercise in empathetic feeling.

As to number (2), one might think that most people are prone to doing this every day, but in fact, most aren't. All too many people feel stuck with the choices they've had to make and don't want to think too much about it. Paradoxically, though, the more you feel for yourself, the more you can feel for others.

Number (3) is equally important. Seeing consequences and destinies and understanding the internal logic of people is not the same as judging them.

All three of the parts of emotional access work are about opening your eyes and ears, listening, and feeling.

The exercises for these three parts are simply to do just what the part states. Take a moment to think about someone in your life and try to understand and feel what it feels like for them. Take some time to view and feel your own life and think about what it means. Consider the consequences of people's acts, their decisions and life courses. Consider what the final consequence — the destiny — would be if nothing else intervened from where you can see things. Think about what a person might be thinking when he does something that you find hard to understand. And speak aloud what you feel (or speak the words of another person with feeling).

Emotional access work can and should be done at any time through this course and beyond it. It should be done as often as you feel comfortable doing it.

Mini-Summary

This marks the end of the separating-out work with separate component skills. Now we move into the beginning of integrative work. However, this work is also comprised of separate components, which are important to understand and master of their own accord.

INTEGRATIVE WORK

Ectypes (Ectypy)

Ectypes ("ects") are the first phase of direct work on archetype discovery and formation. When you are taking the first steps towards forming an archetype you are *not* yet working at the archetypal level. You are merely getting your house in order.

The skill used here is called *ectypy*. I call the use of the skill *doing ectypes* or *ectyping*. It means "changing from specific to general."

The first step in the exercise is to frame a discrepancy sentence, which you will already have done in the discrepancies exercise. If the discrepancy is a usable one, the first mechanical step of archetype formation will be fairly easy. (See the chapter on discrepancies for more information about usable discrepancies.)

(Sometimes you will not know if the discrepancy is usable until you start to do the archetype-formation work. Sometimes you will find that you need to go back and rework the discrepancy sentence or do some of the other component skills work before you find the usable sentence.)

The next step after forming a discrepancy sentence is to *formulate an ectype out of the discrepancy sentence.*

An ectype takes the particular, concrete thing and generalizes it. Thus, if your discrepancy sentence is "Mary says she is on a diet, but she eats constantly," to create an ectype, you would simply change "Mary" into "she" and add the words "is the one who," so that the sentence reads: "She is the one who says she is on a diet but eats constantly."

This mechanical step removes the personal and frames the action in more general terms. It focuses you on the *action-principle.*

This is all there is to this step. It is a simple mechanical act but do not skip this step, as it is crucial.

Isotypes (Isotypy)

Once you have a simple action-principle framed, the next step is what I call *doing isotypes* ("isos") or *isotyping.* The skill is called *isotypy.*

An isotype is something that is similar or identical to the ectype but has a different history or origin.

Here's what you do: Once you have the ectype sentence, you begin to look for examples of *other people who do something that has the same or similar meaning.* This is *isotyping.*

This is a key component of arkhelogy. It is hard work. It requires a kind of jumping back and forth between your original example and other examples, keeping in mind not so much the facts of each but the underlying meaning. It calls upon you to consider all the pieces of each example and ask yourself whether they contain the same or similar meaning, whether they "fit," in other words. In order to engage in this jumping back and forth, you need to repeatedly call forth your original example (and its meaning) to your mind, suspending it there, while you focus on other potential examples.

I like a phrase Proust used: It is "a species of gymnastic which fortifies us against unhappiness by making us neglect the particular cause in order to gain a more profound understanding of the essence."[5]

As you find other examples (i.e., isotypes) of your ectype, you will learn more about your ectype, you will fill it in with other relevant facts that you acquire from the isotypic examples, and you will refine it until it separates itself from all other ectypes.

Arkhelogy

Arkhelogy is a complex process that integrates all the above components and incorporates several additional ones. The skill is called *arkhelogy*. When you are doing akhelogy work, you are *arkheloging*.

The end result of it is that you begin to perceive archetypes in situations and people — you function "at the archetypal level." You will become a full-fledged *arkhelogist*. You see not just what is happening in front of you, but much more. You see an entire imprint of a human being carrying out his or her destiny. You see the beginning, middle, and end. You see *who s/he is* and where s/he is going, what it means, and how it will end. Can you predict the future? No. Because what you see is the imprint itself. You do not read minds and cannot eliminate all paths. This is not a predictive tool. However, because people usually do act consistent with the archetypes they embody or carry, if you discover those archetypes, you will find that your insights about future behavior and consequences are more often correct than not.

How You Start Using It All Together

Although we go into this whole part of the archetypes approach later on, it may be helpful to pause a moment here to see how it works.

The ectype sentence we created earlier is really too broad an example to be of much use in forming an archetype. The larger the discrepancy or unusual the juxtaposition of minute facts, generally, the more suitable it is for archetype work. But again, you cannot always predict what is a genuinely useful ectype.

In order to discover what ectypes are usable and useful, once you form the ectype, your job is to start looking for isotypes, other examples of the ectype in the world around you. You can observe people, read news stories, watch television, look at (read about) historical figures, etc., to obtain these isotypes.

Say your ectype sentence was "she is the one who weighs 98 pounds but claims she is overweight." What would an isotype be? What is the core meaning of this ectype? It is about someone whose image of herself is not consistent with what others see.

Here's another more detailed example. Say you know a man who is impotent and he tells you he grew up in a family dominated by women — a mother, grandmother, and several older sisters. The ectype sentence would be "He is the one who is impotent AND grew up in a family of all women." Note that this is not necessarily a discrepancy. It is a juxtaposition of facts which may or may not have anything to do with each other.

You might be tempted to jump to conclusions here about this person. But part of the archetypal approach is to suspend judgment, remember? So, all you do is simply juxtapose the two facts. Suspending judgment doesn't mean that you don't remain alert to clues. In fact, you will begin noticing more and more clues to character archetypes the more you work with them.

Next you look for isotypes. What could possibly be an isotype for this ectype? What is similar to "impotence" in meaning? What is similar to "growing up in a family comprised of all members of the opposite gender"? Impotence is a physical, sexual dysfunction. What might be similar to that? Frigidity, perhaps. You might even want to do some research into sexual dysfunctional problems. Alternatively, you could try to find something not about sexual dysfunction that is nonetheless similar to impotence. What does impotence mean? It means an inability to obtain physical arousal when you are in an intimate situation. What is similar to that? Would an inability to feel physical pain when hurt be similar? Would an inability to feel emotion? There is no absolute rule about this. However, I counsel students to try to stay as close as possible to the specific original meaning while they are learning the process.

Then look for the isotype for the second half of the ectype: He was raised in a family of all women, all members of the opposite gender, and he was the youngest. What would be comparable to that? Would living in an environment where you are the only one who speaks a certain language be the same? Would being only around adults and no other children?

21

Finally, you need to try to find an isotype which covers *both* parts together. What if you found an example of someone who had effectively shut off their ability to feel physical pain when physically hurt and you also noticed that the person spent his or her early childhood in a refugee camp? This would alert you to investigate further. You might find that the isotype "matches." Or you might find that there really is no relation between the two examples: your ectype and the possible isotype.

Within this process, you may find yourself engaging in using other component skills. You might feel you need to really get inside the head and heart of this person who is your working isotype, in order to determine whether s/he is a genuine isotype that will help you gather the archetype together. You might want to go back and do character facts about both the ectype and the isotype. Or you might want to try an analogue — is there anything in your own life that helps you to feel or experience what this person feels or experiences? Or you might want to select a moment from the life of the person who is your working isotype and "go into it," be "in the moment" in that person's life, while asking yourself whether it really *is* a true isotype.

The more you do isotypes, the more of the invisible world you will see and handle. As we will discuss later, the invisible world is where all the real action takes place.

A Note About Character Archetypes, Stories & Story Archetypes

Character archetypes are not the end result of writing. Stories are — whether in the form of a novel, play, or screenplay, What archetypes work does is to help you find the essence of your characters and the meaning in their lives. We discuss this more fully in the arkhelogy chapter.

Constructing a story is a separate and *reverse* process of archetypes work. Story archetypes come from combinations of character archetypes, but *story construction* is not the same as *story archetypes*. This book does not teach story construction.

Story archetypes are derivable from two or more character archetypes in combination. Character archetypes are also called "secret lives" and story archetypes are also called "the invisible world" (which you may also think of as plural, e.g. "invisible worlds"). This is discussed more in the chapter on "Selves, Secret Lives & Story" in Section Two.

Story archetypes emerge naturally from doing character archetypes. *All character archetypes fit together with a specific set of other character archetypes and it is the interplay between these secret lives that makes the story.* In a sense, every character archetype *carries* an irreducible set of other character archetypes that work together to make the story. Again, this invisible world is where all genuine action takes place.

But, again, it is important to know that story construction is not the same as discovery of story archetypes. Finding character and story archetypes will give you the raw core materials for your story, but has nothing to do with the rules of story construction as a craft. For story construction, I suggest consulting books like Christopher Vogler's *The Writer's Journey* and Robert McKee's *Story*, or something like Evan Marshall's *The Marshall Plan*.

Naming the Skills

The skills in the archetypes approach have never before been identified or named. I have therefore done extensive research to find suitable names (drawn from ancient Greek roots) for the skills or abilities that coincide with the tasks or exercises that make up the archetypes approach. We mentioned these names in passing while introducing the exercises above.

Why have we bothered to name the skills? Because the mind makes a place for something that has a name. Once a skill is named, it is more easily recognized, more frequently sought to be developed, and more likely to come into acceptance and use. As you learn and practice the exercises, you will become accustomed to using the new words. Eventually, you will associate the words with the skills themselves and will find it easier to access those skills by naming them.

The chart at the end of this chapter sets forth the exercises, the associated tasks, and provides the name of the skill or ability associated with the task (and thus used in the exercise).

I also distinguish the tasks and skills from some things that they are not (but may be confused with). The distinctions are not exclusive; almost all of them could be distinguished from any of the skills in the archetypes approach. The selection is merely of those that are most commonly confused with arkhelogy skills.

Be aware that you cannot learn how to use the skills in arkhelogy by simply learning their definitions or by learning what they are not. You learn them through the exercises. The distinctions are just made for your information, as an additional learning tool.

As you read through the book, you will have the opportunity to learn more about the entire process, both on a practical level and a metaphysical level, and to learn more about different ways of working with these components. In the meantime, let me say: congratulations for reaching this point in the book! You've already accomplished a major step forward in your life and in your writing. If you recognize many of these components already, you are among many who do and have a great advantage. If you feel somewhat lost or confused and have nonetheless read this far, BRAVO! You are a brave and remarkable soul. In any case, nothing is lost. Your subconscious is listening!

CHART OF TASKS, EXERCISES & SKILLS

Subject/ Exercise	Task	Skill/Ability Name	Translation or meaning	*Not*
Character facts "CFs"	Identifying relevant CFs & separating out facts from one's opinions	Nos-anthro, nos-anthroing	Knowing people	Judgment, opinion, logical conclusions, adjectival description
Being in the moment "BIMs"	Slowing down and suspending sense of time	Kronobo; kronoboing	Making time sing or roar	Meditation, trance, hypnosis, free association, sensory awareness
Universal drives "UDs"	Discerning the whole life & what drives the person	Nos-amianthy; Nos-amianthing	Knowing the un-extinguishable	Freudian drives (Eros, Thanatos)
Discrepancies "Discs"	Seeing & juxtaposing contrasting things	Parably; Parabling	Placing next to	Critique, criticism, logical deduction, dialectics, devil's advocacy, opposing
Analogues "Anlgs"	Bringing home to oneself what another person feels or experiences	Homopathy, homopathing	Having similar feelings as another	Pitying, judging, psychoanalyzing; using metaphors or analogies to describe
Universes of discourse "UoDs"	Comparing the elements & rules of the dual mind	(This exercise is not about a skill; it is to teach the ways of the dual mind.)		Dialectics, yin/yang, opposites
Emotional access work	Feeling your feelings	Anthropathy, anthropathing	Having human feelings	Emoting, expressing, sharing feelings
Archetypes; Arkhelogy	Perceiving & doing archetypes	Arkhelogy, Arkheloging	Knowing the highest, primary thing	Esoteric arts, astrology, tarot, magic, prophecy
Ectypes "Ects"	Making from specific to general	Ectypy Ectyping	Making general	Generalizing, hypothesizing
Istotypes "Isos"	Finding other examples by meaning	Isotypy Isotyping	Finding things with similar meaning	Finding analogies or metaphors

25

SECTION TWO

Whys & Wherefores

Chapter Three

EIGHT PRIMARY PRINCIPLES FOR WRITING

You, dear reader, have a choice at this point. You can skip ahead to the exercise chapters and start working directly or you can linger on the four chapters in this section to learn more about whys and wherefores. I honestly recommend you do whatever feels right to you at the moment. If you are eager to begin, go directly to the exercise chapters. If you want more information before starting, continue reading forward from here. You can also skip back and forth.

But if you do skip ahead, make sure to come back to these chapters at some point as they explain what's behind the whole approach.

What follows are the main principles that underlie the Archetypes approach.

(1) Writing takes place in the subconscious (a little about the relationship between the conscious and subconscious minds)
Some people view the subconscious as merely a dumping ground for stuff the conscious mind cannot or does not want to handle. Others consider that the subconscious only exists for people who have "problems." They think that if you are healthy, your subconscious will just fall into line with your conscious mind. Neither of these ideas is true.

The subconscious actually operates — in everyone — as an *independent mind*. It perceives, processes, and retains things that never enter the conscious mind at all.

We all have material in the subconscious. In fact, it is where nearly all our material is found, but that material cannot gather itself together, emerge, and become part of a work of art (or our life) unless the conscious mind allows it. If the conscious mind is not ready, there will be no reason for information contained in the subconscious to be absorbed into consciousness or permitted to emerge.

Because conscious objectives are often diametrically opposed to those of the subconscious, *the conscious mind usually acts as a suppressor.*

However, it *is* possible to move the conscious mind gradually towards taking the part of conjurer and collaborator rather than suppressor, asking for material from the subconscious rather than blocking it, and as a bridge for that material to pass into the linear, daytime world and find expression in a concrete product. This is part of what the archetypes approach does.

One's Own Writing

So, why do I say that one's own writing takes place in the subconscious? Of course we can all write consciously. We can sit down to write a report or a letter to the editor and say what we think needs to be said.

Obviously, I am talking about another kind of writing, am I not? I am talking about *your* writing. I'm talking about *your* subject, *your* characters, *your* story: what belongs to you and no one else. These all reside in your subconscious. They already exist and you already "know" them, but at the same time, you don't know them: you may search for others to tell you how to find them, how to write the novel you want to write, how to tell your story. As Proust wrote in *The Captive*: "Every artist is a native of an unknown country, which he himself has forgotten... but remains all his life attuned to."

Part of the reason why people both know and don't know their own subjects is the principle that you must find outside material to substantiate everything inside of you. We'll discuss this momentarily. The other part of the reason is simply that it's in your subconscious. Things can emerge from and disappear back into the subconscious, like ghosts.

There are several components of the archetypes approach that utilize the principle of *subconscious jurisdiction over your writing*, but the exercise that is intended most directly to teach the student how it works, in a kind of real-time way, is the "UoD" (or Universes of Discourse) exercise. This exercise requires you to watch "UoD movies" from a special movie list. Each of the movies on the list has two "universes of discourse" which work in a similar fashion as the conscious and subconscious.

(2) Your characters already exist within you, but the material exists outside of you

Your characters are already there inside of you but you don't know them fully yet. Once you find an example outside of you of part of one of your characters, you'll instantly recognize it as somehow yours, and the additional outside factual material will fill in and flesh out the character inside.

I could speculate why or how it is that people's characters already exist in them, but it is not necessary. It may have to do with the psychological principle of internalization of parental and other forces on one as a child. This would explain how it is that our characters already exist in us but are not fully formed, since children may not yet discern all the details or nuances inherent in the actions of parents or caregivers, even while they deeply experience the effects of those actions on them. In this way, one's characters are simply the people who had the most effect on one's early life. And further, because as a child one only absorbed the archetypal outlines of these characters, it is the archetype itself that needs to be retrieved and filled in.

Whatever the reasons for why characters exist inside of us and are discoverable through archetype work, the fact has great consequences for writing and it is a major underlying premise of the archetype approach.

(3) Certain activities promote your writing

More than time spent writing, more than novel or screen writing classes, more than advice from established writers or editors, there is a certain set of activities, not apparently related to writing, that will enable your own writing to happen of its own accord.

As usual, these activities are challenging to do. The reason why is because the activities change your entire way of looking at things, yourself and your life, your entire way of relating, of living. It is a more powerful and empowering way to use yourself and your life, but the fact remains that if it is your writing that you want to do, these activities are essential. What are they then? They are the components skills in this book.

(4) Story arises out of character

As noted in the last chapter, character archetypes, when combined, form story archetypes. The story arises from the ways in which the character archetypes interact. Ultimately, this means that there are story archetypes, too, but these are generally found only through working with character archetypes.

It is possible to reach one's own writing through other approaches. Students can benefit from studying characterization techniques, story structure, or Jungian-type archetypes. However, the archetypes for writers approach supplies a major missing link which is not addressed by these other techniques.

The archetypes for writers approach is a *travel guide* through the tangled woods of an intimate personal journey, a *tool* for training the dual mind, and a *method of construction* of that for which the hero's journey and story structure provide blueprints: characters and stories.

(5) In order for you to write your own writing, there must be at least one other person who recognizes expressions of your own writing and wants you to do it
That's my role and this book carries it to you.

(6) You are naturally drawn to your subject matter and the process of finding and working with your subject matter is a healing and transforming process
Learning to listen to your subconscious is part of this journey. When you do learn to listen to your subconscious, you'll find that it will lead you. There are many barriers to doing this work. This method is designed to help you navigate around those barriers and learn to listen to your deep Self.

(7) One's own writing is an expression of the Self and thus all work that is intended to enable one's own writing must be to organize one's daily life to enable Self-expression
It is not merely about sitting down and writing. Whatever you do to enable the expression of your Self will enable your writing.

(8) Writing connects one with forces greater than oneself
Writing is not only about getting in contact with your subconscious or deep Self; it is also about coordinating oneself with that which surrounds oneself. It means accepting and working with the world as it is. Human

events and conditions are shaped by many things: the push and pull of collective and individual human desires, physical laws and forces, the force of life around us, personal and collective history, and so on. Ultimately, writing is about everything, not just human interactions. And ultimately, because writing focuses us on things both within and without ourselves, those things become incorporated into our work.

Because of this, writing is greater than any individual. While the self is not lost and selfish drives are not dissolved, the writing is for something other than self gain. Considerations of "the greater good" may or may not arise in your conscious mind, but they must exist on some level if the writing is to be anything more than merely personal and autobiographical — that is, if it is to become universal.

CHAPTER FOUR

WRITING & THE SELF

You can take me down
To show me your home
Not the place where you live
But the place where you belong.
— Toad the Wet Sprocket (Glen Phillips), "Something to Say"[6]

Every artist is a native of an unknown country, which he himself
has forgotten... but remains all his life somehow attuned to.
— Marcel Proust, *The Captive*[7]

Note to the reader eager to get started: Again, feel free to skip this chapter and the following two chapters to go directly to the exercise chapters, but please come back to read these at some point. They contain important information.

Most people would acknowledge that there is a difference between one's *own writing* and writing one does for someone or something else, between writing that comes from some deep core place in oneself and writing done for external purposes. One's *own writing* is not dictated by some external requirement, form, or structure. It is dictated from within — yet with a special interplay between one's internal world and the world outside. As Elizabeth Barrett Browning wrote:

Trust the spirit,
As sovereign nature does, to make the form;
For otherwise we only imprison spirit
And not embody. Inward evermore
To outward, — so in life, and so in art,
which still is life.[8]

THE SELF

In order for writing to happen this way, from inward to outward, even where prompted by outside events, a process of dialogue and dictation must arise from somewhere inside, carrying some internal imperative. What is this place or thing? From where does the imperative arise? Probably the simplest way to identify this place or thing is just to call it "the Self." One's own writing arises simply from the Self. Or, put another way, it is the Self that engages in one's own writing. Proust writes:

> What we have not had to decipher, to elucidate by our own efforts, what was clear before we looked at it, is not ours. From ourselves comes only that which we drag forth from the obscurity which lies within us, that which to others is unknown.[9]

Although it is somewhat redundant to define one's own writing as a central act of the Self, this step has important implications for a writing approach. That the Self exists must be a given. If we did not acknowledge that the Self exists, we'd have to make up something else that would be equivalent.

No matter what the ultimate source of the Self, whether God-created, a biological phenomenon, genetic, intrinsic, or paradoxically self-created, we must acknowledge that something exists that creates our will and our sense of who we are. While the Self may or may not be consciously "self-aware," each of us nonetheless has a "sense of self" from which we operate. Only the Self can legitimately express or define itself. We certainly may define others, define what we think are other people's selves, but the only one who can say what is so in each of us is our Self. Only you know what you feel, what you know, what you experience. No one else can define this but you.

EXPRESSION OF THE SELF

Your Self may only be able to define itself by the act *of* self-expression. In other words, any act of self-definition *is* an act of self-expression and any act of self-expression is an act of self-definition. Only by self-expression can the Self realize itself. Silence or lack of expression is not self-realization. Realization requires an act.

The Self must therefore be allowed the freedom to engage in expression in order to realize itself. Because the Self is realized by fulfilling its own chosen structure or form, any externally imposed structure or form, any external restriction, limitation, or requirement will necessarily exclude some part of the Self and will prevent its full realization.

The purpose of the archetype approach in this book is to show you how to arrange things both internally and externally in such a way that the Self may engage in self-expression and self-definition. That is what archetype work is about. For, while the Self will constantly attempt to express itself through whatever means it finds, if there is no way to capture and make concrete its expressions, they will dissipate and be absorbed into the outside world of other possibilities.

Archetypes work is not about imposing character or story archetypes onto your psyche. It is about helping your subconscious to articulate the archetypes that are already contained in it.

This definition of one's own writing as the ultimate expression of the Self is the difference between the approach in this book to one's own writing and other approaches to writing. It is not that other approaches do not or cannot "work," whatever one means by that. It is simply that the archetypes approach is wholly grounded on the concept of the expression and realization of the Self.

THE ELUSIVE SELF

However, even so, any approach depends on the diligence of application of the practitioner. You must continuously do the work. Furthermore, the Self is elusive and unquantifiable. The reason for its elusiveness is the same as the reason that the Self does not find automatic expression in the world, the same reason that there is an inherent struggle for each and every Self to express its core being: The vast world is not arranged in its sole service. Each of us has good reason for why we hide our Self behind masks and smoke screens. It is a dangerous world out there. There is no automatic ground staked out just for the realization of you and your Self. The task, thus, of realizing the Self belongs exclusively *to* the Self. As Proust wrote:

> As for the inner book of unknown symbols… if I tried to read them[,] no one could help me with any rules, for to read them was an act of creation in which no one can do our work for us or even collaborate with us.[10]

There is yet another reason for the elusiveness of the Self that plays into this equation: the Self largely functions in the subconscious.[11] This fact has an enormous consequence for writing. Let me pose a string of suppositions to which I must ask your temporary indulgence in order to make a difficult point: Because one's own writing comes from one's Self and the Self resides in the subconscious, if I, the teacher, am to reach your Self to enable writing, I must *speak directly to* that Self, which means speaking to the subconscious.

I have found this to be the case. Now, it may be true that in order to reach the Self, one does *not* need to speak directly to it. Perhaps one can reach the Self by other means. Let me simply say that in my twenty years of experience teaching this approach, and over forty years using and talking about it, I have never found a way to reach the writing Self without speaking directly to it, which means speaking to the subconscious.

Paradoxically, however, speaking to the subconscious requires what feels like "slanted" speech. Since each person is aware only of listening with his or her conscious mind, speech directed at the subconscious will seem "off" in some way.

SPEAKING TO THE SUBCONSCIOUS

How do I know when I'm speaking to someone's subconscious? The answer is: when the subconscious answers.

The subconscious/Self, as I discuss in subsequent chapters, has unique ways of communicating that are identifiable and can be learned. What is important for the reader to know here is that there are two levels of communication in archetype work: the conscious and the subconscious levels. These two minds will not at first be on the same page.

Preparing the Way

I am providing your conscious mind with much information and many tools. These will prepare you to allow your subconscious to do its work. As the conscious mind listens and acquires new tools, it is struggling and learning, while the subconscious mind, in contrast, is beginning to feel recognized and starting to communicate. But, because you essentially have "two brains" working at once as you read this book, you may feel at one minute that you fully understand what you're reading and the next minute you may feel confused or lost. There is no "correct" way to work through this. You need to do what feels right for you at the moment. But don't worry if it is not all instantly clear to you.

Twofold Approach

You will learn more about the way these two minds work as you go through the book. The approach I developed is twofold:

First, the conscious mind must be presented with something it can understand and can do, something that will occupy and distract it, or allow it to permit the subconscious mind to engage uncensored. Thus, the concrete, practical exercises, the terms you can learn, and the tasks set forth herein. These tasks must not be merely diversionary, but they must paradoxically be to the purpose of training the conscious mind to be willing to relinquish itself to the subconscious. In other words, the conscious mind must be gradually trained, with its permission, to suspend itself or allow itself to be put into a kind of sleep.

Second, once the conscious mind is occupied, I speak to the subconscious mind.

Although, as we shall see later, the conscious mind does not and cannot handle material that arises from the deep core Self and it cannot therefore handle the whole truth about the Self, whatever that may be, unless and until those facts emerge into conscious awareness from within (and sometimes not even then), it is nonetheless important to say true things about the process to the conscious person.

Although I speak to both minds, I do not make any effort or engage in any practice to get anyone to suspend his conscious mind or judgment. In other words, I don't hypnotize you or play tricks on your mind. Rather, I teach *you* how to do the work yourself.

In theater training, teachers will often tell students to "trust the process." This has always seemed risky to me. Why should anybody choose to trust someone or something one knows little or nothing about? Certainly a teacher who has spawned great actors will garner trust from incoming students who seek his or her guidance, but beyond that, asking someone to "trust the process" seems comparable to asking him to jump off a cliff. The conscious mind needs anchors, while the subconscious needs to be free of those anchors. In other words, they have opposite needs. We resolve this dilemma by the dual approach set forth above.

NAMING & THE WORK OF THE WRITER

Another important element of getting the conscious mind to relinquish control is "naming." The early tasks in this approach are consciously completely engaging. It is important for you to consciously know and choose what you are doing. This was something that was hard for me to grasp for many years. One must have something concrete that one can consciously identify, name, and know how to do. If one does not have those parts in place, the action and its purpose will be lost. Without a name and an action, we cannot know what has really happened, cannot return to it or repeat it.

But a name in itself does very little. The name must be *attached to the activity*, and where the activity is not commonplace, where it is not something that we do every day and can easily point to, especially when it uses a skill that is not generally recognized or understood, a mental/emotional skill that is not readily visible, it is very important that the name be provided both immediately *before* and *after* the action is first performed.

Thus, the manner in which I teach the archetypes approach is (1) name the task or skill; (2) have the student do the exercise using the skill; (3) discuss the exercise, point out examples of the skill the student succeeded in using; and (4) again name the skill she used. Additionally, while the parts of the approach are not sequential, I will often explain to students how later exercises connect or relate to earlier already-learned skills.

The conscious mind learns to work in service to the subconscious, to the whole Self, while continuing its primary function of dealing with daily life. It is a balancing act that takes time to master and integrate into one's life. As the subconscious is able to gradually express and find place for more and more of its content (which are the archetypes it carries), and the conscious mind is able gradually to accept and give place to that content, so the person, immediate environment, and those in it can adapt to the changing person.

Ultimately the Self makes a place in the world for its whole Self where one did not exist before. This is the great work of the artist. It is monumental. It is not just about writing a book, which is a large enough task in itself, even merely in terms of pure factual organization. The work of the writer is about the rearrangement and reorganization of the inner workings of the dual mind, the reallocation of tasks and adaptation to new ways of handling perceptions and work (ways that enable self-expression), it's the gradual restructuring of both the internal world and the external one: it is the creation of an utterly new thing, a new being, a new life form. In a way, it feels like the creation of the Self — because until the Self has made a place in the outside world, it exists completely, as it were, in the dark, invisible and ineffable, silent, secret, unseen, and unknown, like a ghost, a vapor, a dream. Thus, writing appears to be truly an act of Self-creation, a task almost as great as or greater than birth, a miracle of achievement in a world of denials. In the modern world, this is even a more monumental accomplishment, since nowhere in our society is the fulfillment of this inner journey encouraged or rewarded.

THE POWER OF STORIES

The process I describe above is a description of an internal journey. There is no single manner in which this journey may take place. Indeed, the act of writing stories itself may impel the Self onto this journey.

CHAPTER FIVE

ARCHETYPE WORK, THERAPY & THE GREATER GOOD

ARCHETYPE WORK VS. THERAPY

Some students of the archetypes approach have commented that it seems much like therapy to them. In a certain way, this is an accurate comparison. You do dig into and inspect your own past, your own feelings, and the people and relationships that turn up regularly in your life.

However, the differences between therapy and the archetypes approach are numerous and significant. Although the archetypes approach does raise awareness and enable greater insights into oneself and one's relationships, it is not intended to help you function better socially or professionally. Sometimes, in fact, the increased awareness that comes from doing this work can make it harder to "adapt" to and tolerate situations where one's insights may not be helpful or welcome.

The method is not intended to assist you in overcoming your "problems" either. Rather, it is intended to get you to channel your energies into productive writing work and to get that work to reflect the real life you live (which I will discuss further below under the section on Secret Lives).

Arkhelogy gives you a method for excavating and interpreting your own material and it provides a way to acquire and organize information you receive from and about others for the purpose of writing about people.

WRITING AS A GIFT AND FOR THE GREATER GOOD

Sometimes it is helpful to view the nuggets of information one acquires as *gifts*. It is amazing, once one is able to engage in non-judgmental listening, how much information people will simply give you. These are gifts given to us by those people and by the forces in ourselves that have enabled us to have patience and open-mindedness enough to listen. These gifts are likely to be hard-won and hard-maintained, too.

We must learn to respect and cherish these gifts and to use them well and for the greater good or we will lose them. Respecting those who tell you their inmost secrets (sometimes even secrets of which they themselves were not aware until you elicited it from them) is crucial to this work. If you treat others with disdain because of their foibles, ignorance, problems, or failings, you will lose the privilege of their confidence. This is one reason why writing is always an act of respect and love for our fellow humans.

No single person has the right to acquire all that information about people without the willingness and consent of those people and of the greater good. Of course, no person has the right either to determine for everyone what *is* for the greater good. Thus, one must ask and then wait. It will either drop into your lap or it won't; you will either run across it or you won't. If you can't determine what is best, stay still.

I consider this a very important part of the work. It is a relinquishment to the work, to its larger reach, that elevates it beyond the personal. Because you are asking to know so much more than most people know, more than you might need for your own personal ends, it is important to be respectful and thankful for the power you are given and to dedicate yourself to using it for a higher purpose than personal use.

Chapter Six

SELVES, SECRET LIVES & INVISIBLE WORLDS

In character work, there are some other terms I use that I have found assist writers. These are: Character Selves, Core Self, and Author Self; Secret Lives and the Invisible World.

CHARACTER SELVES

One of the basic premises of the archetypes approach is that your characters already exist within you. You need only learn how to discover their contours, let them speak and live out their lives (without taking you off the course of yours), and find their places in the great story that involves them all. (Everyone has a great story in them, a *chef d'oeuvre*, whether it be one single long story, or many medium sized or shorter ones, whether in the form of a novel or screenplay or poem or play or some other form. Whether you think of yourself as a writer or not is irrelevant to this fact.) If your characters exist within you, they are part *of* you. Thus, you contain all your Character Selves within your own psyche.

Some Character Selves are genuine parts of *you*. Others are introjected from important people in your life (usually your early life). An easy way to look at this is to think about someone who continually gets him or herself into abusive relationships. While the individual may in fact always be the victim in these abusive relationships, s/he carries both character selves: the victim self and the abuser self. (The same is true in reverse.)

Another way of thinking of this is that the victim self, itself, contains the template for the abuser self. They dovetail. The victim self, then, is a genuine affirmative part of the victim person and the abuser self exists as a space, like a missing puzzle piece. (Although the victim/abuser template implies complementary opposites, selves that fit together can be of any type or shape. It's better to think of them as puzzle pieces than opposites, since opposites limits the range.)

Just because Character Selves already exist within you, however, doesn't mean that writing work is just about archaeological digging in one's own psyche. That is probably the most difficult way to do the work. The archetypes approach is all about how to find your characters and stories *outside of yourself*. The techniques used are based on the premise, then, that you are naturally drawn to your own subject matter and to your own characters. In other words, once you start using this approach, it causes you to focus differently and move naturally towards your own material. Not only that but once you are aware that your characters are actually walking around in the world for you to find and you are actually listening and looking for them, you will find that *they will come to you* and will speak to you out of the mouths of people you know.

AUTHOR SELF

All these characters are *your* Character Selves. But, in order for you to write their stories, you need to develop an *Author Self*. The job of the Author Self is to tell the entire story of ALL the selves. The Author Self accepts all stories, all selves, as they are, not as the Author Self (or anyone else) might want them to be. The Author Self is not devoid of feeling for these Character Selves. It feels everything, but it also understands that it cannot change what will happen or what a Character Self feels compelled to do. The Author Self knows the entire story, the story of each individual, his/her destiny, and the overarching story that encompasses all of the characters.

The Author may become embodied in your writing as author omniscient, or as a participant in or witness to events, or as a narrator to whom the story was dictated. She may be a named person who speaks like another character (which then means there is someone who writes her as she speaks — an invisible author omniscient — but who does not have a separate function or existence), or she may speak in the first person. She may be reminiscing or speaking about events transpiring in the present. Or she may simply be embodied in the story and force of narrative.

There is a mysterious element of the Author Self: it is you, but it is also something beyond you. It is the "extra-temporal being" that Marcel Proust talks about. If it knows everything, the whole story and the destinies of all the characters, it exists, in a sense, outside of you and outside of time.

The Author is also objective in the sense that it sees all dispassionately. Because the Author knows the end as well as the middle or the beginning, nothing is surprising and all parts are intrinsic to every other part, although the Author is fully aware of what needs to be told and what has and has not yet been told.

People do not automatically develop an Author Self, even if they are writing novels or screenplays, but it is essential to develop this if you are to write the lives and stories of *all* your Character Selves, to write your whole story. An Author Self may of course develop even in those who are not working on their writing. But in practicing arkhelogy, you will move towards developing the Author Self.

While the Author Self is just a term that helps us to think about our central work as a writer, it is my belief that it is actually a real phenomena, perhaps caused by the use of different neurons in the brain that results from arkhelogy work. The Author Self is genuinely able to see all ends or destinies and these do in fact exist outside of linear time. Think about it: If all your characters are already inside of you, you already know the whole story of their lives and interactions. This is not to discount learning or experience, but the real learning comes from getting to know oneself.

An Author Self is a way you use your mind to oversee everything in your life. In order for a person to achieve this, there must be a connection to something greater than oneself, if only to an inspiring role model. The simple intention of connecting to something greater than oneself is sufficient, since it requires looking beyond oneself and seeing oneself as part of humanity and part of forces beyond one's control. The intention itself acts like a lightning rod to draw into oneself whatever can assist one in understanding better and realizing one's own work. Rather than working for one's own solitary ends against the great magnitude of humanity that is working towards other ends, or against the very turning of the heavens, one learns to work *with* others, with the tides, the seasons, the course of human events, and so on.

AUTHOR SELF vs. CORE SELF

Inside of you there is also always your Core Self, which is not the same as the Author Self. I do not attempt to define the Core Self to any extent. I simply distinguish it from your Character Selves and the Author Self.

The Core Self must, by definition, be you at the core. The Author Self does not necessarily include the Core Self, although it does include something beyond you.

The Core Self may not know all the stories of all the Character Selves, but the Author Self does, including that of the Core Self.

Yet, the Author Self is not greater in value than the Core Self. There can be no replacement by the Author Self or otherwise for the Core Self.

The reason, then, for naming the Core Self is that the simple act of naming it permits it to exist and find its place. Naming it signals to your conscious mind that there is some deep part of you that it should be your goal to realize.

One's Core Self is known to one's own Core Self but probably not to one's conscious mind. The Author Self must make room for all the selves, most especially the Core Self.

The purpose of using the term Core Self is only to make space for what we might otherwise not, simply because we don't know it exists or what it is. One way to think about this is to imagine it is like keeping a special, secret place (or closet, cave, mountain top, forest, whatever image suits you) for some invisible and secret creature to use to put himself and his things in, whenever he might see fit. It may take a long time before this creature will trust that the space belongs to him and that the stuff won't be removed or filled with stuff he doesn't want, or worse, with stuff that is dangerous or poisonous to him, or that it is a safe place for him to dwell.

The best thing for us to do is to leave that space where it is and to simply acknowledge that we have a place for that part of ourselves.

SECRET LIVES & THE INVISIBLE WORLD

What you discover from arkhelogy is a kind of subliminal world that is operating all the time. When you apply the approach to one person, you will begin to discern a *secret life* in that person.

Although a character archetype is not synonymous with the person you are observing, the secret life you discern is nonetheless quite real and substantial in that person and it is what enables you to construct the archetype.

It is not that the person is purposefully hiding this life from everyone. It is simply that there is always a difference between how people present themselves to others and the archetypes within them. It's like two parallel universes and you are seeing both at once.

The secret life is the one from which come all impulses, all motivation, all actions. This explains how it is that you hear people say about someone who suddenly began shooting people in the street one day: "He was always so quiet and polite! Such a nice man! Who would have thought…?" It is because social behavior does not necessarily provide the information that the secret life does.

The *Invisible World* is simply any combination of Secret Lives that you observe happening together in relation to one another. It is the ability to see the Invisible World that enables some people to appear to be prophets or seers.

But it *is* possible to learn how to discern secret lives, and that is a great part of what arkhelogy is about. Thus, while this approach is for the concrete purpose of providing writers with a way to work with and develop their characters, it is also much more than that. It is a set of tools and skills that can be useful in many ways and contexts.

SECTION THREE

The Exercises

CHAPTER SEVEN

CHARACTER FACTS
(Nos-Anthro)

I cannot stir a step aside from what I feel to be true in character. If anything strikes you as untrue to human nature in my delineations, I shall be glad if you will point it out to me, that I may reconsider the matter. But alas! Inconsistencies and weaknesses are not untrue.

— George Eliot to her publisher

Character facts are simply any and all facts that have to do with people. First of all, it is important to realize that, as writers, even when we are writing "fiction," we must use facts. (Even fantasy and science fiction must be fact-based in order to be plausible.) At first this might sound harsh and academic, but once you understand this key thing, it really becomes a lot of fun handling facts about people.

The skill this exercise develops is the ability to differentiate between subjective observations, opinions, or conclusions (such as "She's a jerk") and demonstrable, objective facts that can be seen or heard by anyone (such as "He rides his bike to work every day"). The purpose of doing character facts is to whittle away at one's own preconceptions, to separate one's pre-judgments from phenomena that exist outside our self-references — i.e. to *see and hear* better.

This exercise is hard, but great fun! It really shows me how much I add into a "factual" description. I can't believe how much I intentionally slant the facts!
— Debby Haney (student)

Like most of the "Archetypes for Writers" exercises, character facts are simple, but they are not easy. The character fact exercise limits what you can use and how, but it is not the basis for the entire method, so don't worry too much about not being able to do all the "writer" things you may be used to doing.

THE EXERCISE

Each of us has a "little life" — a life that is less than that which we are capable of understanding Yet, writing is not about NOT having that little life. It is about accepting that little life in ourselves and in others, and giving oneself and others permission to be human and experience all those "little" things, but at the same time, watching oneself and others and noting one's own and others' patterns and rhythms, and loving oneself and one's life, such as it is, and others and their lives, as they are.

Choose a person you know, either superficially or well, and write down character facts, circumstances, and questions about him or her. Concentrate on a person and on facts that you find interesting. Do not try to write a story or a character sketch. Focus on what the person *does*. Have fun!

This is what we do in this exercise   This is not *what we do here*

Character Facts	Story/Character Sketch
ଈ things the person does	ଈ narrative or story, with a
ଈ things the person says	beginning, middle, and
ଈ physical description only	end, or
in the context of actions	ଈ free association in any form
ଈ avoid use of adjectives	but without the restrictions
ଈ avoid modifiers	of character facts
ଈ avoid conclusions and	ଈ adjectives & opinions acceptable
opinions	ଈ back story acceptable
ଈ avoid imputing emotions	(education, occupation, etc.)
ଈ context can be stated	ଈ imputing emotions acceptable
	ଈ context is usually created
	within narrative or story, or
	not provided if using free
	association/back story (or
	may be inferred or imputed)

I start students off with a short list of "rules."

THE RULES

1. **Always use facts**. A fact is anything that is demonstrable. Rely on anything observable, demonstrable, literal, and concrete. Do not rely on abstractions or speculations, to the extent they can be avoided. An abstraction is anything general, vague, or unverifiable.

   Concrete: She has a PhD in physics. She tells me she likes the ocean.
   Abstract: She has identity problems. She has low self-esteem.

2. **Avoid imputing emotions to people**. Don't say "She feels angry." Say, instead, "She says 'I'm angry!'" or "She shouts at him."

3. **As much as possible, avoid using adjectives, qualifiers, or modifiers** (such as great, beautiful, terrible, bad/good, excessive, unfortunate, etc.). These words PRE-characterize and prevent you from finding deeper, more revealing things. Use words describing physical characteristics (big/small, fat/skinny, etc.), *only if* they are necessary to the readers' understanding of the person and the situation you are talking about. Always ask yourself if there is another way (other than using adjectives) to describe or portray whatever it is.

4. **Focus on what the person *does***. Instead of saying, "She's a volatile person," try to state what she does that makes you think she's volatile. For example, one person I consider volatile — an attorney who practiced at home — began abruptly shouting on the phone at a court reporter because transcripts were late.

5. **Stick to the character facts**. Character Facts are those which tell us things about the person. Thus, "He lied to his mother!" is a character fact (if you can verify it). "She wears only black." "They are going to the New School." And so on.

6. **Use character circumstances**. These are the surrounding events and environmental conditions that may affect the person. Sometimes these are self-chosen; sometimes they are outside of the person's control. For example: "He lives in a wealthy neighborhood," or "Her mother just died," or "They grew up in South Africa." Include them if you think they are somehow important to understanding the person.

7. **Use character questions**. These are very valuable in working on character facts. "Why did she shout abruptly at the court reporter?" is more valuable than "She's a volatile person," or "She's got problems."

8. **Avoid opinions**. Stating your opinions or conclusions, or the opinions or conclusions of others, is not absolutely forbidden in this exercise, as long as you separate the opinions from the facts. You may, for example, say "This guy did such and such, and I think he's wrong!" or "*He said* 'She's really nice!'" (If you have trouble sorting out your conclusions/opinions from the facts, try physically separating them into two columns: one for facts and actions, the other for your opinions and conclusions.)

9. **State the context**. It helps sometimes to choose a context, but avoid writing the character facts as a story. The context can be an incident, a time period, an episode, a place, etc. The context should simply be stated, not woven into the other facts.

SUSPENDING JUDGMENT

The character facts exercise develops your ability to suspend your judgment. Instead of concluding someone is racist because he sent invitations to only white persons, you simply note the action and hold your conclusion in abeyance. This is HARD to do! But it is important — if you really want to understand someone from the inside. Pre-conclusions and opinions interfere with getting inside of a person's head and heart. Also, when you suspend judgment, you will be in a state of continual inquiry and expectation, watching for more material, more information, and often the people you are observing will sense what you are silently asking to know and sometimes they will tell you. (It sometimes happens that a person will provide you with a missing piece of their puzzle without ever having thought of it consciously before themselves. This is because, as we discussed earlier, the material is in the subconscious, but the subconscious is always "listening.")

Suspending judgment is also a kind of Zen-like brain activity. Over time and with consistent use, the practice changes you in subtle ways. You see people and things differently, you feel different, you breathe differently, you move through your life differently, you even make choices differently. It is a personally transforming practice.

Developing your ability to suspend your judgment does not mean you lose your ability to judge people according to their conduct. You may, naturally, still conduct your social and professional life based on your assessments of people's behavior — for example, you may choose not to hang out with someone who is rude to you — but if you want to know for purposes of your writing, you may hold judgment in abeyance and dig deeper. Again, you may not care to do this with all people you encounter. The skill simply becomes one you can use to expand your range of understanding for purposes of developing yourself as a writer — and of gathering better, deeper material.

Moreover, suspending judgment is only the first step in gaining the skills that together enable you to do archetypes in your writing, but it is a crucial one, without which you cannot attain the global skill.

EXAMPLES: WORKING THROUGH THE EXERCISE

When students do this exercise in class, they usually do it a couple of times, with my feedback in between. In addition to my feedback, there is a lot of interaction between students in class and this can also be a very valuable source of feedback. If you are not in one of my classes when you read this book, it may help if you can find one or two people who would like to try doing the exercise themselves and then you can all share and discuss your work, focusing particularly on how closely each of you were able to adhere to the rules of the exercise.

EXAMPLE ONE: "Eric"

Let's look at a detailed exchange between me and a student I'll call Steve. This is an actual exchange with a few modifications for ease in reading. The names of the student and the subject of his observations have been changed (here and throughout the book). This is what Steve submitted as his initial character facts assignment:

Eric is a large, slightly paunchy, young man of about 26. He has a bushy black ponytail, a long goatee, and tattoos. He is dressed in black jeans and a black tee-shirt. His expression is emotionless and flat. It strikes me as ominous. Yet, when I speak with him, I find that he is soft-spoken, with a gentle round voice. I ask him about a book and he is quick to help and, it seems, eager to please.

Having seen Steve's initial work, can you identify the adjectives, adjectival phrases, modifiers, or qualifiers that Steve uses, without reading ahead? (To see the answer, see below.[†])

I pointed these out to Steve and explained that

I am not trying to find every single adjective. I am trying to make you aware of how much you rely on these descriptions. Many people construe a request for facts as a request for a character sketch. But I asked for character facts without adjectives or qualifiers. What this means is that you should not describe the person; you must instead rely on what the person DOES. That means you must focus on an EVENT. Thus, for example, instead of writing "she replenishes the wine frequently," you write "I have seen her replace the wine several times." You need not write "she is a very active person" if you have shown the activities she engaged in. The reader can draw his or her own conclusions.

Adjectives pre-conclude and limit what the reader sees, and they also limit YOUR own ability to see more than what you have pre-concluded. When you use adjectives, you are paradoxically seeing LESS.

I then asked Steve "What are the important facts about Eric?" Steve replied:

The important facts about this man are that he's adopted an unconventional appearance that would tend to place him outside the general population where he works. (I supposed I should have mentioned where that was geographically.) Yet, his inner attitudes and values are very much the opposite of his externals, in that he is hard-working and wants to please

---

[†] Answer: large, paunchy, emotionless and flat, ominous, soft-spoken, gentle, round, quick to help, eager to please.

and be liked. When he receives attention, he lights up, notwithstanding the fact that he initially puts up a distant, somewhat ominous front.

I responded to Steve that he was anticipating another exercise: discrepancies. (Steve described a discrepancy between Eric's appearance and his behavior.) But I told him that now I was trying to get him away from description. I preferred he simply tell me what he noticed about Eric. I told him that he had to some degree done this. He wrote back that he did not feel he had given me facts; rather he felt he had provided me with an analysis of the demonstrable facts he had earlier presented. My response to Steve:

When you note that the store clerk has an "ominous front," you are using an adjective where you should be saying WHAT it is that makes him seem ominous to you. You did, of course, say that his expression (emotionless and flat) struck you as ominous. However, this is merely moving the adjective to a different place in the sentence. How can you get around this? One possible alternative way to say it could be: "His face did not show any emotion." This places the focus on the noun (emotion) rather than the adjective "emotionless" or "ominous."

Let's take a look at the word ominous. The first time you used it, you wrote: "It strikes me as ominous." The second time, you wrote that he "puts up a distant, somewhat ominous front." The way you used the word the first time was as a description of how YOU felt. The second time, it became a full-blown adjective in front of and modifying a noun (front). You have transferred your internal feeling about him into an external description of him, but you still have not described what he did that made you feel this way. This kind of locks you up into yourself. It also locks up those you observe, making them into what you've already decided they are.

So, again, what can you do? In the example you chose, you have to determine what exactly he DID that made you feel he was ominous.

In this inquiry, we can discover that, in fact, the word ominous doesn't describe HIM at all. It describes YOUR feeling, but, at the same time, it doesn't. YOU don't feel ominous. You feel HE is ominous. What you, yourself, appear to be feeling is dread or fear. (Ominous describes what you think of how he makes you feel.) Why do you feel dread or fear? There were two reasons you gave: his face did not show any emotion and his appearance, hair in a pony-tail, black clothes, etc.

Ask yourself what he DID that made you feel whatever you felt that made you say he seemed ominous. His face didn't show emotion, he didn't smile, he was not responsive to your greeting, etc. What else? He dressed a certain way, kept his hair a certain way, and did something to his body (tattoos). These are actions of his. Notice how I have changed them from physical descriptions into actions. His size may also have affected you, which is not something he did. It is an immutable characteristic, something he could not immediately change. But large people may use their bodies differently. Some large people may hover over smaller people in a way that could be perceived as threatening or invasive. Others may seem to fade into the wallpaper. What did he DO?

Finally, you said he was "paunchy." Rather than using an adjective, what can you say about this? This is a difficult one. It is certainly a fact that he is paunchy (I don't doubt your observation). But what do you mean? Does his belly hang over his belt buckle? Does he look like he doesn't exercise at all? Is he physically imposing in an unpleasant way? Does he take up more space than others?

See how many different things you were doing all at once?

Let me briefly revert to your question about facts versus analysis. When you spoke about the clerk's "inner attitudes and values," you were doing analysis (in the sense I think you mean it). But do you now see the difference between facts which rely on adjectives and those which rely on what a person does?

You can see how fine the distinctions can be drawn on this exercise! The most important thing is to engage your mind in the work of separating out your opinions from the observable facts. The actual final product is not as important as the *doing* of the brain work.

The remaining examples below are set forth in the form of conversations between myself and the student. Student's work and my responses are indented and labeled. Any comments or discussion I have added is set back at the original margin.

EXAMPLE TWO: "John"

Annie's work, and the exchange between Annie and me about it, is instructive because even though Annie was immediately able to change from working in a story format to writing character facts, she then left out the most important piece of information. Her explanation for this illustrates how easy it is to merge facts with attributions or inventions.

This is Annie's work.

> He comes to the office exactly on time and marches right up to my desk. He's wearing a navy suit that is a little too snug for him. His belly hangs over his belt like an apron. Looks uncomfortable. Tight. His face sags. "Appearing older than his stated age" as the doctor might say. Before I can say anything to him he says: "I have a 3:45 with the doctor, my name is Mr. Smith, I called you about 2 pm." He peers over the desk trying to read my papers upside down. "I remember your call Mr. Smith, the doctor is running about 15 minutes late, would you mind taking a seat over there? Here is the questionnaire she told you about, you can fill that out while you are waiting." I hand him the clipboard and a pen and he heads over to the bank of chairs to wait. He is alone there, the last patient of the day. On Thursdays we close early so the doctor can dictate her reports.
>
> He sits down and puts his hard-sided maroon briefcase on his lap and hunches over it, using it as a desk, on which he fills out the form. His cell phone rings and he puts the clipboard on the chair beside him. He opens his briefcase. "Yea, I'm here in the doctor's office now. I can't believe this Jack, that bitch. What a piece of work." He is starting to shout. "Yes I'll stay cool, I'm focused, I'm focused," he said. "We went over everything." He snaps the cell phone shut.
>
> Hunched over his briefcase he's reading through legal papers, divorce papers, I look over and see him lingering over photographs placed between the pages of the white double-spaced legal briefs. I feel sad for him. I know why he is here. He does not move when a

messenger stops by with a delivery, he stays, bent over his briefcase, staring at what's inside.

He does not move when the doctor comes out. Suddenly he sees her standing beside him and he jumps up, the briefcase and papers go flying. "What a klutz," he mutters. He stoops down and in a single movement, sweeps everything into the jaws of the case and clicks it shut. "Lead the way, doc," he says, and follows her into the office.

I see he has left the clipboard on the seat. I get it and put it in his chart. John Smith, born in 1958, New Rochelle, MBA, Columbia, Goldman Sachs. Married 12 years ago. One child, Amy, 13 years old. Wife Yvonne left him two years ago. I think: "Typical custody dispute. He says/she says." I remember the daughter, Amy. These things get nasty. I remember the wife, he was right, a "piece of work," cancelled twice and came late. Not like him. Poor Amy, the children always get the worst of it. I wanted to take that girl home with me. Doc said the same thing. I put his papers in his chart for later.

I hear a cell phone ringing. Must be his. It's on the floor of the waiting area, under his seat. Beside it is a photograph, face down, a Polaroid. At first, I can't quite figure out what it is. It's a naked girl, bent over, wearing only her white knee high socks, exposed, made up, starring over her shoulder, back at the camera. It's Amy.

I responded to Annie:

Annie, you've written a wonderful story here. Very interesting and sad. Shocking. My problem with it is that you did write it as a story. I just want the character facts. There are all sorts of assumptions you've made here, which usually would be appropriate for writing a short story. Although you've written facts, the assumptions are there, if masked. One assumption, for example, is within the voice of the narrator. Any narrative, whether in the first person or author omniscient or whatever, contains assumptions. The author asks the readers to accept these as givens. What you ask us to accept here is that you, the narrator, embody a standard. You convey that standard by setting the scene and through your portrayal of Smith. You judge him without saying so. You've also set a whole scene, which we are asked to accept as given. The time, the place, the circumstance. All those things which rightly belong in stories, but not in this exercise, except in service to a fact you offer to us about someone (not within the context of an already given story).

All these things you've mixed in together here do belong in a finished story, but I do not want finished stories here, for the very reason that they do contain a mixture of things. We are doing separating-out work. We are not producing stories or written products in this class.

Annie wrote back:

I wrote the story about the incest perpetrator and in your response you indicated that essentially I had simply told a story, and had not stuck to facts. Your response was clear.

Here are John's facts: He is a 41-year-old caucasian male, separated from his wife of 13 years for over two years, engaged in a custody dispute with her that has gone on for two full years. Recently, following disclosure in court that she had been arrested and charged in relation to an incident in which she was allegedly driving a car under the influence of alcohol, she accused her husband of having had an incestuous relationship with their 13-year-old daughter, since she was about seven years old. The couple had been sharing custody up to this point.

He is about five feet eight inches tall and weighs about 200 pounds. His hair is short — a crew cut. He wears expensive suits but since he has not purchased a new suit for some time, his pants are very tight. He works as an investment banker in a well-known New York firm, having graduated third in his class from Columbia, achieving his MBA in record time. His parents are both still married to one another, and live in his family home in Westchester. He is their only son. He has never been arrested. He does not smoke. He denies use of illicit drugs. Since the custody dispute began he has "one or two" drinks every night. His drink of choice is vodka and tonic, and of course, wine with dinner. He has it delivered by the case from the local liquor store. He shares custody of his daughter. She is with him on alternate weekends and holidays, and on Tuesday and Thursday nights. She waits at home alone for him to come home.

I complimented Annie on heeding my directions closely but noted that she had left out a fact which I would consider pretty important: the naked picture of his daughter which she found.

Annie responded:

> I thought about that, but I was not sure how to introduce this since we are looking at him from the outside and he is not exactly advertising the fact that he is an incest perp, without resorting to a situational narrative, which is what I thought I did wrong in the first place! Seriously, when you speak about facts, can we go into his internal life? I suppose I could simply state, that in his briefcase were the usual pens and supplies, as well as hundreds of pages of legal briefs. Attached to some of these pages were Polaroid photographs of his daughter, naked, sexual, which he looked at whenever he needed to distract himself from the stress of the world around him. He knew the risk he took in carrying them around, but he needed those pictures, they made him feel so good. When I write this though, I think I am violating some of the rules you set us with regards to his need to distract himself, etc., or perhaps not.

I told Annie:

> You do not need to write a narrative in order to record your observations. When you write that something made him feel good, that is a statement of opinion. You are attributing feelings to him. You can't know his feelings, unless he tells them to you. If he tells them to you, you can say that he said so. If you see that he obviously feels good, note what signifies that. Is he smiling? Rubbing his hands together? Or does the mere fact that he carries these pictures around signify his preference? How do you know he looked at the pictures of his daughter "whenever he needed to distract himself from the stress of the world around him"? You do know he carried the pictures in his

briefcase. You know they are pictures of his daughter. You know she is naked and in sexual positions. You do NOT know why he does this or what needs it fills. Keep that inquiry separate. After we do analogues, we will do universal drives and you can think about what he gets out of doing this. At this point, though, you CAN write down what you actually see and hear him do. I dont want you to speculate about his internal life, but you can go into any background or peripheral facts in your knowledge.

I could find no record in my files of further work on this by Annie, although she may have continued further with the exercise and I may simply have lost the file. Do Annie's comments and my final instructions to her help you to see how she continued, even after changing from a story to CFs, to merge facts and attributions? Annie expressed that she felt she was not allowed to "go into his internal life," but the point is not that you cant look into the internal life but that you have to have a substantial basis for coming to a conclusion. The point is to look at the reasons for your own conclusions.

EXAMPLE THREE: "Hal"

A student named Frank submitted the following character facts. As you read, see if you notice any points where Frank makes opinions/conclusions, uses adjectives, or where you might want to know why he says what he says about Hal (where he gets his information from).

Frank wrote:

> Character Facts: He's six feet tall, 190 pounds, has dark features, tan, pearly white teeth that show when he smiles. He wears shirts too big for his body, designer labels only, a Tag Huer watch, fine leather shoes. Hal is jobless but manages to play golf five days a week by living off his father's money. He claims he's just not ready to work yet. He also exercises five days a week, eats well (fruit, vegetables, water), but binges on chocolates once a week. He's an ex-athlete at the collegiate level for the sport of lacrosse. Hal has a bad temper. Hal blames other

people for his troubles. Hal's driver's license was suspended for the second time when he drove his truck into a ravine (and blamed a motorcyclist). He hates to read and study but can talk his way out of a jam. His charm used to make you feel like the luckiest person in the world. Hal has been diagnosed with clinical depression and an anxiety disorder. Hal takes medication for both of these illnesses. Hal loves to watch television — especially sports. He's addicted. He won't share the remote with anyone. Hal has other addictions: pills, alcohol, pot, crack cocaine, heroin. Hal sleeps with prostitutes when he's not getting laid on his own. Hal was molested at the age of eight at a day camp. Hal has been in several drug rehabilitation facilities (and kicked out of a couple of them). Has used to settle all his disputes with his fists. He was the high school bully but also the popular athlete. Hal used to live the high life and work on Wall Street in the late '90s. Hal hated Hebrew school although he claims that he's very proud to be Jewish. Hal spent Memorial Day two years ago in a mental hospital for suicide watch. They found a gun in the back seat of his car. Hal's mother has manic episodes. Her side of the family has bouts with drug addiction, alcoholism, and mental illness. Hal has never gone longer than eight months since the age of 14 without using some type of drug.

When doing character facts, some writers, especially those trained to write screenplays or scripts, may find themselves looking for potential conflicts between the character and his environment or other persons. Many people find themselves identifying discrepancies (such as Hal eats healthy food but binges on chocolate once a week — a possible discrepancy), which is another component skill in the archetypes approach. If you find yourself pegging potential conflicts or discrepancies, go ahead and note those things, but if just learning how to do CFs now, simply save them for later when we do discrepancies work.

So, now, with Frank's assignment, before you read my questions and comments, see if you can make a list of your own.

If you intend to make your own list, don't read further until you're done.

Note, for example, where Frank imputes emotion to Hal ("Hal hated

Hebrew school…"), where he labels him ("He's addicted…") or makes claims about him without really saying what happened ("He was molested…") or where he concludes something without saying what it is ("He used to live the high life…").

JVB's Comments & Questions to Frank:

Frank, the last sentence — "He also exercises five days a week, eats well (fruit, vegetables, water), but binges on chocolates once a week." — is a discrepancy.

What do you mean by: "He's an ex-athlete at the collegiate level for the sport of lacrosse. Hal has a bad temper"? What is a bad temper?

The statement: "Hal blames other people for his troubles" is a conclusion/opinion.

You write that Hal "hates to read and study but can talk his way out of a jam." How do you know what he hates?

You write: "His charm used to make you feel like the luckiest person in the world." What is charm? What does he DO?

You say that "Hal has been diagnosed with clinical depression and an anxiety disorder. Hal takes medication for both of these illnesses." You call them illnesses. Is that a fact or an opinion/conclusion? Whose?

You say that Hal "loves to watch television — especially sports. He's addicted." What makes you say this? What does "addicted" mean?

You mention that Hal "won't share the remote with anyone" and "has other addictions: pills, alcohol, pot, crack cocaine, heroin." Not all of these are physically addictive. Define it. I think there are more sentences in there about this. What do you mean?

You say that Hal "sleeps with prostitutes when he's not getting laid on his own." How do you know this? This is in the indefinite (ongoing) present. Be specific as to time. Does he ALWAYS do this? For how long? Since when?

You note that Hal "was molested at the age of eight at a day camp." How do you know? What do you mean by molested? What happened?

With respect to your statements that Hal "has been in several drug rehabilitation facilities (and kicked out of a couple of them)... used to settle all his disputes with his fists... was the high school bully but also the popular athlete... [and] used to live the high life and work on Wall Street in the late '90s," what is "the high life"? What are disputes? What is popular?

You write that Hal "hated Hebrew school although he claims that he's very proud to be Jewish." This would be another discrepancy except that there is a huge time difference between one and the other.

With respect to these statements: "Hal spent Memorial Day two years ago in a mental hospital for suicide watch. They found a gun in the back seat of his car. Hal's mother has manic episodes. Her side of the family has bouts with drug addiction, alcoholism, and mental illness": all these Character Circumstances are very good. They all seem important and relevant to understanding Hal. What are "manic episodes"? Drug addiction, alcoholism, mental illness? Very broad statements.

After Frank read my comments, he responded: "Thanks for the comments — I can see the difficulty I'm having with being too general and vague on some points. It's a classic problem I've always had."

You can see that my comments and questions were meant to get Frank thinking about his own internal processes as he worked and to get him to be more specific and concrete. Can you think how Frank might have answered some of these questions?

EXAMPLE FOUR: "Fred"

This is Robert's work:

These are character facts and circumstances for a friend, who shall be called Fred. Fred is over six feet, about 190 pounds. He has a squarish chin that juts out and a protuberant nose, plus a deep, almost harsh voice. He leans forward slightly while speaking, emphasizing his words with short and swift gestures. He exercises regularly, plays squash, and trained (in his forties) for a grueling physical competition where most participants were military men in their twenties (my own view is that it was an idiotic idea, and thankfully he couldn't actually compete).

Fred has a PhD in international politics and is a tenured professor. He professes to love teaching, to love the attention, the theatrics during classes, the opportunity to shape young minds. He gets excellent evaluations from his students and often expresses his pride in his work. He keeps in contact with his students, following their careers and occasionally helping them (right now he has a former student staying in his house with his family).

He occasionally takes on what appears to me as a professorial tone with his friends, in the sense of asking basic questions that seem to be geared more towards instruction than eliciting information. For example, a mutual friend once said that foreign policy should be based solely on a country's interest (a fatuous statement in my view because it doesn't define "interest"), and Fred came back with a barrage of questions, such as "what do you mean by 'interest'," "aren't ideological goals important to nations," "can a country pursue an effective foreign policy without moral benchmarks." Each question was asked in a quiet tone, with a nod of the head, a puff of Fred's pipe, and a short pause. Each question followed the other without providing much time for an answer.

Fred often devotes considerable time to helping his friends, for example spending hours working on one friend's boat or another's dock. He has helped me move, repair and paint a porch, and rebuild another porch. He often goes out of his way to drive me places, for example driving a half hour to pick me up at a subway stop so I could join him for a baseball game.

Fred is often late. Several times he was supposed to meet me for lunch at my office, and called 15 or 20 minutes past the time to say that he would not arrive for another half hour. Once he missed a Christmas season celebration with me and my wife, he said (and I believe him) because he was confused about the date. Several times I have mentioned an appointment we had, for dinner or a play, and he has forgotten the date. He also has had a hard time meeting writing deadlines. It took him six years to get his PhD after finishing his masters, and he often would describe writing projects that he was supposedly working on, but later it turned out he didn't finish or finally submitted well after the due date.

Fred's mother was sick, more on than off, from the time he was a teenager until her death when he was in his thirties. He spent many hours seeing her in hospitals and taking care of her at home. He has what I would describe as a courtly manner towards women (girl-friends and wives), in that he orders for them in restaurants, holds their coats and opens doors, addresses them as "dearest," helps them with work and studies. But his first wife said that she divorced him because he went off to work abroad for a year despite her objections, while expecting her to leave a good job to follow him. He has said that he lived in a fool's paradise while married to his first wife, without a clue as to her feelings and resentments.

JVB's Comments & Questions to Robert:

Robert wrote: These are character facts and circumstances for a friend, who shall be called Fred.

Fred is over six feet, about 190 pounds. He has a squarish chin that juts out and a protuberant nose, plus a deep, almost harsh voice.

JVB's comments: This is all fine so far, but let me ask you something: are the facts about his chin, nose, and voice important to understanding who he is, why he does what he does, what makes him tick? If they are, they are CFs. Notice that I distinguish CFs from facts one might use in a "char-acter study" or sketch or backstory.

Robert: He leans forward slightly while speaking, emphasizing his words with short and swift gestures.

JVB: Again, are these facts which relate to or help explain who he is, why he does what he does, what makes him tick?

Robert: He exercises regularly, plays squash, and trained (in his forties) for a grueling physical competition where most participants were military men in their twenties (my own view is that it was an idiotic idea, and thankfully he couldn't actually compete).

JVB: This seems to me to be more of a real CF, because it reveals something about how he views things. It is an early clue to what makes him tick.

Robert: Fred has a PhD in international politics and is a tenured professor. He professes to love teaching, to love the attention, the theatrics during classes, the opportunity to shape young minds. He gets excellent evaluations from his students and often expresses his pride in his work. He keeps in contact with his students, following their careers and occasionally helping them (right now he has a former student staying in his house with his family).

JVB: Good. To me, these seem to be important facts to understanding him and who he is. (Mind you, this is not to say that the facts I question above, his nose, chin, etc., are not relevant, but there is nothing here that shows how they could be.)

Robert: He occasionally takes on what appears to me as a professorial tone with his friends, in the sense of asking basic questions that seem to be geared more towards instruction than eliciting information. For example, a mutual friend once said that foreign policy should be based solely on a country's interest (a fatuous statement in my view because it doesn't define "interest"), and Fred came back with a barrage of questions, such as "what do you mean by 'interest'," "aren't ideological goals important to nations," "can a country pursue an effective foreign policy without moral benchmarks." Each question was asked in a quiet tone, with a nod of the head, a puff of Fred's pipe, and a short pause. Each question followed the other without providing much time for an answer.

JVB: Great example. Interesting and revealing — shows something about who he is, what he does, how he thinks.

Robert: Fred often devotes considerable time to helping his friends, for example spending hours working on one friend's boat or another's dock. He has helped me move, repair and paint a porch, and rebuild another porch. He often goes out of his way to drive me places, for example driving a half hour to pick me up at a subway stop so I could join him for a baseball game.

JVB: Also a very significant fact.

Robert: Fred is often late. Several times he was supposed to meet me for lunch at my office, and called 15 or 20 minutes past the time to say that he would not arrive for another half hour. Once he missed a Christmas season celebration with me and my wife, he said (and I believe him) because he was confused about the date. Several times I have mentioned an appointment we had, for dinner or a play, and he has forgotten the date. He also has had a hard time meeting writing deadlines. It took him six years to get his PhD after finishing his masters, and he often would describe writing projects that he was supposedly working on, but later it turned out he didn't finish or finally submitted well after the due date.

JVB: Okay. Even though I'm not sure this indicates or explains anything "important" about him, it is at least indicative, slightly tantalizing, makes one wonder more about him, about why he does this, what it means about him, etc.

Robert: Fred's mother was sick, more on than off, from the time he was a teenager until her death when he was in his thirties. He spent many hours seeing her in hospitals and taking care of her at home. He has what I would describe as a courtly manner towards women (girlfriends and wives), in that he orders for them in restaurants, holds their coats and opens doors, addresses them as "dearest," helps them with work and studies. But his first wife said that she divorced him because he went off to work abroad for a year despite her objections, while expecting her to leave a good job to follow him. He has said that he lived in a fool's paradise while married to his first wife, without a clue as to her feelings and resentments.

JVB: Interesting. Excellent work, Robert.

Sometimes students become too mechanical doing CFs. It is important to remember to try to figure out which facts are relevant to your understanding of a person. The idea is to figure out what makes him do things the way he does. Later on, in the universe of discourse exercise, we consider what drives him, and in some respects the questions I asked Robert here were in anticipation of that work.

Robert subsequently posted some follow-up questions:

> I can see that my description of Fred's physical aspects wasn't tied to a personality trait. If I were to say that Fred's height, build, and gestures added up to a physical presence that helped him dominate conversations, and show examples, would that be closer to a "character fact" in your scheme? That is, are character facts only about what determines "who he is, why he does what he does, what makes him tick" or can they also help to explain the effect he has on other people, or what characteristics (physical or personality) he uses to get what he wants?
>
> I was puzzled that you didn't feel that Fred's inability to meet deadlines and his forgetting appointments explained anything important. I would think that the ability to achieve goals on schedule and fulfill commitments is critical. So perhaps I am still confused about what exactly is, and is not, a "character fact."

I responded:

> Thanks for your comments and questions. First of all, my judgment about what is "important" or relevant is not the deciding factor. It (my judgment) is only significant to the extent that I am able to get what you are doing. So, to that extent, you have to be able to show me, in the same way that you need to show any reader (although, of course, I am looking for different things at this moment than I might were I to simply read for enjoyment). I am asking questions to get you to think, be aware, and delve further. I agree with you that Fred's tardiness is significant for the reasons you mention. And, yes, CFs "can… also help to explain the effect he has on other people, or what characteristics (physical or personality) he uses to get what he wants." As to the first (explaining the effect he has on other people), since we are not concentrating on other people but only on him, it is important only if it means something about him. As to the latter (what characteristics he uses to get what he wants), yes, that is prima facie important, and we will be focusing more on what the character wants when we do Universal Drives. But, it also makes me ask, how do you know what he wants? And how do you know what characteristics he uses to get what he wants? This may be obvious to you (or even to your classmates), but I would like you to parse it out.

As you can see, I focus on different things at different times with students in their CF work. Always I'm trying to get students to stretch their minds and to be specific in their assertions. To some extent, this is very strict and disciplined work. At first, it seems so "hard" to have to spell everything out and explain why one arrives at each and every opinion, but after a while it becomes fun.

Robert was incorrect that I meant that "Fred's physical aspects [weren't] tied to a personality trait." I do not use either term: "aspects" or "personality trait." Nor do I require that people tie physical aspects to personality traits. Nor do I ask students to identify traits and then describe them. That is not what CF work is about.

Nor would the various combinations that Robert delineated (that he believed would add up to a physical presence, showing how Fred dominated conversations) be a "character fact," as Robert concluded. Robert cannot be faulted for looking at "character" as something the writer "creates," since this is what many writing classes require. But character facts are not part of the process of "creating characters" or constructing a finished novel or story. They are a deconstructing process which is part of the larger, global arkhelogy skill set that leads to *discovery of one's own characters.*

EXAMPLE FIVE: "Riga"

This is David's work. This is one of the most extensive examples of CF work.

1. Riga is forty-five years old. Her waist-length hair is dyed black and often gray roots are visible close to her scalp. Her eyes are almost black and are set deeply into her head. Her skin is pale and dull. She has a deep and abrasive voice and speaks in a mixture of broken English and Bosnian with a strong Slavic accent. She uses the most vulgar and profane words in both English and Bosnian in the course of every conversation. She is five foot nine and about 160 pounds.

2. Riga is Serbian. She has lived all her life in an ethnically diverse village in Bosnia. Now, after the war few Serbs remain there. Her immediate family is dead except her brother who

emigrated to Canada just after the war. They were very close. He left with his Croatian wife and Riga's three-year-old niece. Riga stares at her niece's picture often. She has extended family hundreds of miles east in Belgrade (now another country), but refuses to move. "Tuzla is home whether they want me here or not," she says.(referring to former friends and neighbors). She keeps a baseball bat by the door.

3. Riga lived alone throughout the war. When bombs fell on the city Riga would fill the bath tub with water and completely submerge herself, breathing through a tube from the washing machine. Now that the war is over she sometimes still does this.

4. Riga has never been married. Occasionally her friend Nicoli visits from a town near Sarajevo. They drink Serbian whiskey and have sex. He stays for only a few hours.

5. Riga hasn't worked since before the war when she was a chamber maid at the one hotel in town. The only money she has is from her father's small pension and rent from the occasional boarder.

6. She rises early and cooks and cleans throughout the day. She moves from room to room in her small apartment arranging pictures, rearranging rugs and polishing things. She is always noisy. During the day she bangs pots around, slams doors and drops things often. At night she snores loudly. She chain smokes throughout her waking hours. Riga had heart surgery about eight years ago. Because of the war she couldn't continue her checkups in Belgrade. Now she says she won't go back to the doctor again.

7. She usually lives alone, but sometimes takes in boarders. When she does take on boarders, she sleeps in the kitchen under the table next to the heater. Her phone rarely rings. When it does it is usually relatives in Belgrade or her brother in Canada. She cooks every day. Every day she leaves her apartment to deliver

food that she has prepared for her Muslim neighbor upstairs whose husband died in the war. A few times a week she goes to the store two blocks away to get cigarettes and food and every evening, weather permitting, she sits on the stoop of her building for about a half an hour.

8. Whenever she leaves the apartment she takes the handset of her cordless phone with her even though she knows it probably won't work.

9. She spends most evenings alone listening to old songs on the radio or reading the pages of a weekly gossip magazine from Belgrade.

JVB's Comments & Questions to David:

1. JVB: Why did you choose these facts? How do you think they are relevant? What is important about them? What do you mean by deep, abrasive? Vulgar, profane? Why did you choose Riga? Does her age matter in terms of what makes her who she is, what makes her do what she does? Does the length of her hair matter? What do you mean that her eyes are set deeply into her head? (Did you try not to use adjectives?)

2. JVB: This seems to be more character circumstances. What is significant to you about these CCs?

3. JVB: What is the significance of this? It's very interesting (to me, one of the most interesting CFs you listed), but I would like to hear from you why you chose to mention it.

4. JVB: Same question as above.

5. & 6. JVB: Same question. Why are these CFs important? From this character sketch of Riga, I get a feeling that she is "war-torn," angry and depressed. You list many interesting facts. Which ones do you think are most revealing or important?

7. JVB: It is spelled "boarders." [David had consistently spelled the word as "border."] It is an interesting spelling error, since the subject is a woman who lives where the country's boarders have often changed and where personal boundaries have been violated.

7 & 8. **JVB**: This seems to illustrate again the state of depression or hopelessness she's in. Was that your intention? Remember that the task at hand here is not to portray someone, but to think about what facts are genuine facts and which ones you think are most revealing about who a person is, and to practice not using adjectives and to watch how you use language and how your own biases may manifest themselves.

9. **JVB**: Again, why do you choose to mention this? How do you know all these things about Riga? Did you follow her around? Did she tell you? How, for example, do you know she cooks "every day"? When you write "usually" or "rarely" or "every day," these things need to have a foundation. What leads you to that conclusion? It might help to rewrite this in the definite present, rather than in the indefinite present. But, first I need to know where you got the info from.

Conversation between David & JVB:

David: You mentioned that you wanted to know where I got these facts about Riga. I lived with her as one of her boarders for over a year.

JVB: Okay, explains much. This is something that was missing. Obviously a reader can and will accept that the author is omniscient, if the author writes that way, but here our work is to look at everything, and in this exercise, to substantiate (among other things).

David: I am a little confused though because I felt that everything I wrote about her was objective and factual. You asked my why certain things were significant. Doesn't age or appearance play an important role in a person's character?

JVB: Yes, you largely succeeded in writing facts, although you did use adjectives that I did question, because an adjective is a judgment or conclusion, and you need to (at least here) substantiate or explain it. Age and appearance may certainly play a role in a person's character, but I need to know why you choose the facts you do. The reason is to get you to think and to pull all the reasons and thoughts you have out of you onto the page.

David: I couldn't say she was aggressive or lonely because that would be my own perception. So I wrote down what I thought were the facts.

JVB: My observation about her seeming angry and depressed was not intended to say that you should have used those words. I'm drawing my own conclusion there, but I am not asking you to endorse or copy it. I am offering it so you can see how your words affected me. Then I ask you to tell me which of the many interesting facts you list, you think are most revealing or important.

JVB's responses to David's questions:

This is David's response to my earlier question about his CF work.

David: I told you that I had lived with her. I chose these particular facts because I feel that although they are physical characteristics, they are also a reflection of what is going on inside her head. I suppose it is up to the reader to draw their own conclusions about the kind of woman Riga is. But because I know her better than the reader, I can choose facts and circumstances which I think reflect her character.

JVB: Thanks for explaining. This explains what I think is amiss here. You have chosen facts which you think reflect her character, so you have already decided who she is and are only listing what supports your conclusions. Remember that we try to avoid conclusions? If you decide in advance what you think her "character" is, you create a closed loop, outside of which you will not see. Also, recall that I do not use the term "character" in this way.

Now, bear with me as I try to explain the difference. It isn't easy. I use the term character only to describe anything that relates to what makes a person do what they do. I never decide in advance what I think someone's "character" is and then try to support my conclusion with facts. That would not be doing character facts. Character facts are those items which you observe which relate to why they do what they do.

Now, you have done this on the surface. You have in fact listed items which relate to why Riga does what she does. However, you have added the assumption that you should select only those facts that support what you think of her, and that you should decide what these facts mean about her before listing them. Remember my injunction against making conclusions? So, how do you observe without concluding? And if you are not to use your observations to make conclusions, then why observe? When you observe without concluding, you heighten your awareness and alertness to other details. You will use your observation powers in other ways in this method (for example, to discern discrepancies). More comments below.

David: Am I to describe her voice? Perhaps it is less subjective. I know you asked us to try not to use too many adjectives if possible. I felt that the adjectives I chose were very close to fact. I mean black is black, right?

JVB: Abrasive does seem more like opinion. But, it is not just a matter of finding a more objective adjective. See if you can do without the description. Of course, since you have already determined what is important, you will find it difficult to do without the description. Obviously, the way her voice sounds is a perfectly good character fact, in itself, if you were to use it without having already decided what it means.

David: I chose the CCs I did because each one of them has an important influence on her character as I perceived it.

"Riga is Serbian. She has lived all her life in a ethnically diverse village in Bosnia. Now, after the war few Serbs remain there. As a result of this she may feel isolated and alienated. But we don't know for sure."

JVB: Okay, again, we're not looking for what "influenced" her "character." You are using the term "character" differently than I do. In my opinion, one can NEVER decide what IS another person's "character" (to the extent that that term, when used that way, can even be defined). I don't ask you to "see" another person's "character" and then list facts about them. This brings us to a very fine point, which I will try to make clearly. I ask you to list facts which you think relate to what makes a person do what they do. So, how do you determine what makes a person do what they do, if you do not have some sense of their "character" (as used the way you mean it)? The answer is twofold: First of all, you simply ask yourself "Why do they do that?" and you gather facts which might explain it. Secondly, the skills you develop by using the other techniques in this class (as well as some beyond this class, which build on these techniques) will give you other, more powerful ways of determining meaning, of discovering what makes a person do what s/he does.

David: "Her immediate family is dead except her brother who emigrated to Canada just after the war. They were very close. He left with his Croatian wife and Riga's three-year-old niece. Riga stares at her niece's picture often." The fact that her family is gone and she stares at her niece's picture might indicate to us that she is lonely. But I didn't want to say that directly even if I might think that.

JVB: Again, you base your choice of facts on your pre-conclusions about what they might mean. I'm glad you wrote that you didn't want to say it directly. Writers are often taught to "show, not tell," and I don't have a problem with that advice generally. The problem is that it is still used to support a totally closed system of judgment about people, which cannot see outside of itself, or outside of what society wants it to see. What really is at issue here is how to really see.

David: She has extended family hundreds of miles east in Belgrade (now another country), but refuses to move. "Tuzla is home whether they want me here or not," she says (referring to former friends and neighbors). She keeps a baseball bat by the door.

These facts could lead a reader to conclude that she is stubborn and feels threatened. All of the facts above could have a very strong impact on a person's character. I could have added that she smokes a particular type of cigarettes and that too could be telling, but in a much more subtle way. For example if she smoked Drina cigarettes, the brand of the former Yugoslavia, it might reflect something different than if she smoked West or Camel or rolling tobacco for that matter. But the meaning of these differences would be difficult for the reader to identify. So I stuck with common ground material like her appearance, etc.

JVB: Eh eh eh, David, this is the best paragraph you've written here. Because the particular type of cigs she smokes is relevant, even if we don't know what it means. That IS a good (an excellent) CF.

David: Forgive me for rambling slightly, but I always feel compelled to explain culturally or politically relevant details when my character happens to be foreign or a scene is taking place in a foreign context. Then when I reread the piece, it sometimes feels unnatural and condescending. I want to just write and assume that everything will be understood but at the same time I'm afraid readers won't "get" it.

JVB: I agree that cultural and political facts are relevant. As to the condescension, I think that is caused by the fact that you have prejudged her.

David: That for many months after the war finished and probably still today, she continues to submerge herself. Well, although I feel it speaks for itself and is better left to the reader to interpret themselves, to me it reflects her desire during the war to escape to a more peaceful place. It became a kind of coping mechanism, one which she continues to employ in a time of external "peace." I think I mentioned it because it's slightly bizarre and at the same time it makes perfect sense in many ways. I tried to highlight defining characteristics which would stimulate the formation of an image or an idea of this woman in the minds of readers.

JVB: I think the reason why I asked you about this was because I sensed what I've mentioned above, that you are pre-concluding. The ability to see the meaning in an action is absolutely one of the abilities a writer must possess. However, another subtle distinction: the act of writing is not (in my opinion), at its best, about representing something to readers. While a writer must certainly be conscious, on some level, of how to reach readers, how to affect them and, as it were, get inside of their heads and hearts, writing is not a mere manipulative device (I'm sure you didn't intend to say that it was — mind you, I am taking your point to the extreme — a typical lawyer tactic). What must first happen is an INTERNAL event, which the writer must then translate to the readers. The internal event (in you, the writer) is what this course is about.

David: With the bit about Nicoli and Riga's sex and whiskey visits, he was just a friend at best, but more importantly, he was Serbian as was the whiskey. This has everything to do with identity.

JVB: Hm. Do you want to guess what my comment is here?

David: You mention that you get the feeling that Riga is angry and depressed. For me Riga is what she is. It wasn't my intention to make her sound any particular way. I was attempting to present facts and let the reader draw conclusions.

JVB: I don't think so. Yes, I think you intended to show, not tell, but you wanted the reader to draw the conclusions you wanted to put in their minds. That may be what many writers want to do, but it isn't what we are doing here.

Notice how David continued to speak about how to get readers to conclude what he wanted them to conclude. He said he didn't talk about what cigarettes Riga smoked because "these differences would be difficult for the reader to identify." He said "I'm afraid readers won't 'get' it." Riga continuing to "submerge herself" was "better left to the reader to interpret themselves." He noted that he "tried to highlight defining characteristics which would stimulate the formation of an image or an idea of this woman in the minds of readers." And after all this, he says that "It wasn't my intention to make her sound any particular way. I was attempting to present facts and let the reader draw conclusions." But this is disingenuous, for almost all of David's remarks show that he was in fact trying to get the reader to see in his portrait what he wanted them to see, and that his entire focus was on this objective. In other words, his objective was not to simply find the character facts that might answer his own questions about Riga, but to make others see or feel what he wanted them to see or feel, which was, of course, what he had already concluded about her.

While it is of course quite possible that David's conclusions were absolutely correct — clearly, David is a very observant person — he was NOT doing character facts. He was therefore not using the Nosanthro skill (at least not in front of me — he might have used it to arrive at his "pre" conclusions, but there is no way I could know that since he had already made those conclusions).

What this exchange reveals, too, is how subtle the ways may be in which people avoid doing the fairly straightforward task of CFs. Because David had long ago been taught to believe that his entire goal in writing should be to "show not tell," he was unable to absorb or follow my simple instruction that this assignment did not involve writing something for readers to consume. Although he did not exactly write a story and he did try to stay close to facts, he nonetheless still attempted to write something of a finished piece the goal of which was to affect me as a reader, rather than to find facts. One of the most revealing factual items was the matter of which cigarettes Riga smoked, but he left that out only because his main concern was whether the reader would "get it." So David's facts were subtly interwoven with his abiding concern about audience perception, rather than being concerned with what facts might reveal things to him about the person.

Perhaps it is easier to think of character facts more as questions. I see a very thin homeless man on a street corner with a sign that says, "Everybody needs help some time." But I note that he has a beard nearly two feet long. What does that mean about him? Where has this man been? How long has he been homeless or out of work?

ADDITIONAL READING

Along with the character facts exercise, I also suggest students refer to the following books.

- Anthony Weston's *Rulebook for Arguments* (Hackett, 1992) gives a lot of great examples of how to use facts (although they are not character facts).

- Melissa Bruder's *Practical Handbook for the Actor* (Vintage, 1986) shows very succinctly how to concentrate on "do-able" (and therefore observable) actions. It is, of course, from the actor's point of view, not from a writer/observer.

- S. Loraine Hull's *Strasberg's Method* (Ox Box Publishing, 1985) and the Introduction in Charles McGaw's *Working on a Scene: An Actor's Approach* (Holt, Rinehart & Winston, 1977) give some helpful tips on handling character information. Clearly, these are intended for actors, but the questions "What is he doing? Where is he?" "When did he get there?"

The big problem is that in trying to embody ourselves, we change what we are into something we aren't, something we think we ought to be, etc., and we lose the simple being-ness of being ourselves. So the trick is to be ourselves, to read ourselves accurately, and to transcribe ourselves as we are, while still being (and not losing) our sense of self. This is as true of our own selves as with other selves, other persons we observe.

or "What happened before he said this?" "What is her emotional condition? What is his relationship to others in this situation?" are all character questions that can be applied to people in real life and help in obtaining usable character facts.

CHAPTER EIGHT

BEING IN THE MOMENT
(Kronobo)

[T]here is… a consciousness which is capable of temporarily arresting, both conceptually and perceptually, segments of the universal continuum. This objective consciousness might be seen as a reduced velocity of the universal consciousness, and has as its instrument the cerebral cortex of man.
— Robert Lawlor, *Sacred Geometry: Philosophy & Practice*

Being in the moment is essential to archetype work. At its simplest, "being in the moment" means being present, feeling your feelings, experiencing everything in that moment as fully as possible. Sometimes being in the moment is referred to as "being mindful" or "living in the now."

Part of being in the moment is slowing yourself down to a point where time seems to be nearly suspended. Being in the moment means that you stop believing that every next moment is the moment you need to be in, that somehow the moment you are in is only valuable as a prelude to the next moment. It means acceptance of where you are. Being or living in the moment could also be termed "letting the moment happen." This is a technique that actors can use to great benefit in their performances. The actor works to just experience each moment of the scene as s/he moves through it, letting each moment happen each time afresh.

Suspending time means taking "being in the moment" to such an extreme that you do not sense time passing. Those who engage in drawing or painting often experience this suspension of time, and it is this almost detached but heightened state that is central to archetype work.

Suspending time is what writers must do when they recreate a moment: First they must stop the moment in their minds' eye, look at it, turn it over again and again in their mind, think about it, feel it, and relive it, as they recreate it.

The ultimate purpose, then, of being in the moment, from the writer's point of view, is to suspend time. Of course, we are not talking about actually stopping the universal flow of time. We are just talking about suspending our *sense of time*. The Being in the Moment (BIM) exercise is simply the conscious attempt to slow down one's sense of time and to maintain a sense of hovering above a moment of time.

The benefits of the exercise are multifold. One definition of archetypes is "still moments revealing a continuous, timeless, universal action." (See discussion of Being in the Moment in Chapters 2 and 17.) Thus, archetype work can be seen as the work of finding those "still moments" that reveal a continuous, timeless, universal action. The more you are able to be in the moment, the better you will discern the universal, archetypal patterns.

Secondly, in order to experience what another person experiences, you must ultimately be able to go into the moment in which that person lives and feels. (In this exercise, however, you will be going only into your own moment. We will use the analogue exercise to step into the shoes of others.) So, the exercise works to help train you to attain a state of readiness to other states. Thirdly, the exercise trains you to stop, watch, and experience. It works to heighten awareness. Finally, being in the moment assists in attaining the meditative or trance states which accompany highly creative work.

Being in the moment work is work that can (and, from a writer's point of view, should) be done nearly all the time. It is a fundamental, underlying component of all the rest of the techniques in this approach.

THE EXERCISE

It is helpful to break down this exercise into segments.

(1) A Moment
First, write down what you consider to be your experience of a moment. I prefer you use the moment you are in, rather than hunting for another

moment, because I don't want you to be using memory, or to try to select one moment over another. Those actions use different brain functions and I don't want you diverted. So, just write down what is going on in this moment.

(2) Replay & Slow Motion (BIM Questions) — Hovering

Second, try to zoom in on one instant of the moment. For example, I am sitting here at my desk, typing this. That is my moment. Ordinarily, I would not be aware of anything but what I'm typing (unless something distracted me). But, when I try to zoom in, I must ask myself what I'm feeling, what do my fingers feel like on the keyboard, where am I in space and time, what is going on around me, what IS this act I am doing?

In asking these types of questions of yourself, two things should happen. First, you will need to replay the moment over and over again in your mind. Second, in order to replay the moment, you will need to slow everything down in your mind.

If you do these two parts (writing out the moment and then replaying, slowing down, and zooming in), you will have completed the assignment.

(3) Going Between — Trance

The third phase — trance work — is not part of the exercise because it usually cannot be attained consciously since it is part of the process of setting aside conscious control. So generally it is better attained through peripheral work, through working with discrepancies and juxtapositions, which are described later in this book, or in doing combinations of the exercises, which you can begin to do after you master each skill separately. I discuss it here, however, to show that it is part of being in the moment.

In the third part, you begin to go *between* the events you experience, go between the spaces within the moment. This "going-between act" can only be achieved in an altered state of consciousness, in a trance state. In such a state, one's sense of linear and logical thinking shifts into "trance logic," which utilizes what is known as "both/and" thinking, a mental/emotional state in which the mind is able to accept and process discrepant and contradictory things. (See Chapter 19 for more on trance logic.)

For now, focus on eliciting, replaying, slowing down and zooming in.

VIDEOS

There are several videos that you can watch as additional BIM work. The pilot episode of *Quantum Leap*, if you can find it, is a good example of the "presentness" of being in the moment — in that case, the experience of Dr. Sam Beckett, who travels not only into a different time but a different body and life. He cannot draw on any history or background, at first, but must depend solely on his in-the-moment impressions.

Another old movie, *Final Approach*, contains over an hour of in-the-moment experience by a pilot who finds himself in some place after a plane accident he can't recall. Everything he knows, once again, is what he derives from the moment.

Another film, *Fearless*, with Jeff Bridges, contains an example of the hovering over a moment when Bridges' character is in a plane crash. Similar to other movies that expand a moment by drawing it out in slow-motion (like the car chase scene in *Mission Impossible 2*). Movies with slow-motion fight scenes, car accidents, or near death scenes do this, and are helpful in making you aware of how much can go into a moment. *Jacob's Ladder* is an entire movie about the dying moments of a man, who experiences a whole bizarre series of events in his mind as he's dying. Similar to this is the *Star Trek: The Next Generation* episode "The Inner Light," in which Captain Picard experiences an entire other life as another person on a long-dead alien planet as he is lying unconscious on the Enterprise, having been zapped by a mysterious "probe."

READING

There are several articles I compiled over the years which I feel have some interesting discussion or expressions about being in the moment. Most of these are impossible to find now, but two of the best of these are available. One is an excerpt from a book, *Diary of a Baby*, by Daniel N. Stern, which is available on Amazon. The other, an article by John Wren-Lewis, "A Terrible Beauty," can be found at *www.nonduality.com/hl1755.htm*, towards the bottom of the page.

Diary of a Baby focuses on what a baby experiences in the very first moments. Since babies have no experience to draw upon, they live totally in the moment. It is an excellent example of *being in the moment.* "A Terrible Beauty" is about a woman who emerges from a coma. She doesn't remember who she is, who her children are, etc., so she must live in the moment.

EXAMPLES

Success in this exercise is measured not so much by the *result* of the process as by how much of the process is visible. This means you may see quite a difference between what I accept from one person and what I accept from another. The following are examples from students' work from one semester, with my comments following.

Peter's work:

1) A Moment

I am sitting in my study, writing out this assignment, listening to my dog scream for its ball (no doubt trapped under the radiator again).

2) Replay and Slow Motion

I feel warm: it's humid and hot in Washington, the room is small and gets little air through the single window. I reach up with my index finger to type the b in bmyb. I feel a slight stretch of the ligament in my finger, along with the hardness of the desk against my wrists (somehow I never adopted the recommended hand placement for typing, with wrists raised) and a slight ache in my thighs since this is an uncomfortable kitchen chair, not really suitable for working at a desk. I am looking at the letter appear on my screen. I am slightly irritated, both because I don't really understand the assignment and because my dog has an incredibly loud bark that makes it hard to concentrate. In fact, I tense up slightly with the noise as I type the letter, raising my shoulders and setting my face in a grimace.

I wrote Peter that this was a very good first effort. I added that the replay, however, was really more of an elaboration than a slowing down and internal replay. I instructed Peter to use his original words and work with only them, or around them, not beyond them into reasons and thoughts or explanations, to stay with the initial thing he wrote.

Since I do not have a record of Peter reworking this assignment, let me give an example of how it might have been reworked:

> I am sitting in my study. I sit. I feel myself sitting. What is sitting? What does sitting mean? I am writing out this assignment. Writing. What is this act of writing? My pen is moving over the page.

That would be a slowing down and replay. After this, I would instruct the student to isolate out an instant of the various components of the moment s/he has chosen. So:

> I sit. Sitting in quiet. Air around me. Sitting in the entire universe, on a chair, not on the ground, not squatting. Sitting of all things. I sit. I. What does it mean that I sit? What am I?

This would be about as far as I would want a student to go with this, because the oddity of this work is that the more you go more into the moment, the more it dissolves into everything else! That, in fact, is part of what the exercise teaches. It teaches both how to BE in the moment and how every moment contains every other moment. If you go too far beyond the experience of just being in the moment, you find yourself questioning yourself, your very existence, and the nature of reality itself. I want students to touch this experience but not go too far into it.

More examples of early being-in-the-moment work (see if you can do the second step of isolating an instant with one or more of these):

Mary's work:

As for the BIMs, here is a first go at it:

1) A Moment — this moment
   To contemplate over what is claimed to be a hard assignment.

2) Replay and Slow Motion
   Slow mo — My hands are freezing and people are moving a lot around me. My water is standing still and I have a mess on my desk. I hear sirens coming from outside and the sound of the air-

conditioner blowing out freezing air to cool an empty office. Most people are out to lunch, but I am still here. I have the taste of leftover chocolate in my mouth from the Reeses Peanut Butter cup I ate a moment ago. What I am actually doing in this moment — I am hesitating.

When I say hesitating, I actually am talking about doing the assignment. Mind you I figured this out before I actually started writing to you. So, this assignment was done a moment ago - not right now (as I type).

(Try doing step two on this.)

Alex's work:

Perhaps this is all too abstract… it is what I felt in the moment. Each piece is like a layer of what I felt although each thing might not have been recognized consciously during that moment until I replayed it over and over after it had passed. I don't think I added something which wasn't there.

Being in the Moment
I sit in front of my computer fighting distracting thoughts. My stomach gurgles from the coffee I drank. Birds chirp outside and a plane passes overhead. I pause, think, type, pause… delete.

My mind flashes, darkness, light, lists, faces, anxiety, tension, hollow stomach. Blood pulses inside my ears, fingers. My heart beats. Impulses and electricity, my finger taps the key.

(Or this.)

Leonora's work:

I have been struggling with this exercise. Every time I sat down to do it, it seemed like it was more of a mental exercise and I wasn't in the moment. Rather, I was outside the moment trying to see the moment. So this morning, when I first woke up, I had the idea to try and record a moment with a handheld tape recorder I use for work. Then I came in and typed word for word what I spoke into the recorder.

A Moment

I am standing on my blacktop paved driveway, with a small tape recorder in my left hand, speaking into the tape recorder, trying to record a moment of my life. In my right hand, I am holding a sprinkler hose watering my newly laid down grass seed. It is 7:30 am, with a slight chill to the morning air.

Replay and Slow Motion

I hear the softly gentle cascade of the water as I watch it emit from the hose. A few drops of water slide off into my hand. I think, maybe I better replace the hose washer, so it doesn't leak.

Then, I re-notice the water and watch the light of the morning as it comes through the stream from the hose. It seems to take me to a moment of reflection, as I try to sense what it feels like to be "in a moment" without being mental about it. A multitude of songbirds whistle off in the distance, interrupted by the coo, coo, cooooo of a mourning dove. The sounds make me notice the silence more.

The air feels crisp, almost alive, fresh, after last night's storm. There is a slight breeze rustling the leaves of the trees at the perimeter of my lawn. I glance over at them.

I breathe in and out, trying to zoom in, and ah! just for a moment feel that I am right here with a hose, a tape recorder, the chill of the morning, the birds, the breeze, and the silence.

(Or this.)

Alex's work

Here is my shot at BIM, actually something I think I'm very good at. In some ways the here and now is everything — at least what really matters to me.

I'm sitting at my computer in my office trying to capture the present moment in words.

Trying to sort out this moment in words, I'm losing attention, focusing on the light rain falling in the high desert in front of my window. Storm clouds are building to the west, dead center in my window. There's the gentle tapping of rain on the roof; a sound that makes me sleepy; the cottonwood to the left of my window glistens with droplets, leaves swaying in time to some distant beat; the pine to my right seems to smile. I imagine the smell of desert creosote and the feel of coming storm winds on my drying flesh. All is as it should be, as I embrace it all, forgetting the computer. Then, the distractions are no longer distractions, and I am comfortable.

(Or this.)

Alex also posted a poem:

I'd like to share lines from one of my favorite poets/singers/musicians, Joy Harjo, a Creek Indian from Oklahoma and New Mexico, that affirms BIM:

"I don't imagine the turquoise bracelet the dusky wash makes,
or the red hills circling the dreaming eye of this sacred land.
I don't imagine anything but the bracelet around my wrist,
the red scarf around my neck as I urge my pretty horse home."

Sorry, Jennifer, for taking up time, but I find these lines that probably best belong in my Indian class to capture the moment exquisitely.

(I agreed with Alex. The poem is very much about being in the moment, but of course it is a description of being in the moment, rather than the experience of it.)

My comments on all posted so far:

I think all of you who have posted so far have been fairly successful in the first stage of BIM work. What I look for in your work here is whether I can see you trying to slow down and replay. I am not looking for elaboration, but it is hard to show slowing down and replaying without some elaboration, I think.

So: Bill writes "I feel warm: it's humid and hot in Washington, the room is small…" "I feel warm" is an elaboration of "I am sitting in my study." However, it is part of his experience of the moment. He simply didn't say so at first. But, when Bill writes, "it's humid and hot," these are explanations to the reader, which are unnecessary to this exercise. "I reach up with my index finger" is, I think, a replay, although Bill didn't mention

93

it in section (1), A Moment. "I feel a slight stretch" and pretty much the rest (except for necessary explanations) seem to be replays.

Most of you have some linear cognition going on, which can be left out, such as "Most people are out to lunch." Or in Leonora's, the mental frame of mind which is behind writing "softly gentle cascade of the water" or "water... slides off my hand." These are evocative and descriptive, and probably also expressive, but because descriptive, not in the moment. In order to make that descriptive statement, you must think about it enough to write it. (Maddening distinctions, eh? Of COURSE, you have to think about it! You have to think about any of it, don't you, to write it!)

But, my point is that I want you NOT to describe so much as JUST to experience. There is a very subtle shift inside the brain when you explain or describe, which takes you away from the state of being.

I don't want to dwell too much on these choices, just point them out. Although I rarely pick favorites, I do want to point out how raw David's piece is. There is some description in the first paragraph ("I sit in front... My stomach gurgles... birds chirp"), but the second paragraph contains largely momentary impressions which David does not attempt to explain or describe. Mind you, this sort of "free association" type thing can also become representative, but I don't think David is doing so here.

Most important, I felt that all of you experienced the first stages, if you will, of being in the moment. As I noted earlier, and as the Proust excerpt above explains better, the experience "outside of time" is most likely to occur within the experience of a particular sort of juxtaposition (which Proust later calls "the miracle of analogy" but I think that phrase is misleading — not all analogies will bring one to this state — more on this soon).

Let's try out some second step work with another one of the above examples. Let's use Mary's. Mary identifies the moment as "to contemplate over what is claimed to be a hard assignment." That is not really a moment. It's a task. In her replay, she describes her sensory impressions and her thoughts. She concludes that she is actually hesitating.

How would we isolate a moment from Mary's example? Because Mary describes a series of sensory impressions, it is hard to tell what the moment IS. So, let's simply pick one part to focus on. This is my version of the second step:

Hands freezing and people moving around her. What does it mean to have freezing hands? What does it mean in the universe? Freezing hands at a desk in a city of millions on planet earth in the solar system. Freezing hands and people moving around her. People moving, hands freezing. What are the hands doing here with people moving around them? What are the people doing here with these freezing hands?

Every being-in-the-moment work will be different. The idea is *to NOT move forward*. The idea is to stay put where you are in your mind, in time, and in physical space. How can you do this in actuality? You *hover*. You simply hover over yourself in that instant. You stay with one little act in time and you replay it, as if you were rewinding a tape and playing it again and again. If you did that, if you watched your own action — just a single one in time and place — what would you perceive? You might think all sorts of things but the point of the exercise is not to think. It is just to BE in that moment.

I have found that asking ontological questions — questions about existence or place in the universe, the meaning of it all — help a person to stay in the moment. You ask the questions but don't answer them. Just stay with them. Stay with the wondering. Stay with the impression of that moment.

There does not need to be any great meaning assigned to what you elicit here. In fact, if you try for meaning, you will go beyond the exercise and effectively undo what the exercise does. The meaning is just the existence of you, there, in that moment, in the midst of all else.

As I noted above, this effort can lead one to question one's very existence or the existence of any and everything else. But the point of this work is not to convince you that we are all figments of our own imaginations or that everything is relative or that meaning cannot be obtained from our lives.

There are actually many reasons why this exercise is a crucial one. It teaches you to get beyond or outside of the idea that everything must happen linearly and that all truth is found in sequence. It teaches you how better to experience yourself and it gives you a tool for how to go into the moment of another person's experience (which we will use in analogues and other parts of this approach). It also teaches about the "being that exists outside of time" that Marcel Proust describes in his novel. It teaches that there is a part of you that exists, as it were, outside of time, that knows everything. This is the part I call the "Author Self." It is this part that will eventually guide your journey in writing.

For now, try hovering with the present moment in your life and see what you experience. Write it down.

CHAPTER NINE

UNIVERSAL DRIVES
(*Nos-Amianthy*)

Universal drives are basic drives that all humans share. Every person is driven by one or another of the basic human drives. Every action we take arises out of these drives. It is obvious that the writer's awareness of universal drives (UDs) is crucial to characterization — what character can be believable without drives? But the skill of identifying UDs is rarely acknowledged or encouraged. We call the skill of finding UDs *nos-amianthy*. (See below for discussion.)

This chapter will help you to develop that skill.

The three most basic drives are the drive to survive and the drives to love and be loved. Most other drives upon closer consideration collapse into one or more of these three. However, other possible UDs are the drive to become one with the mother/universe (return to the womb); the drive to protect/nurture (maternal instinct); the drive to procreate (sex drive, reproduction); the drive to accomplish (love of accomplishment, will power); the drive to realize the Core Self (which includes acknowledgment by others of one's Core Self) (this drive may also be synonymous with the drive to create, ambition); the drive to be free of pain and the drive to feel pleasure (the pleasure principle).

Other possible drives may be the drive to conquer, to hold territory (ambition? survival?); to attain sustenance (survival?); to pair bond (mating drive, survival?); to form and participate in a social group (drive to socialize? survival?); attain rank or power within a group (ambition?).

What is important in this inquiry is to do the work of boiling down every action to the most basic, fundamental *modus operandi* or drive. It is not so much the end result as much as the *doing*, the *using of the skill of nos-amianthy* that is important.

THE SKILL OF FINDING UDS: NOS-AMIANTHY

Because there is no English word for "the skill of finding universal drives" and because it is a unique mental activity without a name, we have created a word out of Ancient Greek roots to describe and label the skill: nos-amianthy.[12]

Nos-amianthy is a kind of a backward process. You work backwards from character facts and goals to UDs. The reason why I say this is backwards is that once you find the UD, you can see that the character goals and the character facts all flow from the UD, but the UD must be found *through* working with the character facts and goals.

Yet, as one develops this skill, one is increasingly able to keep possible UDs in mind while one works through the character facts and goals, until the nos-amianthy integrates with and absorbs the skills of identifying character facts and goals.

Nos-amianthy is related to the analogue skill. The analogue skill is simply the ability to bring home to oneself what another person feels or experiences (empathy). In nos-amianthy we do more than use our empathic skills; we try to see the person within the context of his entire life, imagine what struggles the person has had and continues to have, consider the possible origins of those struggles, and try to imagine what keeps him going, what is behind all he does, and where it will all lead him to (destiny). This is the start of arkhelogy work in one way, by starting to work with the larger questions.

But it is also a discrete, unique skill of its own that exists separate from yet included in arkheloging and has existed in humankind for at least many hundreds if not thousands of years, and likely from the beginning of our existence. Without this skill, the ancient Greek playwrights could not have written the powerful dramas that still come as alive on stage as they did three thousand years ago.

THE EXERCISE

1. Choose a monologue from each assigned book.

I ask students to choose a character in a monologue or scene from one of two collections of plays, and then afterwards, to choose another from the other collection. The reason for starting this way is that it is easier to isolate and define the relevant character facts, and easier to identify and confirm the character's goals, both their overarching goal through the play and their specific goal within a scene or monologue. Once character goals are identified in this limited context, UDs can be more easily discerned.

There are two books I have used for years for this exercise: Ginger Friedman's *The Perfect Monologue* and Stefan Rudnicki's *Classical Monologues*. Friedman utilizes contemporary plays and Rudnicki, of course, classical plays. Yet each contains a tremendous range of material.

Friedman's book contains selections of scenes from modern plays and her explanations of each character she chooses. The book is intended to show actors how to create "the perfect monologue" by creating one out of a scene. In the process of doing this, Friedman shows the student how to identify what drives the character, since the successful condensation of a dialogue into a monologue requires an understanding of what drives the selected character, according to Friedman. Thus, Friedman includes the full scene, a condensation into a monologue, and her discussion of the drive(s).

Rudnicki's book gives excellent short summaries of each set of characters and period of history, where applicable (as many of the classical plays are historical), and with the monologues from ancient Greek plays, Rudnicki has selected his favorite translations, the texts of which he has broken up to make them easier to understand and work with.

2. Read through the monologue and/or scene and any other information provided about the character and circumstance.

3. Write a sentence or two about what you think the character's goals are in the monologue/scene.

4. If you know it, write a sentence or two about what you think the character's main goals are for the entire play. If these are the same as for the monologue or scene, simply say so. If the character's larger goals are different (and if you know what they are) from the monologue goals, articulate how these goals are different.

5. What drives do the goals satisfy? If the character's goal is to win an election, what drives him or her to win that election? If you find that the overall drive is not any of the UDs identified above, ask yourself whether the drive can be subsumed one of the UDs. Ask yourself which UD above applies.

I also ask students to read portions of G. Clayton Viddler's *The Principles of Seduction*, in which the author explains the drives behind falling in love.

SOME HELPFUL OBSERVATIONS ABOUT UDs

UDs are larger than an individual moment or situation. So someone being in love with someone cannot be a drive. A specific feeling of love for someone is not the same thing as the drive to be loved or to love.

Articulate in the affirmative (can't be an avoidance of something).

UDs are generally not conscious on the part of the person whom they drive.

They underlie all else. The bottom line.

Grief is an emotion. Emotions can drive a person, and although emotions are universal, they are not the same as UDs. Emotions may arise from attempts to satisfy a drive, however.

The need for absolution (guilt?) is not a UD. Not guilt, not exoneration, not rage, not grief. Guilt is an emotion, not a drive. Wanting exoneration is similar. Rage and grief are emotions.

The drive to merge with the mother might be a UD. This is the same as the drive to merge with the universe, which may be found in some instances of suicide or the creation of works of art.

To be free of pain? Possibly a UD.

Protective instinct? Possibly.

Power and control are not UDs. I do not believe that the drives toward power or control are really about the drive to survive or be loved. They usually arise out of a feeling of LACK (lack of security, lack of love — although it could manifest as a lack of money, lack of recognition, etc.).

Destiny does not take action out of a character's hands. It puts it inevitably into her hands.

Medea: to kill her sons — rage, hatred, because she isn't loved, rage against the Gods, against her lover, against her destiny, because all she wanted was to be loved, and not to be loved gives her too much pain to bear. She must stop the pain. She kills its source.

Tyrell — making oneself important, getting your way, earning esteem, having your place are specific goals or needs behind the UD. The question of why Tyrell can only feel loved by bullying is separate from the question of what drives him.

Exonerating oneself is a reaction, not a drive.

Lear's drive — he abandons his drive to survive as he was — his new drive is to merge with the mother (universe). (Thus, a character can switch UDs. This does not mean one UD becomes extinct. All UDs exist at all times in everyone. But a different UD can come into play or prominence in a person's life.)

A conscious belief in love is not = drive to be loved or to love.

Killing oneself can be the drive to survive because it is a desire for a new life. Grief is behind it. Grief is confusing because grief can drive some-one to kill himself, but it is actually the drive to survive or be loved, or free of pain, the sense of loss from loss of all that one feels one is (survival) or the loss of love or a loved one. The circumstances that lead to an action do not necessarily reveal the UD. For example, the loss of a loved one may cause one such grief that one decides not to live, but what is actually driving that person is not grief, but the need to be loved.

How do you find the UD, then? You work backwards.

Suicide may be a genuine attempt to save oneself from some sort of perceived annihilation of the Self. To live = not living. To live = to die. Cannot bear her grief so living is a living death; dying is the only way to keep herself safe and intact. Go to a better place, preserve her truth.

The drive to love presupposes TOTAL love, love that cannot be erad-icated, love that equals the extent of one's existence. It is not = obsession. It always exists — is sometimes projected onto a love object.

Objectives or goals are doable things.

Drives underlie objectives/goals.

EXAMPLES

Prisoner of Second Avenue:
The Drive to Survive

Let's start with a monologue Friedman condensed from Neil Simon's play, *The Prisoner of Second Avenue*. This is Mel's wife Edna, talking to Mel.

> Has something happened? Have they said anything? Nothing has hap-
> pened yet, Mel. There's no point in worrying about it now. And what
> if they did? We'd live, we'd get by. You'd get another job somewhere.
> All right, suppose something *did* happen? Suppose you *did* lose your
> job? It's not the end of the world. We don't have to live in the city. We
> could move somewhere in the country or even out West. The girls are
> in college now, we have enough to see them through. We don't need
> much for the two of us. We could move to Europe. To Spain. Two
> people could live for fifteen hundred dollars a year in Spain. You could
> work there, get some kind of job. What is that they have here that's so
> damned hard to give up? What is it you'll miss so badly, for God's sake?
> What kind of life is this? You live like some kind of caged animal in a
> Second Avenue zoo that's too hot in one room, too cold in another,
> overcharged for a growth on the side of the building they call a ter-
> race that can't support a cactus plant, let alone two human beings. Is
> this what you call a worthwhile life? Banging on the walls and
> jiggling toilets? I will go anywhere in the world you want to go, Mel.
> I will live in a cave, a hut, or a tree. I will live on a raft in the Amazon
> jungle if that's what you want to do. Just don't look at me like I'm
> insane. I am trying to offer reasonable suggestions. I am not responsible.
> I am not the one who's doing this to you. What do you want from
> me? *What do you want from anyone?*

Before reading further, ask yourself what Edna's UDs are. Friedman writes about this scene/monologue:

> So, you are at your wit's end. Your husband, whom you love dearly,
> seems to be cracking up before your eyes. He is terrified about losing
> his job, and it appears as if nothing is working for him, right down to

the smallest thing. You are now very frightened by his behavior. This is not normal. This is not your Mel. You've seen this coming, but the way he is acting right now is downright nightmarish. *You are fighting for the rest of your life.* Mel is the rest of your life. You love him and want to do anything in the world to help him and you want to help yourself too so that you don't lose him — and this is a comedy.

Friedman uses the facts presented by Edna's own words to zero right in on her UD: Edna is fighting for the rest of her life. What UD is this? The drive to survive. This drive is often called the survival instinct, which is somewhat misleading for character work. The term survival instinct has more of the flavor of what one must possess to survive in the wild. It is, of course, sometimes applied to surviving in the business world or the asphalt jungle, but really with the same flavor. But the drive to survive is not just a primitive instinct. It is a very real operational drive in every human being and it pops up in the most ordinary events which don't appear to implicate survival at all. Thus, Edna's drive to survive is "triggered" by Mel's panic over losing his job.

Now let's look at another scene later in the same play, in which Edna reveals that she too lost her job. This is, again, Friedman's condensation of the scene into a monologue. Edna is again speaking.

We went out of business today. The business that I'm in is out of business. There is no business in that place anymore. If *they're* not staying, what do they need me for? They went bankrupt. They overextended themselves. One of the partners may go to jail. I had no inkling. I did, but I was afraid to think about it. What's happening, Mel? Is the whole world going out of business? I thought we were such a strong country, Mel. If you can't depend on America, who can you depend on? I don't understand how a big place like that can just go out of business. It's not a little candy store. It's a big building. It's got stone and marble with gargoyles on the roof. Beautifully hand-chiseled gargoyles, Mel. A hundred years old. They'll come tomorrow with a sledge hammer and kill the gargoyles. You know what I thought about on my way home? One thing. I only had one thing on my mind. A bath! A nice, hot bath. And now the water went out of business. *I want my bath! I want my water! Tell them I want my bath, Mel!* Bang on the pipes. Tell them there's a woman upstairs who needs an emergency bath. If I don't sit in some water, Mel, I'm going to go crazy. Bang on the pipes. *I banged for you, why won't you bang for me?* I don't know what I'm saying anymore. It's too much for me, Mel. I have no strength left, Mel. Nothing. I couldn't open my pocketbook on the bus, a little boy had to help me, Mel, who's going to take care of us? *You,* Mel? Let's leave, Mel. Let's give up and leave! Let them have it! Let them have their city! Let them keep their garbage and their crooks and their jobs and their broken gargoyles. I just want to live out the rest of my life with you and see my girls grow up healthy and happy and once in a while I would like to have some water and take a bath. Please, Mel. Please!

A student in one of my classes identified Edna's goal in this scene as follows:
"Edna's need is to be comforted. However, since she sees herself as the care giver, she has a hard time accepting care or trusting anyone can be there for her." The student listed Edna's life goal as "To take care of her family. To lead a peaceful life away from the hassles of the city." And Edna's universal drive as: "Edna wants to take care of and be taken care of."

This student was not wrong about Edna's needs, but compare to Friedman:

> Edna is wrought up from *before* her first line of dialogue. The important thing to remember is to communicate *very* strongly to Mel. That is the way to approach the hysteria. You need to tell Mel, your partner and lover in life. He must be there to help you. You've helped him. Now he *must* help you. Make it more important than it appears on the page. She is frightened for herself, them, and the entire country. She is afraid that Mel will not be able to take care of her. He simply must. With all her fears, she too has an awareness of the absurdities and ironies of life. So must you.

Notice that Friedman identifies the same need for Edna as my student did: the need to be taken care of. But notice the difference between "need to be comforted and taken care of" and "[Mel] *must* help you" or "she is frightened." While Friedman advises her readers to "make it more important than it appears on the page," this is not because she advocates exaggerating or wants to denigrate Edna's fears or needs. It is because drives *are* fundamentally larger than any given situation. Again, drives are in play in every situation, no matter how ordinary and inconsequential that situation may appear, and drives should never be underestimated in trying to understand or explain human actions. They are the most powerful forces in human beings.

Taking another quick look back at my student's work on this scene, notice that the student adds something not in the scene at all. The student says that Edna "has a hard time accepting care or trusting anyone can be there for her." Now, this student may have read the rest of the play and made this determination or she may have just deduced it from Edna's panic, or projected it from her own propensities, but it is not a fact evident from the scene itself. None of these potential reasons for adding that statement are particularly bad ones, but it is important for the student to decide which it is. It is very important to stay close to the facts. It is equally important to keep deductions within close range of those facts.

Additionally, neither having a hard time accepting care nor having a hard time trusting anyone is a universal drive.

Finally, notice the relative weakness of a drive to be comforted/be taken care of versus a drive, in essence, to be saved. Edna is pleading with her husband to save her. What drive does that involve? The drive to survive.

When looking for drives, look always for the strongest reason, even if it seems exaggerated. Why is this so? Because drives are not the intellectual gloss we pile up on top of our childhood fears: they are the fears and needs we have right from birth, when our lives actually do depend on those most basic things: being loved and being fed and protected. Without that most basic care, infants do not survive and thrive, and within each and every one of us those needs and drives continue to exist behind and underneath everything we do and strive to do. Our adult intellectual minds try to water down those drives — to diminish them and make them seem less important — because we are, every day, trying to conquer them. Even admitting we have those drives means we are vulnerable still. Thus, doing UD work takes tremendous courage and insight. It also must never be done out of spite. It requires deep empathy for ourselves and fellow human beings.

Madame Rosepettle in *Oh Dad, Poor Dad*:
The Drive to Be Loved

The full title of this hilarious and frightening farce is *Oh Dad, Poor Dad, Mamma's Hung You in the Closet and I'm Feelin' So Sad*. The play is by Arthur L. Kopit. Madame Rosepettle is, as Friedman says, "the ultimate protective mother... you might say 'monster mother'!" In this scene she is talking to another equally bizarre character, Rosalie, who is 15 years old, wears bright pink dresses, and tries to seduce Rosepettle's 18-year-old over-protected son, Jonathan (but whom Rosepettle insists on calling Albert), who can hardly speak he stutters so much, and who is dressed like a ten-year-old. Rosepettle, by the way, keeps the corpse of her husband hanging in her closet. I have not used the monologue as Friedman condensed it from the scene but have created my own version.

> Two warnings are enough for any man. Three are enough for any woman. The cuckoo struck three times and then a fourth and still she's here. May I ask why? I'm talking to my son, harlot! Harlot, I called you! Slut, scum, sleazy prostitute catching and caressing children and men. Stroking their hearts. I've seen you. Blind man's buff with the children in the garden. The redheaded one — fifteen, I think. Behind the bush while others cover their eyes. Up with the skirt, one-two-three and it's done. Don't try to deny it. I've seen you in action. I know your kind.
>
> Life is a lie, my sweet. Not words but Life itself. Life in all its ugliness. It builds green trees that tease your eyes and draw you under them. Then when you're there in the shade and you breathe in and say, "Oh God, how beautiful," that's when the bird on the branch lets go his dropping and hits you on the head. Life, my sweet, beware. It isn't what it seems. I've seen what it can do. I've watched you dance. I've

watched you closely and I know what I see. You danced too near those men and you let them do too much. Don't try to deny it. Words will only make it worse. It would be best for all concerned if you left at once and never came again. Good day.

Why don't I let who out of his room? Who? Jonathan? Who?! My son? You mean Albert? Is that who you mean? Albert? Is that who you mean, slut? H'm? Speak up. Is that who you mean? *I don't let him out because he is my son.* I don't let him out because his skin is as white as fresh snow and he would burn if the sun struck him. I don't let him out because outside there are trees with birds sitting on their branches waiting for him to walk beneath. I don't let him out because you're there, waiting behind the bushes with your skirt up. I don't let him out because he is *susceptible*. That's why. Because he is *susceptible*. Susceptible to trees and to sluts and to sunstroke.

I came and got you because, my dear, my stupid son has been watching you through that stupid telescope he made. Because, in short, he wanted to meet you and I, in short, wanted him to know what you were really like. Now that's he's seen, you may go.

And if you choose to stay? (*Softly, slying.*) Can you cook? How well? Fairly well? Not good enough! My son is connoisseur. A connoisseur, do you hear? I cook him the finest foods in the world. Recipes no one knows exist. Food, my sweet, is the finest of arts. And since you can't cook you are artless. You nauseate my son's aesthetic taste.

Go, my dear. Find yourself some weeping willow and set yourself beneath it. Cry of your lust for my son and wait, for a mockingbird waits above to deposit his verdict on your whorish head. My son is as white as fresh snow and you are tainted with sin. You are garnished with garlic and turn our tender stomachs in disgust.

I throw you out! I toss you into the garbage can! I heard everything, you know. So don't try to call. The phone is in my room — *and no one goes into my room but me.* (Exits and returns.) One more thing. If, by some chance, the eleventh child named Cynthia turns out to be a Siamese cat, give it to me. I, too, pay well.

Even though I didn't use Friedman's version of the monologue, her comments are still worth reading. Remember that Friedman writes her comments for actors.

Well, here we have the ultimate protective mother. You might say, "monster mother"! But do not play her as you think of her when first reading the monologue. Do not play her as you think of her as actress when you read the entire play and make more discoveries about this woman. Get into her shoes and underwear. *You* may think she is a monster but *she* does not think she is one. Therefore, she is not! She seems strong and invincible. She is fighting like hell to protect her son from the cruel world. She knows only too well how cruel the world can be. She is actually very frightened for herself and for her son. She knows that she alone will never do harm to her son. But others will. And Rosalie will eventually. This Madame knows so she *must* protect her son. And she needs her son to be near her at all times. She is alone. She is very jealous of Rosalie or any woman who comes near her or her son. So she is not so strong and invincible.

Now, there is no love on these pages. So where are you going to find it? You need to have opposites. You are insulting [Rosalie] and demanding that she remove herself from your life and your son's life. You are communicating very strongly your contempt for her. You've got to find the love. I don't mean that the opposite of what you are saying is true. I mean that you are fighting for [Rosalie] to help you protect your son. You need her cooperation. She must not fight you on this. But you have to have opposite feelings for her other than all that contempt. She is young, pretty, and seems to care for your son. She is the object of your son's desire. It is of course threatening to you if he strongly desires a woman. His love and his need for you *must* be stronger than his desire for a woman. With all your contempt for her, try to make her understand that you *must* protect your son.

Can you figure out what Rosepettle's UDs are? Friedman identifies several possibilities. She notes that Rosepettle is "fighting like hell to protect her son." She adds that "His love and his need for you *must* be stronger than his desire for a woman." And she exhorts you to "find the love." Is the drive "to protect"? Or is it "to be loved"?

Viola in Shakespeare's *Twelfth Night*:
The Drive to Be Loved

Now let's look at a monologue from Shakespeare, *Twelfth Night*, the part of Viola. Before Rudnicki discusses Viola, he mentions Portia in *The Merchant of Venice*, who "covers her simple vow of love with a binding care, a legalistic shrewdness to which attention must be paid" by the actor playing the role. Then Rudnicki says that it is Viola in *Twelfth Night* "however, who is the complete mistress of subtext… [D]isguised as a man, she obliquely expresses her love for [and to] her patron, Duke Orsino." Here is the monologue. I have modernized the language and modified the text and spacing slightly to make it easier for those not accustomed to reading Shakespeare. Remember that Viola is pretending to be a man talking about women, but she is really talking about herself.

> I know too well what love women may owe to men:
> In faith, women are as true of heart as we men.
> My father had a daughter who loved a man,
> The same as it might be, perhaps, if I were a woman,
> That I would love you, Duke.
>
>   And what's her history?
> A blank, my lord. She never told her love,
> But let concealment, like a worm in the bud,
> Feed on her rosy cheek. She longed in thought,
> And with a green and yellow melancholy,
> She sat like Patience on a monument,
> Smiling at grief.
>
>   Was this not love indeed?
> We men may say more, swear more; but indeed
> Our shows of affection are more than will, for still we prove
> Much in our vows, but little in our love.
>
> Sir, shall I [go] to this lady [and deliver your message to her]?

What is Viola's universal drive here? One student wrote in class that Viola's "scene goal" was to "secretly find out who Orsino desires," that her "overall theatrical goal" was "to tell Orsino that she is in love with him," and her "motivation" was "her desire for Orsino and willingness to hide in drag to find any and all information about who he loves."

Do you agree? In thinking over your answer, note that the student did not identify a UD at all. In effect, even if Viola's goal were to find out who Orsino desires or to tell Orsino she is in love with him (which is not manifest in this monologue) and even if her overall motivation is her desire for Orsino or her willingness to find out information about who he loves, it does not describe her universal drive. I agree with the student that Viola wants to find out who Orsino loves, although that is not the goal represented in this particular monologue. I also agree that Viola wants badly to reveal herself to Orsino, although again it is not manifest in this scene. But what does this monologue reveal about Viola's universal drive?

The line before the last, which happens to be the hardest to understand, I think, happens also to be the most significant. Men prove much in their promises, but little in their love. In other words, Viola, pretending she is a self-aware man talking man-to-man to the Duke (with whom in reality she's in love), admits that men make lots of promises to women, but do little to actually prove they really love them — or little in showing their love to them. (It is typical of Shakespeare to use a word in two or three very different ways in the same sentence, to show irony or humor, or tragedy. Here the word "prove" has two very different meanings. In the first half of the sentence, the meaning is closer to "try to prove." In the second half, the implied repetition, "men prove little in their love," means they actually fail to prove. While this is not a course in Shakespeare, learning to pay close attention to different uses of words is extremely valuable in characterization work.)

So what does Viola really mean to say? She is saying *"Love me!"* She is saying that she loves the Duke and he should love her, and should show her that he loves her. She is making him think about how he does not show his love. She is making him aware that women may conceal their love, too, but that does not mean that men are up front. Men say a lot, declare a lot, "swear more," but it doesn't really prove their love. Of course, at this point in the play, Orsino cannot possibly know that Viola loves him or that this man is actually Viola in disguise, but that does not change the fact that Viola is crying out for his love. Nor does the fact that she cannot admit it to him openly change her drive. There are lots of reasons why she might not be able to profess her love, but again her drive is the same.

Clytemnestra in *Electra* by Sophocles: The Drive to Be Loved

Clytemnestra narrates this monologue and is addressing her daughter, Electra. Clytemnestra has murdered her husband, Electra's father. Clytemnestra's goal in this monologue is to win back Electra's love and acceptance. She gives several reasons for why she has killed her husband in an attempt to explain and justify the murder.

So you are out loose again.

You only do it because
Aegisthus is away.
You harangue everyone
With tales of my cruelty.
You are all malice and venom
But I am not an evil woman.
Before people pass judgment
They should first check their facts.

Your father, I killed him:
It is true and I do not deny it
But it was not me alone.
There was another with me:
Justice, Justice did it.
I will say it once again:
Your precious father
Was brutal enough to murder
Iphigenia, your sister.
Her throat was cut
In front of the whole army.
Why did he kill her?
For the Greeks or for Menelaus?

I don't know what the truth was
But one thing is certain:
He was cruel and a coward.

Yet for all that
I would not have killed him
But he had to bring home
A mad girl, a prophetess,
Flaunting her before me.
Two brides. One bed. He did that.
You would not still love him
If you really had known him.
He was a self-deceiver
Who always blamed the gods
For his own mistakes. He talked
Of doing what is right
But he never did it. No,
He always did the wrong things,
The selfish, the mean, the easy.
He thought he could steal from Apollo
His so-called "Virgin Priestess";
He thought he could bring her home
And be sweet with her in front of me.

O can't you understand?
Nothing in the world
Hurts a woman more
Than to love and to be hurt.
When a husband looks for love
Outside his marriage
Shall we not do as he does?
Why are women blamed for it
But never our guilty husbands?
I have no regrets, And if you think me evil
Look into your own hearts
Before you judge another.

I include this monologue because of its straightforwardness and simplicity. Students should not be afraid to use ancient Greek drama. As this translation/adaption shows, it is very accessible, down-to-earth, and feels utterly contemporary. And these plays get right to the bottom of human nature. They are both simple and complex at the same time, because so recognizable — although few of us would otherwise know what it might feel like to murder one's husband — but the sense of hurt a woman feels from a cheating husband is recognizable.

A student wrote:

> Her universal drive is the need to feel justified in one's actions, especially when it does not gel with the dominant moral tone of the society. I felt that the other drive at work is the need to feel unconditional love by one's own family, especially in the parent-child relationship. This was pretty clearly illustrated when Clytemnestra points to her husband sacrificing her other daughter to win a war as a primary reason for [why she murdered him]. She seems to be telling her daughter, in not so many words, that it was her love and loyalty for her children that drove her to kill him.

What do you think? Do you think that "the need to feel justified" is a universal drive? How about "the need to feel unconditional love"? What *must* Clytemnestra have here? What can she not survive without? Justification? Will her world end if her daughter doesn't understand or believe her?

In my opinion, Clytemnestra's situation will be most easily understood by someone who has mothered a child. I believe she needs to be loved by her daughter, although she never will directly ask for it. What she asks instead is for Electra's understanding. She disarms Electra's defenses intellectually, with words and reasons, with rational thought and justifications. Certainly, Clytemnestra shows emotions to her daughter: righteous anger, sorrow, and frustration. But there is something deeper than these "surface" emotions or intellectual rationales. Clytemnestra knows she won't completely convince Electra. First she chastises her for being "all malice and venom" and passing judgment without checking her facts. Then she admits openly that she did kill Electra's father and goes on to explain it to her. It is a woman speaking to a woman, not a woman speaking to a child. Her tone is respectful towards Electra, drawing on a strong bond they've clearly shared. It is this undertone that I feel carries the universal drive: the drive to be loved — here, by her daughter. I wouldn't say it was a "need for unconditional love," however. That is a slightly different thing. She hasn't asked for anything unconditionally from Electra, nor do I see her as demanding love — which the term "unconditional" implies, to my mind. Nor do I think that Clytemnestra's argument to prove her love and loyalty to her children illustrates either her need for unconditional love or the drive to be loved. Nonetheless, I do agree that the UD is to be loved. Read the monologue over and see what you think. (Better yet, read Rudnicki's synopsis of the Trojan War period in which this play is set, or read the play itself.)

Cassandra in *Hecuba* by Euripides:
The Drive to Merge with the Universe

I include this monologue because it deals with a UD that is not often expressed but that is always present. Cassandra was a daughter of Priam, the king of Troy, and Hecuba. She was endowed with the gift of prophecy by Apollo but cursed by him never to be believed. Here she describes her encounter with Apollo.

> The sun ... I dreamed that the sun
> Came alive in my brain.
> I felt light pour in
> To my skull and I knew.
> I saw a landscape
> Of time spread out before me —
> My kingdom — and I saw
> All things that are to come.
> Then he said, "Now pay me.
> Give yourself now. Let me own you
> And I will give you time to rule
> Forever"... I was frightened.
> I said I would but I could not.

My mind was riddled, scorched
With too much seeing and brightness.
I longed for shadows ... caverns ...
Dim sea-beds ... all I wanted
Was to hide from him, from seeing.
I hid. I shut my eyes.
I wanted so much to be
Alone in the dark.

Whiteness ... his heat is white
And despair is white and madness
And the thoughts which race in my skull.
Please, Apollo, I cannot
Give you myself. I'm frightened.
Then he said, "So be it,"
And he grew quiet and gentle.
He begged one kiss of me.
I gave my lips to him.
And he spat into my mouth
And said, "Keep my gifts.
Keep my brightness in you.
See it all, the truth
About the war and all things
But since you lied to me
When you tell that truth
It will seem to those you tell it
Toys, bauble, babble,
And they will laugh at you."

This monologue reminds me of some of Bernard Shaw's Saint Joan monologues. These types of pieces are often considered beyond the range of most actors, since they engage on a level that few people experience on a daily basis. They are spiritual, rapturous, ecstatic in the sense of religious fervor. Yet, this piece is clearly not religious in the contemporary sense.

This piece also reminds me of Shakespeare's *King Lear*, about which Rudnicki says: "It has been my experience that material from *King Lear* must be treated in a manner altogether different from any more standard approach appropriate to the other [Shakespeare] plays." Rudnicki continues:

> Lear and the others in the story journey across a bleak, forbidding landscape toward revelation and death. In his travels, each pilgrim must divest himself of all the trappings of civilized life until, ordeal by ordeal, he is stripped down to his basic humanity so that he may take on a new, archetypal personality. As the naked person ("the thing itself," as Lear puts it), he may then play out his role in the larger context of history, the elements, the stars, and all of the most primal human and natural forces.

Rudnicki adds that "Lear and his fellow travelers share the awareness of their place in moral and physical matrices in a manner reminiscent of the Greek tragic heroes." He says that this "is a consciousness I find best represented today in the work" of certain science fiction writers for whom "the scale of vision... shifts rapidly from galaxies to grains of sand, and they can relate minute personal moral decisions to monumental images." Rudnicki adds that "Lear not only speaks about — and to — the storm, he creates the very elements with his words and *becomes* the storm himself." Lear's "creation, like most creative acts, cannot be rushed, and the momentum of the [play], although powerful, is slow."

What is Cassandra's universal drive, then? Is it love? No, I don't think so. It is rather, I believe, the drive to merge with the universe.

An astrology writer, Liz Greene, wrote an entire book on the mythology of this drive: *The Astrological Neptune and the Quest for Redemption.* She writes:

> Because they are so vast and elusive, usually lacking human characters and depicting instead the creation of the universe, the[] psychological significance [of creation water myths] seems to be related to primal experiences of which we have only the dimmest awareness. Since all myths are in one way or another the psyche's portrayal of its own processes, these creation stories are, on one level, images of human conception, gestation, and birth, projected out onto the cosmos and envisaged as the birth of the world. Human birth also occurs in more

than one form, for it involves not only the physical emergence of the baby out of the womb; it also describes the birth of an individual identity out of the undifferentiated sea of collective psyche.

Cassandra's monologue is not a creation myth, nor does it invoke images of Neptunian waters or the storm in Lear, but it is of the same genre. Cassandra's story is, like Clytemnestra's, intensely simple. She recounts what happened in the simplest, sequential terms. Yet what she experienced was a "transcendent" state. Although Cassandra explains that she felt frightened and could not make payment to Apollo for the gift he had given her — so it seems that Cassandra was not at all *driven* to experience this "rapture" of "white heat," of "a landscape of time," of "the sun … alive in my brain," and "thoughts which race in my skull" — Cassandra has clearly sought out this experience. What drove her to do so is the UD. The drive to merge with creation, to return to the primal mother, to be more than human, to be outside of or beyond the landscape of time, to know the future, to "see the light," to be born again, to return to the womb and swim in the amniotic sea before time began, and so on.

At the moment she is speaking, Cassandra is in the throes of a this powerful drive.

Richard, the Hunchback
(Shakespeare's *Henry VI, Part 3* & *Richard III*):
The Drive to Survive or to Be Loved

Here is a monologue of Richard's from Shakespeare's *Henry VI, Part 3* (Act III, Scene 2), which is a much more revealing monologue about him than any in the play *Richard III* itself. I have not modernized this one but will discuss it afterwards.

This is a long but powerful monologue. It contains such honest, telling statements by Richard about his ambitions and drives that, despite the linguistic challenges of the Shakespearean English, it is worth studying. Very few people in real life (and even very few character in plays or movies) will be this honest. Thus, it is a very helpful monologue for students. But even so, despite its honesty, the primary universal drive is often missed by students. Therefore, it is an excellent exercise to use as an illustration here.

Ay, Edward will use women honorably.

Would he were wasted, marrow, bones, and all,
That from his loins no hopeful branch may spring
To cross me from the golden time I look for!

And yet, between my soul's desire and me —
The lustful Edward's title buried, —
Is Clarence, Henry, and his son young Edward,
And all the unlook'd for issue of their bodies,
To take their rooms ere I can place myself:
A cold premeditation for my purpose!

Why then, I do but dream on sovereignty;
Like one that stands upon a promontory,
And spies a far-off shore where he would treat,
Wishing his foot were equal with his eye;
And chides the sea that sunders him from thence,
Saying, he'll lade it dry to have his way:
So do I wish the crown, being so far off,
And so I chide the means that keep me from it,
And so I say I'll cut the causes off,
Flattering me with impossibilities.
My eye's too quick, my heart o'erweens too much,
Unless my hand and strength could equal them.

Well, say there is no kingdom then for Richard;
What other pleasure can the world afford?

I'll make my heaven in a lady's lap,
And deck my body in gay ornaments,
And witch sweet ladies with my words and looks.
O miserable thought! And more unlikely
Than to accomplish twenty golden crowns.
Why, love foreswore me in my mother's womb:

And, for I should not deal in her soft laws,
She did corrupt frail nature with some bribe,
To shrink mine arm up like a wither'd shrub;
To make an envious mountain on my back,
Where sits deformity to mock my body;
To shape my legs of an unequal size;
To disproportion me in every part,
Like to a chaos, or an unlick'd bear-whelp
That carries no impression like the dam.
And am I then a man to be belov'd?

O monstrous fault! to harbor such a thought.

Then, since this earth affords no joy to me
But to command, to check, to o'erbear such
As are of better person than myself,
I'll make my heav'n to dream upon the crown;
And, whiles I live, to account this world but hell,
Until my mis-shap'd trunk that bears this head
Be round impaled with a glorious crown.

And yet I know not how to get the crown,
For many lives stand between me and home:
And I, like one lost in a thorny wood,
That rents the thorns and is rent with the thorns,
Seeking a way and straying from the way;
Not knowing how to find the open air,
But toiling desperately to find it out,
Torment myself to catch the English crown:
And from that torrent I will free myself,
Or hew my way out with a bloody axe.

Why, I can smile, and murder while I smile,
And cry, "Content," to that which grieves my heart,
And wet my cheeks with artificial tears,
And frame my face to all occasions,
I'll drown more sailors than the mermaid shall;

I'll slay more gazers than the basilisk;
I'll play the orator as well as Nestor,
Deceive more slily than Ulysses could,
And, like a Sinon, take another Troy.
I can add colors to the chameleon,
Change shapes with Proteus for advantages,
And set the murderous Machiavel to school.

Can I do this, and cannot get a crown?
Tut! Were it farther off, I'll pluck it down.

Richard is jealous of Edward, his brother, who has become king. In the preceding scene, Edward has just boldly won over Lady Elizabeth Grey, a widow whose husband just died in battle, while Richard and his other brother, Clarence, watched. Edward has negotiated with her for the return of her husband's lands in exchange for becoming his queen. At the end of the preceding scene, Edward tells a nobleman to "use her honorably," meaning to treat her well. So, Richard starts out his first great monologue with "Yes, Edward will use women honorably," and adds his own thoughts that he, Richards, wishes Edward were "wasted, marrow, bones, and all," because Edward could father children that might steal "the golden time" Richard looks forward to, when he becomes King instead. He calls Edward "lustful" because Edward has lusted after Elizabeth — meaning Edward (admittedly) wants to sleep with her. Edward's "title," of course, is the crown and the kingdom.

But Richard also notes that standing in his way are his brother, Clarence, and several others (Henry and his son young Edward), and their children ("all the unlook'd for issue of their bodies").

Richard then makes an analogy of his own position, in which he "dream[s] on sovereignty" (i.e. he dreams of becoming king) like one standing on a mountain ("a promontory") seeing a far-off shore he wants to walk on. In the analogy, "his foot [would be] equal with is eye" — meaning, he wishes that what he could see, he could walk on. And he talks angrily to the sea that keeps him from doing so, saying he'd drain it dry to have his way.

Richard determines to obtain that which he is kept from, knowing the quickness of his eye, his strong desire, and the strength of his hand to do what he needs to do. He knows that making his "heaven in a lady's lap" will not happen to him, as he thinks love renounced him even before he was born ("love foreswore me in my mother's womb") and his mother intentionally caused his arm to shrink up "like a wither'd shrub" and made an "envious mountain on my back" (he's a hunchback). He compares himself to "a chaos" or "an unlick'd bear-whelp," i.e. the young offspring of a bear whose mother never cared for it. He says, "Am I then a man to be belov'd?"

So, instead of seeking love, Richard determines to make his heaven by dreaming upon the crown. The images Richard paints of being "one lost in a thorny wood," with thorny bushes that he must separate ("rent") and which tear at ("rent") him, "seeking a way and straying from the way, not knowing how to find the open air, but toiling desperately to find it out," convey Richard's emotional state vividly and prepare us for his cruel conclusion that he can "murder while I smile" and engage in worse endeavors than the many remaining images he conjures:

> drown more sailors than the mermaid shall — mermaids were thought to drown sailors
>
> slay more "gazers" than "the basilisk" — Richard claims he can kill more onlookers than the mythical serpent who killed anyone who looked at it
>
> play the orator as well as Nestor — a hero celebrated as an elderly and wise counselor to the Greeks at Troy
>
> deceive more slyly than Ulysses — the King of Ithaca in Greek mythology, a leader of the Greeks in the Trojan War, who reached home after ten years of ordeals
>
> "like a Sinon, take another Troy" — Sinon was a Greek warrior who devised the stratagem of the wooden horse by which the Greeks ultimately captured and destroyed Troy
>
> add colors to the chameleon — chameleons change colors to blend into their surroundings
>
> change shapes with Proteus "for advantages" — Proteus was a sea deity who assumed various forms

and set the murderous Machiavel to school — Niccolo Machiavelli was the author of *The Prince*, a guide intended to train statesmen how to use power and deceit — Richard is saying he could teach some things to Machiavelli.

So what is Richard's universal drive? Many students conclude that Richard's UD is power, need to control, ambition. But, in this context, none of those are UDs. (Ambition is the love of accomplishment. That is not what is driving Richard.)

I often recommend students watch Al Pacino's film *Looking for Richard*, which is about Shakespeare's *Richard III*. After viewing that film, one student wrote:

Before Hitler or Stalin ever existed, Shakespeare predicted the capabilities of a man [who had lived] without ever feeling loved or respected. Richard is the picture of evil and disgust on a grand level, yet we all feel something for him and connect with his needs... Richard thinks ultimate power and control over the kingdom will give him ultimate love and devotion, and he will stop at nothing to achieve it. He develops a God-like complex and it is much too late for him (crown or not) to ever conquer what he truly needs and originally set out for: To be loved by others. This need to be loved is the driving force that makes him so destructive, and in the end he destroys his ability to love himself.

I agree with this student that Richard's UD is to be loved, although a later monologue (*Richard III*, Act V, Scene 3) shows that Richard, even though self-loathing, was also self-infatuated. (Note: "wherefore" means "why.") He says to himself:

Richard loves Richard. That is, I am I.
Is there a murderer here? No. Yes I am.
Then fly. What, from myself? Great reason why!
Lest I revenge. What, myself upon myself?
Alack, I love myself. Wherefore? For any good
That I myself have done unto myself?
O no! Alas, I rather hate myself

For hateful deeds committed by myself.
I am a villain. Yet I lie, I am not.
Fool, of thyself speak well. Fool, do not flatter.
My conscience hath a thousand separate tongues,
And every tongue brings in a different tale.

Richard ends with: "There is no creature loves me, and if I die, no soul will pity me. Nay, wherefore should they, since that I myself find in myself no pity to myself?"

Despite the thousand separate tongues in Richard's conscience, the universal drive does not change. No creature loves him. "Love foreswore me in my mother's womb." His drive is to be loved.

Now remember what I said about how doing UD work takes tremendous courage and insight? Remember that I said you cannot do UDs out of spite: It always requires deep empathy for ourselves and fellow human beings. So, think about that now. Shakespeare's Richard felt deeply unloved. What drove him was the drive to be loved. This drive exists in everyone. It is nothing new or extraordinary, or unique to Richard. But the drive to be loved does not by life circumstances trump everything else in most people's lives, as it did in Richard's broken life. And, here is the fundamental obligation for the writer: Our job is not to excuse Richard, nor is anyone asking us to live next door to him, but as a writer, we must understand him from the inside. That is what UDs are really about.

CHAPTER TEN

DISCREPANCIES
(Parably)

Discrepancies are perhaps the most significant item in the archetypes approach. **A discrepancy is an incongruity or inconsistency in a person's behavior that reveals something significant about the person.** It points to an internal truth about someone and often holds a secret, a hiding place, or sometimes a lie.

A discrepancy is not a thing in itself. It is always one thing in comparison to another. It could be the difference between saying "I'm loyal to my wife," and winking while you say it. It could be a person who acts differently when alone with you than when in the company of others. It could be a discrepancy in words, gestures, actions, or any combination.

Discrepancies reveal actual (albeit sometimes unconscious) intentions and drives. (In a story or movie, discrepancies make up part of the subtext.) Importantly, in order to interpret discrepancies, you must infer from a set of facts. Thus, you cannot make use of discrepancies without understanding some basic concepts of inference and logic. Deductions or inferences made from any given group or series of facts must be logically compelled and consistent in order to be useful.

The basic skill of doing discrepancies is called *parably*. When you are doing discrepancy work, you are *parabling*.

First let's look at the exercise and ground rules, then we'll discuss interpretation.

THE EXERCISE

Find an example of a simple discrepancy in someone. First write out exactly what you observed, then try to frame it in the form of a two-part sentence. For example, "When he talks about the car accident, he smiles." Another example: "She is engaged to Frank but she's dating other men."

A few guidelines:

1. Do not use an external conflict between two people. (The discrepancy is within one person.)

2. Try to choose a discrepancy that does NOT point to something that changed IN TIME. (Like he did this THEN and that LATER.)

3. Stick to actions and spoken words. (Avoid reliance on your own opinions, as in character facts.)

4. Limit words that a person speaks about him or herself, or what another person says about him or her, unless they were present. ("I'm a good guy!" "She's a liar!") (It might help to think of such spoken words as hearsay or opinion.) If the discrepancy is between what a person says about himself and does, preface the sentence with "S/he says that…")

5. Avoid relying on pre-conclusions, abstractions, or adjectives/adverbs. ("She's a monster!" "Her behavior was monstrous!" "He said it angrily." "She ALWAYS shouts!" "She's smart.") (Adjectives may, of course, on occasion be necessary to the meaning, in which case, include only those necessary adjectives. For example, "He had a red pen which leaked from the breast pocket of his white shirt, prompting him to quip that he was just 'a bleeding heart liberal.'")

6. Be careful with discrepancies or inconsistencies that are not internal to the person. For example, he usually doesn't wear a coat; today it's raining and he wore a raincoat. The fact that he wears a raincoat when it's raining is not an internal discrepancy; it shows an external change or difference (a change of weather). While the fact that he wears a coat when it's raining may show something about him (it certainly is a character fact), it is not a discrepancy.

7. Phrase the sentence as follows in two parts, using a conjunction to connect the two parts: "She laughs *but/and/yet/while* she says nasty things about Sue."

Discussion

This exercise is one of several in the archetypes approach that is intended to get your inside the head and heart of someone other than yourself. This one is like detective work. We're trying to catch someone doing something. But, we are not trying to point the finger of blame. We are only trying to understand what is inside of someone. You should be asking yourself silently, "What does this mean about him/her?" However, we will not try to answer this question just yet. This is another exercise in suspending your judgment. We are simply going to juxtapose two pieces of information which are in some way inconsistent with each other. (If you feel you absolutely must, write on a separate page what you feel is the reason for the discrepancy. You can keep these "opinion" pages for later reference, but make sure to keep them separate and labeled as opinion pages.)

Not all discrepancies are equal. Some reveal more than others. We will discuss this more below. Right now concentrate on doing the exercise correctly and don't worry about finding the most revealing or interesting ones.

> DO EXERCISE: Try to spend a few minutes or hours looking for discrepancies in people you spend time with. Follow the guidelines above. I suggest you use separate pieces of paper that you can later put into a binder. If you find yourself wandering into conclusions or opinions, don't stop yourself — just write them down on a separate page. If you feel like you want to write an entire sketch of the person or a story, go ahead, but remember to keep the discrepancies separate. On the discrepancies page, just keep a list of two-part sentences that illustrate the discrepancies. Don't try to write an entire narrative on that page.

Now let's move on to interpretation of discrepancies.

Interpretation of Discrepancies: Logic & Inference

> "[A]n opinion which does not within its own confines exhibit an awareness of relevant considerations, whose premises are concealed, or

whose logic is faulty is not likely to enjoy either a long life or the capacity to generate offspring."
— Former Illinois Chief Justice Walter V. Schaefer (1904-1986)[13]

Personal opinions, like the legal opinions which Justice Schaefer talks about above, that are not founded on sound premises, good logic, and an awareness of relevant considerations are not helpful to one's own writing. Why is this so even with respect to fiction? It is so because, for one thing, even fiction must be grounded in a credible reality. But it is also so because when a writer does not follow these precepts, when he rather follows the flow of his own biases, he is not likely to see beyond his own closed thought patterns, which in turn means the world of his characters will be limited merely to proving his opinions correct, not to revealing human truths. Logic provides a reliable way to accurately interpret discrepancies.

While the use of logic is a crucial interpretive skill in discrepancy and isomorph work, it is not a core component skill. It is rather an interpretive skill that is applied on top of the core skills.

In addition to being a way to construct arguments, logic is a method of interpretation of facts. It is a largely lost art today which we should all learn. Here, we are concerned with how to interpret discrepancies contained in sets of facts. In this book, when I refer to the use of logic, unless stated otherwise, I mean the use of the principles of logic as I set them forth below, the reliance on sound premises and clear identification of facts, and the application of any other relevant considerations.

An example: In my household, we have four ferrets. One of them bites sometimes. I tell my daughter, who is the main caretaker of these ferrets, that the ferret, named Cheesie, does not mean to be aggressive when she bites; she's just trying to tell us she wants to be taken out for a walk. My daughter says "That's not true, Cheesie *is* aggressive because she bites even if she's already been out." I say, "That's because she loves going out more than anything in the whole wide world and she has no other way to tell you that." Usually Cheesie will sit by the door and wait. If you ignore her, after a while, she'll come over to you and stare at you. If you still ignore her, she will look for some bare skin to bite. This could be considered aggressive, but I don't view it as intentionally aggressive. She is not trying to hurt us. She just wants to go out. And she tries other methods of getting what she wants. If none of those work, her last resort is biting, which she apparently has learned gets people's attention. (We don't reward the behavior, but we're her second owners.)

Okay, see what I've done here is to make logical inferences from the facts with an awareness of relevant considerations. This effort takes time and energy.

In other words, I've provided *context*. However, although the term *context* describes part of what I'm doing (in particular, implying "relevant considerations"), it does not imply logical inferences from sound (not concealed) premises. So, if you want to use the term *context* as a mnemonic, remember that we also mean relying on sound premises, all relevant considerations possible, and making logical inferences.

Of course, you can also see that I am looking at things from Cheesie's point of view. This is a core component skill which we is covered in the analogues work and will also come up in more direct advanced work.

What is an Inference?

An inference is a mental movement from one proposition to another. In order for a conclusion to arise from a logical inference, there must be a reasonable probability that the conclusion flows from facts because of past experiences in human affairs. One judge wrote: "Inferred factual conclusions based on circumstantial evidence are permitted only when, and to the extent that, human experience indicates a probability that certain consequences can and do follow from the basic circumstantial facts."

To most of us, the concept of reasonable inferences is just common sense, but when it comes to actually making reasonable inferences ourselves, it is sometimes hard to act or judge reasonably. Making reasonable inferences is a real mental discipline. In fact, courts prohibit (and on appeal have overturned) jury verdicts that are arrived at by "piling inference upon inference." This happens in a manner something like this: We infer that Cheesie wants to go outside when she runs to the door and looks at it expectantly. And we can infer that when Cheesie bites after waiting at the door, and then running over to us and staring at us further, and being ignored, she does so in order to get our attention so we'll take her out. Both of these are logical inferences. But if we infer that because Cheesie wants to go out (an inference in itself), she hates us and viciously comes after us because of her hatred, it is *not* a logical inference. It is an inference piled on top of other inferences and is neither a compelled conclusion nor a reasonable one.

Thus, when working with discrepancies, it is important to (1) make reasonable inferences, but not to (2) pile inferences on top of inferences.

Types of Logic

There are two kinds of logical reasoning: deductive and inductive. In a valid deductive argument, if the premise is true, the conclusion must be true. **Deductive reasoning** moves by inference from general to particular: (If all ferrets bite, then Cheesie must bite.) In a broader sense, though, deductive reasoning means drawing a reasonable conclusion from any set of facts. Thus, one can deduce that Cheesie wants to go out by the combination of her behaviors. In this sense, the terms deduce and infer are synonyms.

Inductive reasoning is the opposite: from particular to general. In induction, the connection between given pieces of information and another piece inferred from them is not a logically necessary connection and the conclusion is not necessarily true; it is more probably true than not. (Cheese bites and 50 other ferrets I know bite; thus, all ferrets probably bite.)

Reasoning by analogy is another logical form. It relies on similarities and differences between two particular things. (Wolves bite. Wolves have snouts, sharp teeth, are carnivores and predators. Ferrets have snouts, sharp teeth, are carnivores and predators. Thus, ferrets probably bite.) Analogies, of course, only go as far as they go. Ferrets in captivity usually don't bite. Do wolves raised in captivity bite?

When we work with discrepancies, it is very important to be aware of which kind of reasoning we're relying on. Generally, it's best to use close deduction when working with discrepancies. This is because other parts of the archetypes approach require other forms of mental discipline that work in the opposite way from deductions. They require mental leaps, so we want to make sure the foundation is solid.

Discrepancies are a major foundational component. Discrepancy sentences are used to construct the archetype sentences.

Close deductions are those that stay very close to what the facts imply. It is reasonable to conclude that Cheesie standing by the door means she wants to go out. She has been taken out that door many times for walks and it is reasonable to infer that she knows that is the way out and it's reasonable to infer that her standing by the door means she wants us to take her out. That is a close inference or deduction. A wide (and unfounded or unwarranted) inference or deduction would be to conclude that her standing by the door means she expects the doorbell to ring. There is no basis to conclude that. It's an unwarranted, non-purposeful leap. Later we will make purposeful mental leaps that are carefully selected and placed in a set of skill activities to arrive at the highest results possible for this kind of work. But here, we need to build our foundation.

Variations of Discrepancies (Simple vs. Complex; Ordinary vs. Extraordinary) & Juxtapositions

We start with learning the mechanical steps of creating discrepancy sentences, because we construct the archetype sentences in the same mental format. (Since the process of constructing archetypes is considerably more complex than discrepancy sentences, even complex ones, you will not actually use a two-part sentence in constructing archetypes, but it is essential to start the discrepancy step with the act of physically separating the two parts on the page so that you mentally grasp the format.) But the mechanical step can only be used for basic, simple discrepancies.

It is easy to find basic discrepancies in almost anyone but they don't really show much about a person. Discrepancies, to be useful, are not simple or ordinary and they must be used in batches and combinations — in context, in other words — to be meaningful.

Another type of two-part sets is the brother of discrepancies: juxtapositions. A discrepancy is a set of any two things that don't seem to be consistent with each other. Juxtapositions are any two things, whether consistent or not, juxtaposed — or laid side by side. Discrepancies are actually a subset of juxtapositions. Juxtapositions, to be meaningful, must also contain all possible relevant considerations and close logical inferences.

The reason we begin with discrepancies and not juxtapositions is because discrepancies reveal the most amount of information the quickest. Juxtapositions are equally as valuable but take considerably more time and skill to master and use in archetypes work.

The following example illustrates both discrepancies and juxtapositions and shows how they gain meaning by being considered together in batches or combinations (where, separately, they would have very little meaning). The subject here is a young man we'll call Richard.

Richard, aged 18, was dating Elizabeth, aged 16. Richard had a friend, Lawrence. When Richard first started getting to know Elizabeth, he communicated with her via an internet blog/chat site but had never met her in person. After moving on to using instant message, and eventually the phone, Richard's friend, Lawrence, suggested that he and Richard drive to Elizabeth's house, which was about 45 minutes from where they lived. Lawrence offered to drive and Richard agreed.

Richard and Elizabeth started dating and soon called themselves boyfriend and girlfriend. They arranged to go to Richard's prom together (which cost Richard a few hundred dollars), and became physically close. Once this relationship was established, Richard was so busy completing school and attending to other things in his life, he had very little time to drive down to visit or spend time with Elizabeth. Even when they talked on the phone or via instant messenger, he often fell asleep during the talk or forgot he was talking to her while playing a PS-2 game or playing music with friends who were visiting him. Elizabeth got angry at him. At first Richard denied everything, but eventually he admitted his neglect and promised to try to pay more attention, not fall asleep, visit her more, etc. Richard told Elizabeth he was serious and that she was a "quality girl." He did not say he cared about her or loved her.

In the meantime, however, Lawrence had been spending a lot of time hanging out at Elizabeth's house. The times that Richard came down, it was Lawrence who usually picked him up and drove him down, or brought Elizabeth up to Richard. Richard had a car and he drove but he just didn't feel like making the trip very often.

Inevitably, Lawrence and Elizabeth developed a physical attraction and shared some passionate kisses. Elizabeth did not want to tell Richard and Lawrence agreed not to. She wanted to keep dating Richard to give him a chance, even though she was angry at him for neglecting her. However, she felt bad about getting involved with Lawrence, and finally decided she had to tell Richard.

Elizabeth and Lawrence sat down one day and told Richard. Lawrence explained that Elizabeth and he had kissed. Richard wanted to know "What kind of kiss?" Elizabeth told him that she didn't think Lawrence needed to tell Richard what kind of kiss it was, that what mattered was what Lawrence and Elizabeth felt about each other. Richard disagreed emphatically. He said that it *did* matter to him, that his relationship was "sacred." Despite saying this, Richard did not manifest any concern for Elizabeth's feelings whatsoever. He did not show concern that he had neglected or disrespected her, or any awareness that it was her feelings of being neglected that pushed her towards a physical relationship with Lawrence. He did not ask her how she felt or what she wanted. Richard did not show any concern about how Lawrence felt either. His main concern was with the fact that his friend had betrayed him and made him look bad.

Richard suggested that the three of them go to his home and talk with his brother, Frank, and brother's girlfriend, Mary. Richard and Frank had been friends with Lawrence for many years. The resolution of this talk was that Elizabeth and Richard would continue to date until two weeks after his graduation and then would reassess their relationship.

Shortly after the prom, Richard and Elizabeth broke up by mutual agreement and shortly thereafter, Richard began putting on the blog site offensively altered pictures of Elizabeth.

Before reading my list, see how many discrepancies and juxtapositions you can find about Richard.

Discrepancies & Juxtapositions about Richard:

෴ Richard said his relationship with Elizabeth was "sacred" but when they talked on the phone or via instant messenger, he often fell asleep or did other things such as playing a PS-2 game or playing music with friends while talking with her. He also ultimately published offensively altered pictures of her on his site.

෴ When she got angry about being neglected, he did not ask her to explain her feelings so he could understand — instead he blamed her.

෴ He called her his girlfriend but he made no effort to visit or spend time with her.

෴ When Elizabeth asked Richard if he was serious about dating her, he said he was but to illustrate this he described her as a "quality girl" without saying he cared for her or loved her.

෴ He took Elizabeth to the prom and then shortly thereafter broke up with her and put offensively altered pictures of her on his site.

Can you find any more significant discrepancies or juxtapositions? It may seem obvious from reading this that Richard was not a very nice guy, but interestingly, neither Elizabeth nor Lawrence recognized it until he altered the pictures. Lawrence had been Richard's friend for years.

Meaning Interpretation

The above set of facts is all true and personally known to me, who was a witness. Although I was an interested witness, being closely acquainted with Elizabeth, I have tried to present the facts as simply as possible without con-clusion-opinions. I cannot guarantee that the inferences I now draw from these facts are not tainted with bias, but I will offer them and explain the connections I made, so you can see how the process works. Indeed, it is exactly this type of situation — one in which we are personally vested — that is likely to pique our interest most and to spur us to observe and write. After all, it is not the easy situations, but the most difficult, volatile, and closest-to-heart situations that we want to learn to utilize in our writing.

There were several signals I observed that alerted me to something wrong in the situation between Elizabeth and Richard. Some of these were discrepancies and some juxtapositions to my own previous observations and research.

Richard was a very good-looking, baby-faced young man. To me, this indicated he was probably accustomed to attention from women for his looks. (This conclusion was confirmed by Elizabeth.) In my experience, such men often do not have an opportunity to develop relationships with women that grow out of trust and respect. For these men the issue is whether the woman is worthy of his looks.

When I heard that Richard referred to Elizabeth as "a quality girl," when asked if he really cared about her, this indicated to me a misplaced priority. His priority was on her worthiness for him, whether she qualified. His caring was based on this, not on feelings. At least, that was how he chose to frame it; he did not express that he loved her or cared about her.

I felt that his demand to know what type of kiss she and Lawrence had exchanged, rather than to know whether they really cared about each other, was an odd demand. He did not care whether they had feelings for each other. He only wanted to know whether he had been cuckolded. Feelings, either his for her, her for him, or theirs for each other, simply did not enter into Richard's thoughts or reasoning.

When I then heard he said that his relationship with her was "sacred," I could not help but think that this was a completely empty word for him. It held no meaning whatsoever to him. He had learned the meaning of the word and used it appropriately in the context, but given his complete lack of feelings otherwise, I felt he had no sense of what sacred really meant or felt like. He did not feel betrayed because Elizabeth had violated something sacred (which, in fact, he had never shown high regard for, in the first place, having repeatedly neglected and ignored her). He was betrayed because she made him look bad.

This conclusion was borne out when Elizabeth nearly broke up with him before the prom and he asked her to please at least stay his girlfriend until after the prom. He didn't really care that they broke up; he cared that he would go to the prom without a girlfriend.

My overall conclusion, which was admittedly based in part on knowledge that is impossible to imbue the reader with here, was that Richard was a narcissist, seeing everything in the world as significant only to the extent that it had to do with his image. While Richard is young and youth is arrogant, I felt his self-centeredness was more than just youthful arrogance.

Narcissists are a paradox. In their minds, the world revolves around them, but paradoxically they do not feel much, even for themselves. Narcissism is a mild version of psychopathology, in which the psychopath appears to articulate feelings appropriately but has no genuine understanding of other people's feelings because he is really unable to feel his own feelings. The unnecessary cruelty with which Richard posted upsetting images of Elizabeth on his web site after they mutually agreed to break up, confirms Richard's pathology, at least in my opinion. Elizabeth, who had given Richard every benefit of the doubt along the way, came to realize this herself, as well, at that point.

Elizabeth's betrayal of Richard by kissing Lawrence indicates that she was more aware subconsciously of the hurt Richard was causing her than she was able to admit to herself until they broke up.

Hopefully you can see from this interpretation what I mean by close deductions or inferences. Hopefully you can see how important and mean-ingful discrepancies and juxtapositions can be and how central to the writer's work they are. What I have done here is not free association or intuition. Yet, hopefully it contains some insight into these characters. And this is only the beginning.

Embedded or Coded Discrepancies

Discrepancies are usually objectively observable but there is one type of discrepancy that cannot be observed objectively: an embedded or coded discrepancy. This type of discrepancy can only be observed by the intended recipient of the message. In other words, the discrepancy is an intentional one. An embedded or coded message may take forms other than discrepancies as well, but here we are concerned with only discrepancies.

An example of an embedded or coded discrepancy would be something that appeared consistent to everyone else but one person. Thus, if an individual is generally seen by his friends and associates as a calm, easy-going man, but is known to his family as violent, the family will notice the discrepancy if he says "Hey, I'm an easy-going guy!" but his friends won't. The discrepancy is between what he says and what he does.

Of course, recognition of discrepancies is generally dependent upon some level of background knowledge or set of previous observations. Thus, all discrepancies could be categorized as embedded. The difference, however, is that the embedded or coded discrepancy is consciously *intended* to be detected by one person (or by a few select persons) *only*.

Say, for example, the calm, easy-going man had only committed violence against one person. He might want to make sure that one person would never tell, so he might develop a "code" to convey the message to that person that if he ever told, dire consequences would ensue. The code could be anything — a wink, a gesture, a look, a word, an intonation, an act or omission — and would not necessarily be a behavior that contrasted with another behavior, but to anyone else who witnessed it, the meaning could never be uncovered: the discrepancy would remain forever hidden.

The importance, then, of knowing about these types of discrepancies is, first of all, for the benefit of those who have experienced them. For you, you and only you are able to break the code and uncover its meaning for others. There is always a great deal of context for coded messages.

Secondly, for those of you who have not experienced embedded messages, it is important you know about them so you can learn to be alert to their possibility. The magical thing in knowing about things invisible is that once you're alerted to their existence, they have a tendency to come to you. And this is a rich area to mine.

See if you can work with a set of discrepancies and engage in some logical deductions. Share and discuss with a friend.

CHAPTER ELEVEN

ANALOGUES
(Homopathy)

The analogue exercise requires you to record something you saw happen to another person and then to elicit from yourself and record some past incident that, while not similar factually, made you feel how you think the person felt in the witnessed incident.

What you experienced in your self-elicited event is therefore *analogous* to what you think the person experienced in the recorded incident. Because we are concerned with an analogous *experience*, not an event that is analogous factually (i.e. an analogy), we distinguish this exercise from analogies by using the word "analogue."

The skill associated with doing analogues is called *homopathy*. It means literally "to have similar feelings." If you are engaged in doing analogue work, you are *homopathing*.

There are two steps to this exercise:

(1) Write out an incident or event you witnessed or heard about. The event should involve at least two people. An event with conflict of some sort is preferable but not necessary. You will focus only on one of the two people. You should state what the incident is, whether you saw it or heard about it, whether you chose to pick one with or without conflict, and who you are focusing on.

Then:

(2) Find something from your own life which you experienced which you feel enables you to understand what your selected person experienced. This experience of yours is the "analogue." It is analogous to the other experience. The incident should not be identical. What is important is that you were able to feel or experience something similar to what you believe the person in your incident might have felt or experienced.

State a) what you believe the selected person might have experienced, and b) how your analogue is similar.

Example:

(1) A child's father walks in on Halloween with a skull mask on. The child cries.

(2) Your lover becomes suddenly violent and then walks out on you.

a) The child was bewildered and frightened.

b) You feel the same as the child (but perhaps in reverse order).

Here I have written only a single sentence for each but you can elaborate as much as you want. How DID it feel to be that child at that moment? Can you imagine it? Can you put yourself in his shoes for an instant? Then think of something that happened to you which made you feel like that. The more *different* your analogue is *factually* from the witnessed incident (but containing what you think is a closely similar experience, feeling, or state), the better.

Most students find this exercise quite easy and enjoyable. And it is obvious that writers need to be able to put themselves in the shoes of other people and imagine how they feel. The exercise is important because even though most people can engage easily in imagining what another person feels *when that person apparently feels something we find easy and comfortable to identify within ourselves*, it is not so easy for most of us to engage in this activity when the other person is involved in an activity of which we disapprove or involving feelings that we don't readily identify in ourselves.

At first, you may want to try this exercise with easy prospects. You should then immediately provide yourself with examples of people that you find hard to relate to.

The fact is, your characters, the ones you carry inside of you, are not all ones who naturally think or feel like you. Some of your characters are actually ones you would consider your enemies if you came across them in real life. It is not easy to imagine what someone feels when that person is injuring you! If you find that certain things seem to happen to you repeatedly, whether you choose them or not, the persons involved in those events are very likely members of your own cast of characters. Say you always manage to date men who cannot be emotionally or physically present with you. This is someone you should use in analogues work.

When you do analogues work (homopathy), you must necessarily do being-in-the-moment work (kronobo). In considering how the other feels in a certain situation, you have to "go into" the moment you imagine they are experiencing. What is he feeling? What is he thinking? What does he feel when he withdraws from you?

Then you ask questions, like you do with character facts. If he doesn't like you, why does he date you? If he wants to date you, why does he withdraw?

But mostly, for this exercise, you should stick with asking what he is feeling — and then trying to find a situation in your own life in which you think you felt something similar to what it appears he is feeling.

You will notice that *in this exercise*, you must speculate about what another person is feeling. There is no other exercise in the archetypes approach that requires you to speculate like this about what someone feels, and you have seen from the character facts exercise, which is one that grounds all the others, we specifically charge you NOT to speculate. Later on, in the final integration work, you will learn how to work with the material you have elicited by using questions, hypotheses, and logical deductions. And in Universal Drives, you are also asked to imagine what drives someone in a particular instance. But analogues is the only place where you are charged to imagine what another person feels.

The reason why we ask you not to speculate about what others feel in every other context is that it presupposes a conclusion that you have already made in your conscious mind and thus closes the door to you finding out more.

By *not* speculating or concluding, you are suspending judgment. Suspending judgment is an important skill that you started to practice in character facts and is also part of being-in-the-moment work.

But, the skill of bringing home to oneself how another might feel is a crucial skill for a writer. While that skill must not be allowed to supplant the task of seeing what is in front of you, it must be developed also.

EXERCISES

Amy's work:

1. My friend Becky had been dating a girl long distance off and on for over a year. She recently visited her in Philadelphia and came home to California very upset. I asked her over the phone what had happened. She said that she and Fran had broken up and told me that she found that Fran had been dating another girl when they were together for a few months.

2. I invited my friend Pam to my 21st birthday dinner with my mom and a few other friends. She called me the day before to say she wasn't going to be able to make it due to work. I found out later from her boyfriend that she didn't have to work that night.

   a) Becky felt betrayed and deceived. She couldn't believe that she was lied to and had no idea for how long. She reacted with anger and rage towards Katie.

   b) I felt the same. I had been lied to on my birthday and was very upset about it. I turned to her boyfriend to find out why and he didn't know. I got very angry and hung up.

This is a very straightforward analogue. Becky was betrayed, so was Amy. It is good to start with simple examples like this, but as you progress, you should try to find instances that are harder for you to relate to.

Here's an example that shows what *not* to do.

Edward's work:

1. The professor cried out loud after many unsuccessful tries to access his online course.

2. She wouldn't answer the phone, though it was clear she was home.

   a) The professor was frustrated and angry.

   b) I felt much like the professor.

This one contains too little. It is unclear at first who is who. The professor appears to be somebody Edward knows (but in fact, *he* was that person). The second example appears also to be somebody he knows, but in fact when you read b) you realize that Edward was the one calling the woman who wouldn't answer the phone. Thus, Edward was actually comparing his frustration to his frustration. It is also not a good example because Edward assumes a fact: that she was not home. He does not explain how he knows this.

Third example

Ben's work:

1. When I was 10 years old, my 18-year-old half-brother kicked in my bedroom door early one morning and cursed under his breath. He told me his real father committed suicide the day before. He kicked the door several more times, his voice cracking, and rumbled away downstairs.

2. A few months ago, my younger brother phoned to tell me his dog (also one of our family dogs) died accidentally the previous night when she wolfed down a pan caked with grease — it somehow stopped her heart — and she died.

   a) My older brother was hurt, shocked and extremely angry.

   b) I was also hurt, shocked and extremely angry (whose fault was it? how did she get into a pan? who left the pan out? etc.) I realize both examples deal with internal conflict more than external conflict between people.

   Also, both examples deal with death — should they have been more dissimilar?

   The problem with Ben's example is that #2 is not something that happened to *him* that enables him to relate to what happened to his half brother.

Working with a student to find an analogue

CM and I did a session on Instant Message. First we talked about BIMs. When we began talking about analogues, CM at first merged the two. First she told a story about an incident in which she experienced increased perception and sympathy for someone. Her description of the incident was something like her going into the moment. She thought this was an analogue.

Thus, she merged the idea of sympathizing with someone, which she thought was an analogue, with BIMs. A description of a moment of empathy for another person is just that: a description of one's empathy for another. It is not an analogue. An analogue is where you describe something that happened to another person, then you describe something not identical that happened to you that enables you to understand what you think that person felt. That's all.

CM next recalled a similar incident that had happened to her daughter that gave her daughter an experience similar to CM's semi-BIM/empathy moment. I told her this was kind of a reverse analogue: almost illustrating how she thought her daughter could relate to *her*, rather than the other way around.

Also, the incident was really more of a parallel, I explained. The experiences were not analogues; they were almost identical situations and results. That is a parallel.

CM then asked me: "What if I picked a moment of awkwardness from my own life [that] enabled me to see the man in the office [whom she empathized with], his awkwardness?" I told her that analogues are not about moments in which you are able to see something you didn't see before. They are about relating to what another person experienced. You have to set forth what happened to the other person and what you think s/he experienced, and then you have to set forth what you experienced and felt and how you think that enabled you to understand what the other person experienced in the other situation.

Finally, CM found something that worked as an analogue. Here is our conversation in which that analogue is elicited:

CM: When I was living in England, my husband told me one night he was working late. That night, Katy got sick, so I called his office around 6 pm. His secretary told me that all the guys had gone out to the pub for a beer. I was shocked I couldn't believe that he hadn't told me. When he came home, I was upset and asked him about it. He said he didn't tell me because I had been home for days with katy and he felt guilty about going out and having fun. I could not understand it, I felt betrayed and shocked. I didn't understand who he was in that moment and whether I knew him or not.

JVB: Can you find an analogue?

CM: Yes. When I was a manager for a bank in NY, I was told by the bank that we had to cut staff 50%. I had to lay off a lot of people, one of them was a friend I had lunch with sometimes. She felt betrayed and shocked to be laid off, by me a friend. I had no choice, I was told who to let go, and couldn't change the decisions.

JVB: It's somewhat different, of course, because you had no choice. Can you find an analogue which would enable you to understand what your husband did, what the feeling was in him? What do you think he thought and felt? Because you seem to be finding a parallel, not an analogue.

CM: Let me think about it from that end — the need to get out, the need to be free, the need to not be tied down just for a moment…

JVB: Okay.

CM: The need to have camaraderie with the guys.

JVB: Good.

CM: Okay, now that I see his need, do I find an experience in me like that? That is harder.

JVB: Yes, you don't need to find a similar experience, just something that enables you to understand. Have you ever needed to be free of your obligations to the extent where you have actually walked out, left?

CM: When I got married, I decided to do it alone without my family because I just wanted to do something without all the tradition and obligation that inviting them would have created, is that similar.

JVB: Was it walking out on an obligation? Does the example enable you to understand how your husband might have felt that made him not be there?

CM: I know my mother felt betrayed by this, and felt that I owed it to her to include her, but I had to do it, I wanted to be free. I got married overseas.

JVB: But did your husband do it just because he wanted to do something without tradition?

CM: Yes, I think it is similar, I made a choice for me, because that is what I needed in that moment, I wanted to be free of obligations and walked out, did what I wanted and he made a choice yes without regard for me, because it was what he wanted.

JVB: Made without regard to how others you loved would feel... Good, then you got it.

CM: Wow, that was hard.

JVB: Yes, but mostly because you were thinking of it the wrong way. Also because it is hard to understand an act like his, but that is what is most useful about analogues, understanding what you might not be able to otherwise.

Notice that the easy examples are usually ones in which somebody was hurt or suffered. It is easiest to empathize (homopath) with suffering.

Now that you have read through several examples, try doing your own analogue and come back and compare it. This exercise does not take long.

If you find it easy, move on to more challenging instances — in which the other person does something you find really hard to understand and relate to. Think about what you might have experienced that could enable you to feel what you think s/he felt.

Here is an interesting analogue, somewhat more challenging to relate to.

This is Mary's work:

I witnessed a brief and volatile incident on the subway platform. A man (Man #1) and a woman were walking along the platform together. She accidentally bumped into another man (Man #2). Before she could apologize, Man #2 yelled "Fuck you!" at her.

Immediately, her friend, Man #1, swung around and pushed Man #2, and an escalating duel of nasty words and physical threats developed between the two men. Man #2 yelled more insulting things at the woman before the three finally separated.

I was paying close attention to Man #2 throughout the incident. He got mad really fast. He was indignant and acted like this woman had intentionally harmed him. I think he irrationally made split-second assumptions about her intentions and lost all perspective. This was a narrow and crowded platform we were on. She was carrying two huge bags and had another bag over her shoulder. She was turning around to apologize as he cursed at her. I think he wanted to blame her and let her know that he was mad and wasn't going to take her abuse.

My analogue took place between myself and a cop who was starting to write a ticket on my car. I was dropping off my boyfriend after a weekend together. My car was double-parked and we were standing on the sidewalk. The trunk was open and bags were next to us on the sidewalk.

I watched the cops pull up and stop and one of them get out and walk towards my car and pull out his ticket book. He saw us on the sidewalk as he pulled up and got out.

I quickly became furious when I realized he was beginning to write the ticket even though he saw us standing there with the trunk open and our bags on the sidewalk. I said many angry things to him and didn't calm down even when he agreed not to write the ticket.

When I saw these cops drive up, I was already on my guard because I am very distrustful and intimidated by cops. I think Man #2 was also predisposed in some way to easily be set off by this particular woman bumping him. I was sure that the cops would keep driving once they saw us on the sidewalk. When he got out and pulled out his ticket book, I "lost it." I said many things you just don't say to cops. I was indignant in an out-of-control way like Man #2 on the subway platform. I felt disrespected and was telling this cop that he had no right to treat me like this. At the point when he agreed not to write the ticket, I kept yelling at him. I had no perspective and felt like he was maliciously targeting me in some way. He was just doing his job and that woman was merely walking down the platform with a huge load.

The hardest analogues, the most challenging occasions in which to engage in *homopathing*, is with your enemies. Try to imagine what it feels like to steal from somebody or to viciously attack a stranger or to cheat on somebody you say you love. Remember that the goal here is not moral (or legal) judgment. The goal is to try to feel what another person feels, to put yourself in his or her shoes and imagine what it feels like. When doing analogue work, you do not go farther. You do not try to articulate that person's thoughts or describe subsequent behavior or actions beyond a single incident. In the archetypes approach, that comes later. But if you find words coming to mind, write them down and save them for later reference.

CHAPTER TWELVE

UNIVERSES OF DISCOURSE

Our normal waking consciousness, rational consciousness, as we call it, is but one special type of consciousness, whilst all about it, parted from it by the filmiest of screens, there lie potential forms of consciousness entirely different. We may go through life without suspecting their existence; but apply the requisite stimulus, and at a touch they are there in all their completeness, definite types of mentality which probably somewhere have their field of application and adaptation.

— William James, *The Varieties of Religious Experience*

We might think of the ordinary state of perception as a building that is our home for most of our waking hours. It surrounds us, protects us, but also confines us. This solid building does not even seem to have any windows, so that the illusion arises that there is nothing beyond its walls. That is not the case, however. We regularly escape when we dream, to what we might think of as another building next door, which is equally ours. It contains a number of separate rooms, of which that of our dreams is only one. The door to the dream room is sleep; we cannot dream unless we sleep. There are also rooms of daydreaming, the hypnotic state, the various meditative states, ecstasy, and many other hitherto unidentified changes necessary to enter it. There may be no resistance when we want to get into the second building, its front door may be heavy, but once inside, it is relatively easy to pass from room to room.

— Felicitas D. Goodman, *How About Demons?*
Possession & Exorcism in the Modern World

The Universes of Discourse exercise is about our states of consciousness. It is about the conscious and subconscious processes of the human mind: the "dual mind." It is one of the most important exercises in the archetypes for writers method, but it is not in any direct way about character. In other words, although you will watch movies for this exercise, you should *not* pay particular attention to the characters in the movies or cross-apply any of the other exercises towards those characters — at least not when you're watching the movies for the purpose of this exercise.

This exercise teaches something quite different from the other ones in this book. It teaches something I call "the two-part principle," which is an undercurrent in all of the Archetypes for Writers work. The two-part principle is useful because it reflects a basic truth about the dual mind and the way it works. It teaches not only about the duality but about the way that duality actually works.

The dual mind is our genetic endowment. However, a certain amount of knowledge does help to enable us to consistently use it. It helps to know *what the dual mind does, why it is important,* and *how to recognize it* at work. But it is not enough to learn these things in theory. It is important for writers to have the benefit of walking through the processes of the dual mind. I have therefore developed the UoD exercise to provide writers with a way to experience the workings of the dual mind through movies that use theatrical or story devices that work the way the dual mind does.

Because we all possess this dual mind, we all know about it intuitively. But, oddly, most people in our culture have great difficulty recognizing subconscious processes in action, or knowing how to work with them.

The UoD exercise is a simple and fun exercise that you can do alone or with friends. In this exercise, you will watch one or more videos from a selected list and do the UoD work, which I will describe in a minute, using the content of that film.

A "universe of discourse" is a realm of experience or existence that is separate and mutually exclusive from at least one other realm or universe of experience or existence. Because the subconscious/conscious duality is internal and invisible, and separated by an invisible, shifting sheath or wall, the easiest universes of discourse are those which are simple metaphorical enactments of this duality and its functioning. Thus, movies about ghosts versus the living; aliens versus earthlings; altered states of consciousness versus the "normal" state of consciousness; the undercover/covert world versus the overt world, etc.

These dualities, you will notice are not necessarily direct opposites. Nor are they mere ideas (good versus evil, light versus dark, etc.). They are two mutually exclusive realms such that where one is in existence, the other is not. Living beings don't exist in the same dimension as ghosts, an altered state of consciousness does not happen simultaneous with a normal state, and so on. This is putting it rather simply since there *are* points and rules of contact, as well as shifts or transformations from one state/realm to the other.

Note that not all dialectical pairs are genuine UoDs for our purposes. So, just because a film appears to have two universes or states does not mean it is a genuine UoD film. Once you learn the rules of UoDs, you will be able to consider other films, but at the start, please use only those films listed here.

There are several reasons for doing UoD work. As I noted above, this work develops your awareness of your own dual mind and its processes. This is crucial in doing archetype work. Secondly, it also helps you to develop the Author Self (which I discussed earlier). Third, it will wake you up to "secret lives" and "the invisible world." These elements are what archetype work eventually uncovers and how such work develops characters and reconstructs the lives of genuine archetypal character shells.

COMMON INGREDIENTS IN UoDS

All genuine UoDs have certain characteristics in common. For example, information flows in *one* direction, particularly at the outset. People in the ordinary world are not, at first, aware of those in the "other" world, but those in the other world can see and hear those in the ordinary world. The other world always starts out being invisible to those in the ordinary world. The other world also has "magical" or extraordinary capabilities not shared by the ordinary one. Sometimes these capabilities are based on access to special information and training (as in spy films — spies know and can do things ordinary humans don't and can't). Other times the special abilities simply are part of the other world (like ghosts, who can walk through walls, etc.) Oftentimes, those who have contact with the other world also gain special abilities (for example, they acquire psychic or healing powers). The invisible, other world is often frightening and dangerous, especially if revealed too abruptly or too soon to those in the ordinary world. Sometimes, people in the ordinary world simply don't believe the other world exists until it is forced on them in some way. In many UoD films, one person experiences contact with the other world, and everyone else around him in the ordinary world thinks he has simply gone crazy.

WHAT'S THE POINT OF UoD WORK?

UoDs accustom your brain to working in a different way than is required in almost any other kind of work or in normal, everyday human interactions. This is not because UoDs are obsolete or ahead of their time. The mode of working embodied in the UoDs work is ultimately the key to archetypes work — which is always about the emergence of your deepest Self.

Here is the exercise. Directly after it, I will walk you through the exercise with two examples. You can jump right in and try the exercise before reading my walk-through, or you can do it the other way around.

EXERCISE ONE: BEGINNING UoD WORK

I've found that the best movies to watch when you are first learning UoDs are ghost movies. Select a movie from the following short list for the first one you will watch:

> (Mostly not scary)
> *Always* (Holly Hunter, Richard Dreyfuss; Dir. Steven Spielberg, 1989)
> *Field of Dreams* (Kevin Costner, Amy Madigan, James Earl Jones, Burt Lancaster; Dir. Phil Alden Robinson, 1989)
> *Frequency* (Dennis Quaid, Jim Caviezel; Dir. Gregory Hoblit, 2000)

    (Scary)

    Ghost (Demi Moore, Patrick Swayze; Dir. Jerry Zucker, 1990)

    The Haunting (Liam Neeson, Lili Taylor, Catherine Zeta-Jones, Owen Wilson; Dir. Jan de Bont, 1999)

    The Others (Nicole Kidman; Dir. Alejandro Amenabar, 2001)

    The Sixth Sense (Bruce Willis, Haley Joel Osment, Toni Collette, Olivia Williams; Dir. M. Night Shyamalan, 1999)

    Stir of Echoes (Kevin Bacon, Illeana Douglas; Dir. David Koepp, 1999)

It doesn't hurt if you've seen the movie already and it might even help. You can watch the movie alone or with a friend who would like to do the exercise with you. Do the exercise with only one movie at a time. You can take notes while watching the movie (and even stop and start it if you want). Or you can watch it through once and then re-watch it and take notes. (If you haven't seen the movie before, you might want to just watch it through first — but read through the whole exercise before doing this, so you know what we're looking for here.)

UoD Exercise: Part One
(Characteristics & Rules of Each UoD Before Contact)

Step One: Scratch List of Characteristics & Rules (Before Contact)

Your first assignment in this exercise is to answer this question: "What are the characteristics and rules of each separate world (the ghost world and the world of the living) *before* they interact?" Write down your answers. Thus, for example, ghosts can usually pass through solid objects; living beings cannot. Ghosts can see and hear living beings but living beings (usually) cannot see and hear ghosts. (This is a good example of a rule that must be established before it can be broken. Make sure you write down the general characteristic or rule before you note any exceptions. Exceptions usually occur as the film progresses and usually belong to the "points of contact" work, below.)

Each movie establishes these characteristics and rules in different ways. List and describe the scenes that establish these things in the movies you watch. For example, if you state that one characteristic of the ghost world is that they can see and hear living beings, also note where and how that is established in the movie. Avoid focusing on how the two realms make contact or interact, just yet. (If you can't help but notice the points of contact, simply record them on a separate sheet of paper.)

Each world is peopled in some way. Who are those people? What do they want? What is their world like to them? What do they spend their time doing? Why do they do what they do? What drives them? Do they have feelings? Families? Are they friendly or hostile? Do you ever see the UoDs separate from each other, or are they interacting immediately? (If there are no scenes which establish each UoD separately, you have to try to deduce what the characteristics were before contact.) What is the UoD like for the character or entity within it? (What is it like for the character/entity who is in the other UoD? Can s/he perceive the other UoD at all?) What does s/he know about things and about both his/her own UoD and the other?

Step Two: Narrative of Each UoD

At first, just make a scratch list of these things. Then, put all the information you have about each UoD into narrative form. Try *not* to just retell the movie's story. The organizing device you are using is *not* the story itself but the two universes within the story. The UoDs form the backbone, the framework of your narrative. So, organize by UoD characteristics and provide examples for each. The narrative is really just the list explained to a listener.

Each UoD has numerous characteristics. Do the characteristics for each UoD separate from the other.

Up to this point, keep the UoDs separate. Don't mix them or consider them together or interacting.

Once you complete the discrete UoD exercise, move onto the second part of the exercise: the points of contact.

UoD Exercise: Part Two (Points of Contact)

Now, go back and figure out what are the first points of contact between the two worlds. How does the first contact happen? For example, what are the first signs to the living beings that there are ghosts there? In *What Lies Beneath*, for example, the first signs are electronic devices turning on or things moving or falling. (*What Lies Beneath* is a good UoD film, but I didn't list it in beginning work because it shifts focus towards the end of the film, which might be confusing.)

Usually, in ghost films, points of contact (POCs) increase gradually until there is direct person-to-person contact or mixing, or even merging of the two worlds. Take careful note of each and every point of contact and how they progress. How does contact start? What is the medium of the contact: electronic devices? moving objects? voices? What is the next phase of contact? Does the contact simply increase or does it shift to a new means or medium? For example, does it start with moving objects and move to a "conveyor" (a reliable means of conveying messages from one realm to the other)?

Finally, what are the later means of contact that lead up to resolution? Is it more direct, relying on less subtle means? Is it less scary or more scary? What resolves the tension between the two worlds?

TWO WALK-THROUGHS
(1) *Hideaway*

For our first walk-through, I am using the 1994 film *Hideaway*, with Jeff Goldblum, Christine Lahti, Jeremy Sisto, Alicia Silverstone, and Alfred Molina, and directed by Bret Leonard. Although the cinematic quality of "good" UoD films varies tremendously and a good UoD film may not be a good movie on any other terms, I chose *Hideaway* because, even though my video guide rates the movie poorly, it is an excellent UoD film and it presents particular problems of interpretation that I can use to clarify UoDs.

In *Hideaway*, Goldblum plays Hatch Harrison, an ordinary man who dies and is revived after 120 minutes dead. This event causes him to "bring something back" with him from the place to which he "crossed over." It brings him a psychic real-time connection with a murderer, who is named Vassago, played by Jeremy Sisto. (Both Goldblum and Sisto are excellent in their roles.)

The story, of course, is far more complex than this, but this is sufficient set-up for UoD purposes. The other world is not the world of the murderer, however; it is the origin of the psychic connection (the after-death realm). The murderer exists in the ordinary world along with everyone else, although he, too, has a psychic awareness — only with the Harrison character, though. It's a simple two-way door. This seems to break one of the first rules of UoDs, which I mentioned earlier, that information flows only in one direction. However, if you remember that the other world is not the murderer but the origin of the psychic connection, you'll see that the rules hold fast, because neither the murderer nor Harrison obtain any further information about that other realm except through a single scene between Harrison and a psychic who does a tarot reading for him. This is when Harrison learns that he brought something back with him when he crossed over and is counseled that he has to trust what is pure and good in him.

Although the realm of the murderer is not the UoD, Harrison's psychic experiences with him are points of contact with the other UoD, because they draw on the psychic realm, and they work the same way as points of contact with more direct UoDs — that is, they develop knowledge in the person who's in the "ordinary" world. These points of contact progress until the recipient masters this new means of acquiring knowledge and resolves the conflict(s) created by the contacts.

It is interesting that most UoD films resolve the conflicts by domination of one realm over the other, despite the genuine development of the contacts and mastering of the means (which logically would make resolution by domination unnecessary and not even sensible). The same is true in *Hideaway*, in which the development of the points of contact is very well written, but the resolution is almost laughable.

There is very little information in *Hideaway* about the other world. What makes *Hideaway* very useful are the points of contact, which are both contact points for the genuine other realm and for the realm of the murderer. (Again, the realm of the murderer is not a UoD because information flows in both directions from and to him and because he lives by the same laws as those in the ordinary world. Thus, his world is actually the same as the ordinary world, albeit a sick, twisted version of it, and purportedly drawing from the genuine other UoD, which in this film is also a divided world of good and evil. Remember, also, that good and evil are, in themselves, never UoDs.)

So, let's look at the points of contact and their development in this movie. The first PoC is when Harrison dies. This is the only genuine PoC with the other UoD. It offers a basis for understanding the rest of the PoCs but in this film, it offers very little information. Harrison goes down a tunnel and sees his daughter who had died in a freak accident the year before. He later thinks she was trying to tell him something.

The first contact after that is spontaneous. Harrison is cutting a tomato and has a vision of himself murdering a young woman. He's in a complete altered state. Soon after that Harrison has a dream of some place which turns out to be the murderer's hideaway. The next day, Harrison sees a picture of the missing girl, whom he tells his wife is dead. The next connection is when he's driving. He experiences the murder of another young woman and calls the police to tell them where the body is. He then dreams of the murderer seeing his other daughter, who is alive and had gone out to a club. He speaks her name in the dream and the murderer thus knows her name. This is where we find out that the connection goes in both directions. This was set up in the opening scene of the movie in which the murderer also dies, although we don't know until later that he was also revived by the same doctor who revived Harrison (who happens to be the murderer's father). So, essentially, both Harrison and Varragos have contact with each other *through* contact with the UoD, although the murderer learns nothing from it.

Harrison, however, learns how to force the psychic contact and use it to find out what the killer is doing. A side benefit of his psychic connection is that although he has to induce pain by cutting or burning himself to make contact, his wounds heal almost instantly. Similarly, a baby who's crying from teething pain is instantly calmed when he touches the baby's cheek.

An interesting scene juxtaposes Harrison, whose contact with the other UoD has given him special knowledge, and his wife, who declares that this is all Harrison's guilt for having lost his daughter. This lack of belief from those in the ordinary world is found in almost all UoD films. Often, the lack of belief is held by the one who is confronting the other realm. Other times, it is held by other characters.

Thus, *Hideaway* illustrates a fundamental way in which UoDs work: the one-way rule. This can help us to discern what the UoDs are. Because the real other UoD is not the one with whom Harrison has the points of contact, it would be easy to get confused over what the other UoD really is. Nonetheless, if one remembers the rules of UoDs, this movie is a good UoD film. If you wish, feel free to watch the movie yourself and use my work as a guide.

(2) *Alias*

Alias is a television series about a woman, Sydney, who has a double life. She is an "Operations Agent" in the CIA. In other words, she's a spy. She goes on missions in foreign countries to retrieve information critical to American national security. She fights bad guys, gets tortured, breaks into secure facilities, steals stuff, escapes, etc., etc. In the very first episode, we learn that she was recruited while in college, which she is still completing. The two worlds are set in relief pretty clearly. In the very first scene, we see Sydney being subjected to torture by Asian bad guys. This cuts quickly to Sydney finishing an exam in her literature class at college. We see her boyfriend propose to her; then we see her going into work — a cover for her CIA workplace — and taking her engagement ring off in the elevator. Right away we see both worlds and we are given points of contact. Her partner, Dixon, notices she has a glow.

Sydney decides to tell her fiancé who she really is. She turns the music up and takes him into the shower to talk to him. She then goes on her next dangerous mission with Dixon (to photograph an odd instrument made from a 400-year-old design). She and Dixon complete their mission, almost getting caught.

Meantime, Sydney's fiancé leaves her a message on her phone, which is, of course, tapped and picked up by surveillance. We were introduced to Sydney's dad, who she says imports airplane parts for a living, when her fiancé called him to ask permission to marry her. However, the two worlds become tangled when we see her boss, Sloane, instruct her father to take care of her fiancé.

Sydney returns from her mission to find her fiancé murdered. She takes time off from undercover work but after she declines to heed Dixon's warning that "If they don't have confidence with someone in as deep as you are, they'll fix that problem," two thugs try to kill her in a garage. After she bests one of them at hand-to-hand combat, her father suddenly drives up and tells her to get in the car. After doing some amazing driving maneuvers and killing the other thug, her father reveals that he not only works for the same undercover group she works for — which is called SD-6 — but SD-6 is actually *not* part of the CIA. It is a segment of "The Alliance," which is an international group of renegade spies.

Sydney refuses her father's assistance (and tells him to stay away from her) and goes to her friend, Will, to ask him for his sister's passport and credit cards. Having obtained these, she goes back to the Orient to get the instrument she had earlier photographed. This is when she gets captured and tortured.

She escapes, gets the instrument, and brings it back to Sloane, who accepts her back into the SD-6 fold. She says she has midterms coming up so she won't be in for a week and she goes to the CIA and becomes a double agent.

The original two worlds are (1) the ordinary life Sydney leads, going to college, dating, hanging out with friends, and (2) the secret life she leads as a spy. Subsequently, her spy life also becomes divided into two worlds. It is rare in UoD films that three worlds are genuine UoDs, but the three in *Alias* are genuine because they follow the UoD rules. Sydney cannot tell her friends about her life as a spy, and she also cannot tell those at SD-6 that she works for the CIA. Some people at SD-6 genuinely think they work for an undercover section of the CIA. Others (like her boss, Sloane, and her father) know they are really working for The Alliance.

It turns out her father is also a double agent, so he shares all three of Sydney's worlds. Otherwise, though, Sydney cannot let anyone know she is now working as a double agent for the CIA spying on SD-6. Thus, the dual CIA/SD-6 world is the "other" UoD in relation to the ordinary world. And the CIA, alone, is the other UoD in relation to SD-6. Notice that UoDs always come in pairs, even when there appear to be an odd number, since a UoD is always in relation to another world. Each of these relationships is discrete and singular in that the UoD rules work through the single pairs only, not in trios or larger groupings. In this case, there are simply two pairs of UoDs in *Alias*. It's unusual but not unprecedented.

The points of contact are abundant, which makes this pilot really fun to watch for UoD work (particularly after you have watched a few of the easier UoD films first). The mechanism for contact between the worlds is Sydney herself. She bridges both worlds. She is both the bridge and the gatekeeper. We see her dealing with this difficult situation and we see the consequences of her breaching the key rule "Don't tell!" Telling people in the ordinary world about the special world brings torture and murder upon the recipient (and possibly on herself, the conveyor).

When Sydney is captured we see another UoD element playing out in another direction: her torturer wants to know who she works for and she says "I got news for you. I am your worst enemy. I have nothing to lose." (He says "You have your teeth.") So, here is the same "Don't tell!" rule played out differently. Those in the special world have to protect their information from falling into the wrong hands — both those of the "good" guys and those of the enemy. In *Alias*, the enemy's world is another genuine UoD, but it is not developed much. (It's kind of a subplot of a UoD.)

The mechanisms for further points of contact outside of Sydney's gatekeeper function are surveillance (SD-6 tapping her phone, her father sitting in a car watching her at her fiancé's funeral), notes (Sydney leaves her friend, Will, a note that she's on the roof of his building), pager (Sloane pages her when he wants her to come in), personal appearance (both Dixon and her father come to her), violence (thugs shooting at, chasing, and fighting her; torturer), cell phones (Sydney's friend calls her in the middle of her escape from the thugs; later her father gives her a special cell phone), and debriefing (she goes into the CIA, writes everything down for them and meets with her new "handler").

All in all, *Alias* is a fun UoD TV series to watch and very educational for UoDs.

EXERCISE TWO: MORE DIFFICULT FILMS

Exercise Two is really "UoD exercise ad *infinitum*." It is an exercise that you can do for the rest of your life and always benefit from it. It is done exactly the same way as Exercise One, except using more difficult films. Make sure that you work on at least two (and preferably all) of the easy films before moving onto the more difficult films listed below. You can continue doing UoD work alternately with the other exercises in this book as you move forward. (In fact, once you learn all the exercises, I recommend you continue to go back and forth between all of them until they are all mastered and merge as a single global skill.)

Many films fall into the "more difficult" UoD category. They have two easily identifiable UoDs but sometimes it seems like there might even be more than two UoDs, or there are other elements that complicate the UoDs. For example, only the first half of the movie *The Insider* is a UoD film. The UoDs do not ever really resolve; the invisible world remains invisible and the original story that involves Wigant's decision to tell all and his being shadowed and harassed transforms into the story of his deposition and how CBS suppressed and then finally aired Wigant's revelations.

I've divided this list up into general categories. There is some overlap between these categories.

(Note: In case you are thinking of watching any of these films with children, kids can do this exercise well and it is usually fun for them, *but*, except for Casper, the ghost movies are not suitable for children. In fact, most of these films are not suitable for children. If you want to do this exercise with your child, choose films from the magic category or family/romance. Also, other than *Communion*, which is scary, the two alien movies are probably okay for kids.)

- More "Ghost" Movies (all scary except where noted)
    Below (Olivia Williams, Bruce Greenwood, Matt Davis; Dir. David Twohy, 2002)
    Casper (Christina Ricci, Bill Pullman; Dir. Brad Silberling, 1995) (not scary)
    In Dreams (Annette Bening, Robert Downey Jr., Aidan Quinn, Stephen Rea; Dir. Neil Jordan, 1998)
    The Mothman Prophecies (Richard Gere, Laura Linney; Dir. Mark Pellington, 2002)
    What Dreams May Come (Robin Williams, Annabella Sciorra, Cuba Gooding, Jr.; Dir. Vincent Ward, 1998)

What Lies Beneath (Harrison Ford, Michelle Pfeiffer; Dir. Robert Zemeckis, 2000)

"Spy" or Covert Movies

Arlington Road (Tim Robbins, Joan Cusack, Jeff Bridges; Dir. Mark Pellington, 1999)

The Bourne Identity (Matt Damon, Franka Potente, Chris Cooper, Clive Owen; Dir. Doug Liman, 2002) (the Bourne movies are really amnesia movies, like *Dead Again* & also like *Communion*)

The Bourne Supremacy (Matt Damon, Franka Potente, Brian Cox, Julia Stiles, Joan Allen; Dir. Paul Breengrass, 2004)

Conspiracy Theory (Mel Gibson, Julia Roberts, Patrick Stewart; Dir. Richard Donner, 1997)

Enemy of the State (Will Smith, Gene Hackman; Dir. Tony Scott, 1998)

The Insider (Russell Crowe, Al Pacino; Dir. Michael Mann, 2000)

Mission Impossible (Tom Cruise, Jon Voight; Dir. Brian de Palma, 1996)

The X-Files (the movie) (David Duchovny, Gillian Anderson; Dir. Rob Bowman, 1998)

Time Bender or Psychic Phenomena Movies

The Butterfly Effect (Ashton Kutcher, Amy Smart; Dir. Eric Bress & J. Mackye Gruber, 2004)

The Cell (Jennifer Lopez, Vince Vaughn, Vincent D'Onofrio; Dir. Tarsem Singh, 2000)

Dead Again (Emma Thompson, Kenneth Branagh (actor & director), 1991)

Dead Zone (Christopher Walken; Dir. David Cronenberg, 1983)

Donnie Darko (Jake Gyllenhaal; Dir. Richard Kelly, 2001)

Final Destination (Devon Sawa, Ali Larter; Dir. James Wong, 2000)

Alien Movies

Close Encounters of the Third Kind (Richard Dreyfuss, Teri Garr; Dir. Steven Spielberg, 1977)

Communion (Christopher Walken; Dir. Phillippe Mora, 1989)

Superman: The Movie (Christopher Reeve, Margot Kidder, Marlon Brando, Gene Hackman; Dir. Richard Donner, 1978)

- Alter Personalities or Other

  Bram Stoker's Dracula (Gary Oldman, Winona Ryder, Keanu Reeves, Anthony Hopkins; Dir. Francis Ford Coppola, 1992)

  Fight Club (Ed Norton, Brad Pitt; Dir. David Fincher, 1999)

  Final Approach (Hector Elizondo, James B. Sikking; Dir. Eric Steven Stahl, 1992)

  Identity (John Cusack, Ray Liotta, Amanda Peet; Dir. James Mangold, 2003)

  The Long Kiss Goodnight (Gina Davis, Samuel Jackson; Dir. Renny Harlen, 1996)

  Primal Fear (Richard Gere, Ed Norton; Dir. Gregory Hoblit, 1996)

  Shattered Image (Anne Parillaud, William Baldwin; Dir. Raul Ruiz, 1998)

- Magic

  Harry Potter & the Sorcerer's Stone (Daniel Radcliffe, Rupert Grint, Emma Watson, John Cleese, John Hurt, Alan Rickman, Fiona Shaw, Maggie Smith; Dir. Chris Columbus, 2001)

  Jumanji (Robin Williams, Kirsten Dunst; Dir. Joe Johnston, 1995)

  Peter Pan (Betty Bronson, Ernest Torrence; Dir. Herbert Brenon, 1924) or (Mary Martin, Cyril Ritchard; Dir. Vincent J. Donehue, 1960) (NOT the Disney animated version or the recent Spielberg version, *Hook*. Alternatively, read the original play by J. M. Barrie.)

- Thriller/Horror

  Gaslight (Charles Boyer, Ingrid Bergman, Angela Lansbury; Dir. George Cukor, 1944)

  Hideaway (Jeff Goldblum, Christine Lahti, Jeremy Sisto, Alicia Silverstone; Dir. Brett Leonard, 1994)

  Poltergeist (JoBeth Williams, Craig T. Nelson; Dir. Tobe Hooper — screenwriter Steven Speilberg, 1982)

  The Ring (Naomi Watts; Dir. Gore Verbinski, 2002)

  Sci-Fi/Fantasy

    Batman Returns (Michael Keaton, Michelle Pfeiffer; Dir. Tim Burton, 1992)

    Star Trek 4: The Voyage Home (William Shatner, DeForest Kelley, Catherine Hicks; Dir. Leonard Nimoy, 1986)

    Star Trek: The Next Generation — "The Inner Light" (TV Episode, Patrick Stewart, Jonathan Frakes; Dir. Peter Lauritson, 1992)

    Quantum Leap — Pilot Episode (Scott Bakula, Dean Stockwell; Dir. David Hemmings, 1989)

  Family/Romance

    Chances Are (Cybil Shepard, Robert Downey, Jr.; Dir. Emile Ardolino, 1989) (not scary)

    Heart & Souls (Robert Downey, Jr., Charles Grodin, Kyra Sedgwick, Alfre Woodard, Tom Sizemore, Elisabeth Shue; Dir. Ron Underwood)

    Kate & Leopold (Meg Ryan, Hugh Jackman; Dir. James Mangold, 2001)

    Mrs. Doubtfire (Robin Williams, Sally Field; Dir. Chris Columbus, 1993)

    What Women Want (Mel Gibson, Helen Hunt; Dir. Nancy Meyers, 2000)

  Spy Television Series (I put these separate from the movies because the quality of the shows for UoD purposes varies from episode to episode. I'd recommend not watching them until after getting well acquainted with UoDs through the movies.)

    Alias (Jennifer Garner, TV Series, 2001- ; Created by J. J. Abrams)

    The X-Files (David Duchovny, Gillian Anderson, TV Series, 1993-2002; created by Chris Carter)

When you first do the UoD exercise, follow the instructions closely to write down your observations of the separate UoDs and POCs, make lists, then narratives. Do this with at least half a dozen films. Even after years of doing this work, I still sometimes take notes on more complex and interesting UoD films. After you do a bunch of films this way, you will find that you don't need to write everything down anymore; you'll just notice the UoDs naturally. You'll become a connoisseur of UoD films. The mental process and understanding will become part of the global skill you're acquiring.

There are many movies you might expect to see on this list that are not UoD films. Movies like *The Matrix*, *The Mummy*, or *Lord of the Rings*, *Practical Magic* (or *The Craft*), *Hocus Pocus*, *Sleepy Hollow*, *Signs* (or *Unbreakable*), *Pirates of the Caribbean*, *E.T.*, James Bond movies, classic television series like *The Fugitive* and *The Avengers*, *The Falcon & the Snowman*, *WarGames*, *North by Northwest*, *2001: A Space Odyssey*, etc. While some of these movies may have elements of UoDs in them, the UoDs are not clear or developed enough to be useful. Others may at first appear to be UoD films because they have two of the realms typical of UoD films: like the covert and overt worlds of spy films, or ghosts, etc. But I do not include these films in my UoD list either because the UoDs don't operate like UoDs or, even if they do, the films simply teach nothing about UoDs. (There are, of course, many movies I have not watched which may be UoD films.) Other films are simply not UoD films, even if they are in the same genres as the selected films.

I would recommend not experimenting with other films you think might be UoD films until after you've watched most of the listed UoD films here.

Chapter Thirteen

EMOTIONAL ACCESS WORK
(Anthropathy)

Writing work is nothing without access to all one's feelings. While emotional work is taking place within each of the components of the archetypes approach, working with one's feelings is also a separate task with its own specific goals. In this chapter, I will discuss some goals and techniques that will help you gain greater access to feelings in a manner that will be useful to your writing.

These can be broken down into the following:

(1) **Empathetic or sympathetic feeling:** Bringing the circumstances of other people to your attention and trying to feel what it would feel like to be in that circumstance.

(2) **Self-observant feeling:** Also can be called "self-feeling." Looking at your own life and situation and seeing what it means and feeling it. Feeling and owning your own feelings.

(3) **Outward-observant feeling:** Also can be called "impersonal or humanitarian feeling." Seeing, understanding, and feeling the consequences and destinies that result from people's actions. Understanding the internal logic of what people do and why, but also what it means about their lives.

The skill is called *anthropathy*. When you are doing emotional access work of any kind, you are *anthropathing*.

Feeling in these ways is a complex and difficult task. Feeling for yourself calls you to experience things you might want to avoid. Feeling for others can be a lot of work, particularly if you don't acknowledge your own feelings or feel recognized yourself, and more so when it is someone for whom you don't naturally feel empathy. Understanding consequences and destinies is the highest goal and greatest challenge.

There is no component of the archetypes method that can replace the work of accessing one's own feelings and feeling for others, and indeed this component binds all the others together, but it is also the most challenging topic to cover in a book. It is easy to set a goal of feeling one's feelings, and it's easy for a teacher to point out the importance of doing so, but feelings are not so easily trammeled. (That's a Shakespearean word for bound, confined, restricted, restrained.)

First, the individual must feel, and if he doesn't feel, how will he come to feel? Can someone else get him to feel? And, anyway, feel what?

Years of working with people has taught me that the hardest thing for most people is to feel for one's enemies. In other words, we may be entirely open to everything else in the universe, but our enemies get not one bit of our understanding.

For each person, there seems to be a genuine point of no return, beyond which one's life can really begin, but which we are prevented from ever reaching by the mere fact that we will not understand certain people. It is odd that most people view this point of no return as a kind of little death. They resist it with all their power and will. They refuse to acknowledge their enemy. If they get so far as to master the rest of this method, they will nonetheless do anything to lull me into thinking they are doing it really well, as long as they don't have to meet this one thing. Sometimes this barrier actually takes form as a literal enemy, a person or persons whom we feel obstruct us (or worse, want to harm us). It may be a single individual from our past, or a group of them. Or it may actually play out in the present. Or it may be an issue or a situation we consistently avoid — or repeatedly encounter, despite everything we do to avoid it.

Whatever form it takes, the archetypes approach will do nothing for you if you only apply it to the easiest situations in your life — to those about which (and about whom) you already possess a good understanding. Indeed, what is the point of acquiring tools like this if you do not use them on the most difficult aspects of your life? After all, it is your life that is your material.

Thus, it is something of a paradox and an irony that in order to do one's own writing, which will, the idea goes, bring you a kind of inner peace and happiness, you must encounter your pain and grief, your sorrow, your humiliation. What this means is that the archetypes approach is *about* such encounters, more than anything else. It is about feeling one's pain, grief, etc. Perhaps this was why Marcel Proust wrote that the people about whom writers write "have quite simply been posing for the artist at the very moment when, much against his will, they made him suffer most."

As such, it is a rare and unique person who is capable of meeting the challenge and gaining mastery. And, also as such, many people confuse this work with a variety of other things, including whatever made them suffer in the first place — for whatever calls up one's suffering is often seen as the perpetrator of it.

I can only caution students not to confuse the message with the content or the messenger with the source.

So, the goal of gaining emotional access is to find one's skeletons in the closet. One must be willing to grapple with whatever is most difficult for oneself, and one must be prepared to feel it from the other side, even the enemy's side.

For example, a woman I know cannot think about her older sister without feeling pain and disgust. Thus, it is very difficult for her to imagine being inside her sister's skin. Yet, in order to understand what happened, why her sister did what she did to her, and to use this material in her own writing, she must enter into her sister's body and mind. A story that did not include her sister in some form or another, would never be complete from the point of view of this woman's own material, and a story that did not fully recreate her sister as a character would be hollow or shallow. To fully recreate any character, you must be able to feel for them, to hear their thoughts in your head, and to live their lives through the writing.

For some people, such material is so toxic that they can carry out these tasks only if they work in the third person with characters whom they never consciously recognize as the people in their own lives who have hurt them. Some people have the ability to invent characters out of whole cloth and work with their inventions without recognizing the deep connections. But even so, for these people, invention may fail where the material becomes too close to home.

In any case, the task of creating one's own archetypes is essentially the same work — albeit a more reliable and consciously chosen method — since you remove the original person one step, by moving from "Sally said" to "she is the one who said" and then finding those like examples of the ectype (the pre-archetype form) that we call isotypes ("who else is like the woman who said…?").

Not only does this process attain the level of archetypes, it helps in unearthing all the material — since, once removed from the original source, it is emotionally easier to handle, but it helps one to reconstruct the entire full-fledged person, since by this process you accumulate multiple examples of all pieces of the character.

But again, the goal for us must be to find the things that bother us most. This does not have to happen at the outset but it does have to happen or the method remains peripheral and ultimately vapid. Similarly, this means we must, if not actively seek out, then at least pay close attention to those whom we dislike the most, even detest, those who have given us the most pain and suffering, those whom we would otherwise wish to avoid at all costs.

This presents us with an odd and troubling dilemma in this work. What if such persons and situations are actually dangerous to us? (Indeed, it could be argued that even if not physically dangerous, every situation we avoid with such fervor is likely dangerous to us in some way, even if only psychologically — that, however, being equally as valid as any other.) How can we pay attention to, absorb, and feel for persons whose purpose is to destroy us? (That's an extreme example, I admit. Not all those we avoid are such mortal enemies, but the example is illustrative.)

It goes without saying that I would never advise anyone to walk into the jaws of danger in order to obtain some potentially useful piece of information for his writing! I advise that if you feel you have toxic material like this, experiences in your life that were terrible to you, first ensure your own safety. This is very important even for those who did not suffer some early trauma but had relatively uneventful childhoods (or adolescences or adulthoods, for that matter), because archetypes work tends to bring stuff up that you might not even have known was there, or sort of knew but didn't really know. The truth is that we all, merely by right of being human beings, have some deep pains. Some of this pain is cultural, some is just the condition of humankind. And it seems that the greatest personal growth is nearly always through facing and learning to handle this stuff.

Our purpose here, of course, is not just to "handle" it, but to create full and deep characters with it, to tell their real stories, to have our deepest inmost recesses seen and heard and to reach into the deepest parts of others to move them, too. This means embracing and *using* those feelings that we most wish to avoid. In a sense, in order to do so, one actually must be using *all* of the resources of the archetypes method.

The method I use for this part of the work is two-pronged. First, I ask the student to try to get into the skin of the person who bothers them most. I ask them to imagine the scenario which is most disturbing to them and then to switch sides, to take the opposite side, to try to view it from the point of view of their enemy. Then I ask them to speak for that person, say that person's words, try to feel why they are saying them and what is making them think as they do. That's the first part.

The second step is that I show them how to do it by illustrating with my own material. This is risky and I do it only when I can't find any other way to get the person to fully engage and get inside the enemy. It's risky because when I am fully engaged, I am also completely emotionally engaged, and whatever I am feeling, I am feeling deeply. Because it is of no use for me to illustrate this work with insipid examples, it is best if I can use something that is affecting me deeply and painfully. The problem is that when people see me engaged like this, they may either become frightened by the power of my emotions or the content of the incident, or they confuse the content with the messenger. Indeed, when I am fully engaged with this work myself, with my own material, I am not at that moment working to make things clear to my student! But this is still the best way to show others how it works and that it can and must be used with the deepest and most painful experiences.

After this (whether using my own experience or not), I ask the student to tell me what she thinks is this person's destiny. Where will that person end up?

In truth, the consideration of another's destiny is deeply wrapped up in the archetypes work, as well, since once you have grasped and constructed a character archetype, it is very easy to see where this life of that character will lead and to what end. So, this exercise is just another way of doing archetypes work. Of course, simply speculating about various destinies cannot substitute for archetypes work as a whole. This technique is meant as a facilitating technique for archetypes work, not a replacement.

After doing archetypes work for some time, you will develop a high level of skill in anticipating destinies. When I say destiny, I don't mean fate. I don't mean either that we can predict outcomes. I am simply talking about what is essentially a form of logical deduction, but within the context of archetypes work.

Ultimately, after a while, you will be able to discern not only potential destinies but also common crucial traits that tend to join with other traits.

CHAPTER FOURTEEN

INTEGRATIVE WORK: ARKHELOGY

INTRODUCTION

Archetypes are *inherent* human patterns, and, thus, are discoverable. But archetypes are not discoverable from a mere series of mechanical steps. One must be actually using one's brain in a particular way to discover and frame an archetype. All those steps that we have covered in preceding chapters form the stepping stones to the archetype, but you must engage in an additional and crucial practice, in combination with all the prior techniques in order to be working at the archetypal level.

Arkhelogy is the work of finding archetypes.

Arkheloging includes the use in simultaneous combination of all the component parts of archetype work, but that skill — the skill of juggling and even beyond that, of resolving the separate movements into a wholly new use and purpose — is also a discrete, unique, separate skill of its own. Imagine, for example, that you made the leap from being able to toss and catch one or two balls at a time to being able to juggle three or four or more balls all at once. This is an accurate but oversimplified comparison to isotype work, described below, but it would not yet be arkheloging. If you could transform the juggling into a new form of propulsion or energy power, that would be comparable to arkhelogy.

The basic remaining mechanical steps for arkheloging, however, involve the construction of an ectype ("the ectype step") and the process of finding and working with isotypes ("the isotype step" or *isotyping*).

Isotyping ultimately transforms and merges into arkheloging. There is not an easy, clear division between the two, but it is important to identify isotyping as a distinct, fundamental final step in arkhelogy.

Let us walk through this wonderful, miraculous process.

THE ECTYPE STEP ("ECTYPING")

An ectype is simply a form or model for something. In the archetypes approach — which we can now call arkhelogy — an ectype is the first step you take to generalize a specific example. This step must precede isotyping.

First, you frame a discrepancy sentence. "Francine says she loves animals but she hits her cat." As we learned earlier in the introductory chapter, all we do in ectyping is change some words in the sentence. We change Francine to "she," and after the first "she" in the sentence we add "is the one who." Thus, "She is the one who says she loves animals but she hits her cat."

You can see that we are no longer talking about a specific person but about any person who does that action. We can call this step "ectyping." It is an incredibly simple but crucial step.

THE ISOTYPE QUEST ("ISOTYPING")

Now we look for isotypes for the ectype. Isotyping involves two steps. The first one is simple and quick. The second, which constitutes the bulk of isotype work, can take years.

An isotype is whatever is similar or identical to the ectype but has a different history or origin.

Using the above ectype sentence, in the first isotype step we would ask: "What would be similar to someone who says she loves animals but hits her cat?" This is the "isotype step" or the "isotype question."

Notice that to find satisfactory and complete answers to this question you might end up going to the far corners of the Earth. Framing the question properly is easy, but critical.

Finding the answer(s) is the process of isotyping. Once you are engaged on a particular isotype quest, it could take days or weeks or even years.

Thus, while the framing of the question — which constitutes the pre-liminary isotype step — is simple, the quest, the isotyping work, involves a great deal more. While every isotype quest is different, I will spend some time in this chapter describing, and walking you through, what this quest may entail generally. Since isotyping, and ultimately arkheloging, involve complex mental and emotional processes that will engage all the component skills as well as involving their interplay, coalescence, and ultimate integration and merging into a new, different skill, every isotyping-arkheloging quest will be different and unique. Along the way, as I walk you through the isotype quest and lead you into the beautiful but tangled forest of arkhelogy, I will point out many features and elucidate many dark corners, while occasionally taking a moment to show the working of various component skills.

Here is the basic outline of an isotyping quest: To look for isotypes, you must keep in mind the ectype and juxtapose it with other similar examples. When you find another example that you feel closely matches your ectype *in meaning* (not factually similar), you draw from it any additional facts or insights that can add to your understanding of the original ectype.

Isotype work may sound sophisticated and complex but it is not really new. Writers describing how they compile characteristics from different people in their lives to create a fictional character are talking about doing isotypes in some manner. Biographers of novelists discuss who were the people in an author's life who might have been models for their characters.

The more isotypes you find to match your original ectype — that is, the more you do isotyping — the more it will take on its inherent characteristics and embody its genuine truths. In other words, the more you do isotyping, the more it becomes arkheloging and the closer your material comes to embodying universal truths about your characters.

STARTING ISOTYPE WORK

Go back to the discrepancies chapter and reread the Richard/ Elizabeth/Lawrence story.[14] What would be the archetype for Richard? We don't know yet. We have to start by framing the ectype.

Remember that Richard called Elizabeth his girlfriend, took her to the prom, and asserted she was a "quality girl." He stated he was upset by her and Lawrence kissing because he considered his relationship with

Elizabeth "sacred," but he continually neglected and insulted her, never told her he cared for her, and manifested his stated upset by demanding to know more about what the kiss was like rather than to know what it meant. (In other words, he wanted the down and dirty details — almost like voyeurism — but he didn't appear to care whether Elizabeth and Lawrence had real feelings for each other.)

How do we form an ectype sentence from this? Mechanically, we would simply go back and write "He is the one who took her to the prom, called her a quality girl, called the relationship sacred, but neglected her and exhibited more interest in private sexual details than in her actual feelings or loyalties." We could add to and subtract from this, of course, but, more importantly, this is where it becomes helpful to start doing what I call "two-column work."

STEP ONE: USING TWO-COLUMN WORK TO FORM ECTYPES

Take a piece of paper and make a lengthwise fold (fold down the middle of the page the long way). In one column, list the first parts of the discrepancy sentence. In the other column, list the second part of the sentence: all the parts that are in contrast to the first part.

This method helps you as you start to deal with complex discrepancies and juxtapositions. One of the great challenges that arises when you work on increasingly complex discrepancies, juxtapositions, ectypes, and isotypes is keeping clear in your mind what is juxtaposed with what, what is attached to what, and what is in contrast to what. It is important to keep the parts separate so you can move them about like puzzle pieces, without merging them, either into each other or into some preconceived notion you have.

The simple process of separating out and juxtaposing is a crucial part of the archetypes approach.

So, our page would look something like this.

He Is The One Who	But
∽ Took her to the prom	∽ Neglected and insulted her (list specific facts — as in original example)
∽ Called her quality girl	
∽ Said she was his girlfriend	∽ exhibited more interest in private sexual details than in her feelings
∽ Said the relationship was sacred	

For the sake of keeping the illustration relatively simple, I'm not listing here every possible derivative from the discrepancies example, but when you do this work, you should list all the discrepancies.

At this point, you should go back to the original narrative and make your own two-column list.

The above list has no spaces. On your page, when you do two-column work, you should always leave spaces to fill in more material if and when it arises. Leave spaces between the lines and after them. Sometimes you will want to add something that goes with something you've already written and often you'll find other things to add after you write down what you've initially noted.

Two-Column Work & Finding the Ectype & Isotypes

Now, finding the ectype and isotypes is not as simple as merely adding up the elements in these two columns. What the two-column work does is engage your mind in the mental process of separating these elements out and thinking about them and what they mean. When you first learn the mechanical steps, you should stick close to what you have on the page, and if extraneous stuff arises in your mind not apparently related to the original discrepancy (e.g., she has red hair), use separate pages to write them down. For example, if you knew Richard and Elizabeth, you might want to list that he's got a baby cute face, is five feet ten inches tall, slim, and blonde, and that Elizabeth is five four, looks something like Cameron Diaz, etc. (Remember that you should work to remove the adjectives, where possible. Sometimes, however, an adjectival description is unavoidable. Just try to be

177

aware of the adjectives you use and to find actions rather than descriptions.)

In fact, the ectype is no longer a single, simple sentence. Could we sum this up in a single sentence? Yes, but it would leave out many of the critical juxtapositions. So this is what we do:

STEP TWO: ASKING WHAT IT MEANS (DIALECTICS & THE SCIENTIFIC OR SOCRATIC METHODS)

Once you have the ectype "sentence" set out on a page in the two columns, you LOOK AT IT, *look at each of the phrases and what it juxtaposes with*, and you ask yourself a simple question: "What does this mean?"

For example, what does it mean that Richard said the relationship was sacred to him? What does it mean that he said this but neglected her? What does it mean that Richard agreed to break up with Elizabeth but asked her if she would at least go to the prom with him before they did so?

Now you can see that the answer to any single one of these questions, separate from the rest, may lead to one conclusion that might not be consistent with the answer to another question. For example, the first question: What does it mean that Richard said the relationship was sacred to him? The use of the word "sacred" is pretty powerful. Richard didn't say that the relationship meant a lot to him. He said it was sacred! Maybe he really meant it! But what then about his neglectfulness? Well, he could really feel the relationship is sacred but just be too busy to give it the time he wants to. Okay, what about the fact that he readily agreed to break up with Elizabeth as long as she still came to the prom with him? Now it seems that Richard might not really have meant it when he said the relationship was sacred to him.

In the process of asking what each fact and juxtaposition mean, you are in a sense asserting various hypotheses ("Maybe he really felt it was sacred") which you then test against the other facts and juxtapositions. This is very much like the method of scientific proofs. The scientist sets forth a hypothesis that he then creates experiments to test. Here, of course, you are merely questioning yourself.

It also resembles cross-examination of a witness in court. A good attorney will go after any discrepancies in the witness's testimony which will lead the jury to a conclusion compelled by common sense. Here, of course, your are only cross-examining yourself!

Another method this step resembles is the Socratic method of teaching. It's the one used in law schools and was developed originally by Socrates in ancient Greece. The method involves asking the person to use his own sense of reason to answer questions. The questions are intended to lead the student to the very limits of his understanding and to discover whatever kernels of absolute truth, if any, remain.

STEP THREE: FORMING HYPOTHESES, REVIEWING, ASKING MORE QUESTIONS

One could conclude that Richard's concern that Elizabeth not break up with him until after the prom indicated that Richard was more concerned with how he was seen by others than with the value or meaning of the relationship itself or with Elizabeth's feelings. This hypothesis is borne out by Richard's other behavior: the times Elizabeth confronted him with his rudeness and neglect towards her and he made excuses and blamed her for it; the time when he showed more concern for the details of her intimacy with Lawrence than the meaning of it; and perhaps the later behavior he showed by posting offensively altered pictures of her on his website.

Now we might want to look back at one of Richard's first behaviors that we listed: his calling the relationship sacred. What does it mean? If Richard had no concern for what Elizabeth felt, how could he consider the relationship sacred? What did he mean by it? Did he mean anything?

Richard appeared serious when he said the word. He did not appear to be intentionally mocking Elizabeth or the relationship, but why would he use that word if he really did not care, if what he cared about was what he looked like to others? Perhaps he thought it sounded cool and sophisticated to say it. But looking at it from his point of view as a writer (go into the moment), the real important inquiry is "Did he feel it?" If he did not feel it and he said it anyway, what does that mean? It means, at the very least, that he used words to get what he wanted even when he didn't feel them. What does this mean?

The other evidence of Richard's lack of regard for Elizabeth's feelings supports the idea that Richard did not feel much. Perhaps he merely didn't feel much for Elizabeth — but then, why was he dating her? Simply because she was pretty? (Is there evidence of Richard doing this with other women?) Perhaps it is only women that Richard doesn't feel much for? Or perhaps it is both sexes? What was/is his relationship like with his mother or other important women in his life? His father?

STEP FOUR:
ADDING INFORMATION: MORE TWO-COLUMN WORK

Here, if you have this information, you can record it on your page. You might want to then use a new sheet of paper, writing down the entire two-part original ectype sentence in one column and the new information in the second column, like so:

Complete Original Ectype Sentence (2 Parts)	New Information
He is the one who took her to the prom, called her a quality girl, called the relationship sacred, but neglected her and exhibited more interest in private sexual details than in her actual feelings or loyalties.	His mother says he is her special son, always coming home to do the dishes or help her around the house.

But Richard also showed disregard for what Lawrence felt, insisting, as he did, that Lawrence come into a separate room alone with him and demanding there that Lawrence tell him the details of Lawrence's intimacy with Elizabeth — information that Lawrence might have felt greater compunction to keep private if Elizabeth were present. (In this instance, Richard merely overrode with disregard whatever compunction Lawrence had.)

You may conclude by now that what I am doing, in a sense, is similar to building a case in court or constructing an argument. Juxtaposing facts and asking for logical conclusions to them is indeed what lawyers do. The difference is that you, the writer, are living the situation that is your material and that you will shape into a book. The difference is that you are inquiring, rather than pre-deciding the conclusion you want others to reach. You are looking for discrepancies and juxtaposing various things that raise questions, which you are then using to answer further inquiries.

STEP FIVE: WHO IS HE? CORE CHARACTERISTICS — STARTING TO PUT THE PICTURE TOGETHER

Where a young man exhibits behavior such a Richard's, where he uses words and phrases like "quality girl" and "sacred," where he shows disregard for her and her feelings (even before she kissed his "best friend"), and where his behavior illustrates that his interests were in looking good to his school classmates and in private sexual details, we can begin to get a picture of who Richard really is. He is a narcissistic man, good looking, concerned about how he looks, pretending to feel noble emotions and to feel for others when he feels neither. This is a man who pretends to feel what he does not. Do we all do this? Is he different from the rest of us? Don't we all pretend these things? Aren't we all self-centered and selfish?

The extent to which the rest of the world does this matters only a little. What we are doing is isolating Richard's core characteristics. But note that we are not doing that by using adjectives or labels. Yes, we can call him a narcissist and that might help us to remember the facts about what he did and does, but the word itself is of no help without those facts.

Once we've isolated Richard's core characteristics, we have the ectype.

SHORT REVIEW

You see that constructing a genuine, workable ectype is far more challenging than it first appeared. There is an entire internal dialogue that takes place, which utilizes juxtaposition and discrepancies. Along with the engagement of that dialogue, you will use the other components of the archetypes approach that you've learned. You will take a look at one moment in this man's life and try to stay with that moment to fathom what it means and what he intended or felt. You will ask yourself what drives him. You will continue to dig up more discrepancies and make more juxtapositions. You will grapple with facts and try to separate out your opinions. You will ask yourself whether you (or anyone you know) ever did anything like he did and what you (or the other person) meant by it and what it means about you (or the other person).

All of this will go on inside of you, even to some extent unconsciously, as you ask yourself what it all means, what Richard means, what it means about Richard, and so on.

But is this all there is? No!

STEP SIX: GETTING MORE INFORMATION — ISOTYPE QUEST

Now that you have a clear idea of who Richard is — that is, not all of who he is but who the man is that does these things (the ectype) — you will begin looking for more information about that ectype.

Say you can see Richard's behaviors as self-centered and egotistical. That's how you view them; that's how you feel about them. Say you know nothing about narcissism, just think it means he's self-centered. How would you find out more about someone like Richard? (Remember that we are not judging Richard himself. We have extracted his behaviors and are now working only with those behaviors, which is working with the ectype. For now, it is easier to refer to this as "someone like Richard," but it is also important to remember that we, as writers, cannot/do not know or judge Richard. All we are doing is working with the ectype.)

One way would be to read up on narcissism. Or read stories about "pretty boys." I'm being somewhat facetious. But the question is "Are all pretty boys self-centered?" They may not be but in the process of reading about them, you might discover similarities to Richard. How can you read up about pretty boys? You could read biographies of good-looking male celebrities. How would you read up about narcissism? You could read a psychology book or find a book on the subject itself.

If you don't like reading about things, try hunting out similar people and situations. If you know somebody you think has similar characteristics, talk to him, observe him, ask him what he thinks and feels about things. Or if you know someone who dated someone like that, talk to her.

There are an infinite number of ways to get more information. Most writers find this process highly enjoyable. If you saw the movie *The Year of Living Dangerously*, you will know what I mean. Some writers compile entire dossiers on people. I would simply recommend that you work with your ectype so you don't violate any person's privacy or personal boundaries.

STEP SEVEN: FROM ISOTYPES TO ARCHETYPES (ISOTYPING INTO ARKHELOGING) — ASKING THE BIG QUESTIONS: RAMIFICATIONS, ENDS & DESTINY

Let's say that we've concluded that the Richard ectype is a narcissist. He fits the description. We look for more information (for isotypes) about this.

Here's a definition of narcissism:

- Excessive love or admiration of oneself.

- A psychological condition characterized by self-preoccupation, lack of empathy, and unconscious deficits in self-esteem.

- Erotic pleasure derived from contemplation or admiration of one's own body or self, especially as a fixation on or a regression to an infantile stage of development.

As we fill in more and more information about the ectype we constructed, we start to ask bigger questions: questions about where this type of person ends up, what are the ramifications of his actions, what are the end results, the consequences. Does the picture we are starting to shape (which is the nascent archetype) lead us to believe in a particular end, a destiny or fate for this person?

One important thing to know about a narcissist is the damage that such a person can do to others because he does not feel for them. But there are other questions a writer might want to ask. What made him this way? What are the consequences of his narcissism? Does it lead to fame and fortune or to failure and poverty? What are the degrees of it? Aren't we all narcissistic? Why can't a narcissist feel empathy for others and how does this affect his life and the lives of others?

What are the most extreme examples of narcissism? What are the components of the most extreme examples? Do the extreme examples embody components that are shared by all narcissists? (An extreme example of narcissism is psychopathology. A psychopath is not able to feel for others. Many, if not most, serial killers are considered psychopaths (but not all narcissists are psychopaths). Psychopaths are unable to be normally emotionally or physically stimulated. They can subjected to extreme pain and have little emotional or physical reaction. Some experts believe that psychopathic killers kill in order to provide some level of emotional arousal that they are normally devoid of. The lack of empathy or remorse in psychopaths is part of the reason they can be extremely cruel.)

A characteristic of narcissists is that they use words to express feelings that they don't have. They know what they are supposed to feel and they pretend to feel it, but they don't actually feel it. To some degree our society teaches all of us to do this. Does this mean that we are all sick or that we are all healthy? For the narcissist, however, these traits are core ones.

These are the types of questions that arise when you start working at the archetypal level, because archetypes raise questions about a type of human being or a pattern of human behavior that to some extent we all contain within us. All archetypes are universal in some way. This is one reason why arkhelogy is so powerful.

But if we were to ask these types of questions outside of the context of a specific example (in a human being we know), they would be mere abstractions, and to ask such questions when we are merely imposing our opinion on someone we've observed would be even worse. Thus, it is always important to work from a specific example.

Through the process of asking yourself questions and looking for more information through isotypes, you will gradually start to arkheloge. Your mind will learn how to engage in all these complex processes at once. You will begin to discern archetypes in people almost instantly.

For example, if you had been observing narcissists for some time, you might have been able to sense that Richard was a narcissist simply from the emptiness with which he stated his relationship was sacred. Thereafter, your work would go considerably faster. His other behaviors would quickly confirm or disaffirm your sense and you would have many other examples and facts to draw on. In your mind, his behaviors would then become isotypes to the other instances you had observed and the archetype would form unconsciously and naturally. You would likely be able to predict his behavior and the outcome of his relationships. You would be able to construct an entire string of episodes in his life and could imagine the people who fell victim to him. In other words, the archetype would lead you not only to the ultimate destiny of the character, but to his entire story. Your remaining task would be only to fill in details and to write what you know.

Many people who have historically been viewed as seers, prophets, or psychics were very likely arkhelogists.

STEP EIGHT: INSIGHTS & WRITING

Let's return for a moment to the Richard archetype. One can imagine that the life of someone like Richard is rather empty. He cannot feel much for others and he likely thinks that others feel little for him (and he may be right). He likely lives in a loveless world. His narcissism saves him from the consequences of that lovelessness. As long as he loves himself and cares nothing about anyone else, he's safe. But his narcissism also prevents him from being loved by another person.

It's a terrible closed circle that imprisons him. How would it feel to live like that? Can you imagine the repressed sadness, the rage, the hopelessness, the emptiness, and the sense of loss (all likely unconscious)? It would be unbearable. And how do you think his life would go? Perhaps he'll eventually catch a pretty little woman who has such low self-esteem that she accepts marriage to a man who cannot feel any love for her, who neglects her, or even actively mistreats her.

See how these insights draw from being-in-the-moment work, from understanding universal drives, from seeing from another person's point of view (which includes analogue work, among other things), and from asking the questions of end results and destiny? But note that these insights are only offered after all the preceding steps have been carried out.

This, however, is where the writing takes place.

STEP NINE: THE STORY

The writing of the story should always come out of the arkheloging, but arkheloging, while it does lead to writing, does not automatically lead to embodiment in a story structure.

There are several ways to approach writing the story. You can simply free associate, getting it down on paper, and later on shape it into a story. Apparently Thomas Wolfe (author of *The Web and the Rock, Look Homeward Angel,* and many more) wrote like this. He did not even separate his writing into chapters. A friend did that and edited it for him.

Or you can decide how to plot your story, based on what you know, and then insert your insights into the story. Because stories that resonate do contain particular structure, this approach appears to be more in vogue today, but it also has its own problems. The story structure can either trigger arkhelogy work in you or it could suppress and supplant it.

Either way, it is important to know that although a character archetype leads inevitably to his story, the task of writing a story (or a novel or play) is separate and different from the archetype work.

SUMMARY

Congratulations! You have now walked through the arkhelogic forest with me. You may not know it yet, but this is a great day in your life. Let the information settle and percolate.

The following section discusses advanced techniques and the last section provides some scholarly information about some of the components. You may read these sections any time, when you are ready or interested in them, but if you have read through the entire book to this point, you have now completed a full reading of the archetypes approach. You will know by now that reading the book will not magically change your life, but you will also know that you have great new tools in your hands that you can use to create and live a real writer's life, and ultimately to write your own writing from inside to outside.

SECTION FOUR

Advanced Techniques

Chapter Fifteen

INTEGRATIVE EXTENSION TECHNIQUES

This chapter covers techniques that are extensions of and integrate the basic component skills. In other words, you need to learn the basic techniques before trying these out and these require you to integrate two or more of the basic components.

JUXTAPOSITIONS

Discrepancies are a form of juxtapositions. To juxtapose means to place one thing next to another, for comparison or contrast. The word comes from Latin: *juxta* = close by, and French *poser* = to place. Using discrepancies is the quickest and most reliable way to frame an ectype sentence, but juxtapositions can also be used. I recommend working with discrepancies for awhile before using general juxtapositions.

Of course, in general, like discrepancies, juxtapositions can be about anything. They can relate to character or not. But as with discrepancies, we are interested mostly in internal juxtapositions of the actions of a human being. By "internal juxtapositions," I mean, juxtapositions of actions that are carried out by a single person — not comparisons of one person to another.

But in contrast to our earlier restriction, with respect to juxtapositions generally, the archetypes approach also has use for some types of external juxtapositions: e.g., he remembers an incident differently than you do. Such things may or may not be discrepant. Juxtapositions can include combinations of things, such as "He was raised by a preacher AND he became a law enforcement officer."

Juxtapositions, like discrepancies, may or may not end up leading to usable ectypes for archetype work. Juxtapositions may just add up to a collection of random traits. The best juxtapositions are those that contain two *divergent* actions (even if not discrepant).

Why do I not use the term "comparisons" when I refer to juxtapositions or discrepancies? It is because juxtaposition work is not the same as comparison work. To compare one thing to another implies judging its value or quality, which is not what we're doing. We are simply setting one thing next to another. As you have learned by working through the basic component exercises, we articulate a discrepancy in order to use it to construct an ectype sentence which we then juxtapose with *isotypes*. The same goes for juxtapositions as it does for discrepancies.

Example:

Here is a nice example of a juxtaposition. A friend of mine told me her recollection of how she made friends with "Fran," whom she later came to dislike. She had wondered aloud, at first, how she could have ever made friends with her, since she came to dislike her so much. She told me that she remembered the first day of school in a new school, she saw Fran and Fran was small, like her, so she thought "Hey, there's someone like me!" and so she went over to her.

However, my recollection of the event is that my friend (let's call her Rebecca) expressed no interest in making friends with Fran at the time. I was actually the one to introduce them. I started speaking to Fran and then to a teacher who was standing with her. I know how Rebecca is about meeting people. If I had suggested she might want to introduce herself to that girl over there, Rebecca would have refused.

The juxtaposition is between how I recall Rebecca having acted and how she recalls it. I am not sure if she actually remembers it differently than me or just tells it that way, but this is the first time I have seen her present herself as this very outgoing person. There is also a juxtaposition, for me, between all the times Rebecca has told me things about how she acted when I wasn't around (she's always the warrior princess) and this combination (how I remember her versus how she says she acted).

In the first instance, the juxtaposition is something of a discrepancy. In the second instance, it merely puts together two things that I never saw together before (her presentation of herself and how she might appear to me). What it means to me is that she either has reason to present herself as more invincible than she actually is (which is not hard to understand — who doesn't have such reason?), and/or she actually believes she is more assertive than she is. (In the latter case, she has picked up some of her self-image by osmosis from my presence in the event (i.e. she merged her memory of herself with her memory of me), or from subsequent events independent of me (i.e. she merged later memories, in which she was more assertive, with this memory).

Now, whenever I hear her talk about herself as being assertive or aggressive or outgoing, I will always wonder. I will always have the image in my head of me introducing a somewhat overwhelmed Rebecca to Fran. In my head, I will always juxtapose those two things. It doesn't mean that I know what Rebecca feels, will feel, or felt — or that I know the truth that Rebecca is hiding. It just enables me to know her a little bit better.

RULES FOR TWO-COLUMN WORK

We discussed two-column work in the arkhelogy chapter. Here, let me talk about it more generally and offer some rules for doing it.

There are many varieties of two-column work and once you learn the technique, you will likely find additional ways to use it. But there are some basic ground rules that are important to use whenever doing any type of two-column work. For example, say that you are listing multiple discrepancies to a common root and in the midst of this work, you suddenly remember a separate set of discrepancies or juxtapositions. **Rule #1 is that you put everything on the page that belongs on the page and everything that is about something else on a separate page.**

Rule #2 is that you do not mix the content of columns. What you decide to put on one side of the page stays on that side. However, if something, say, that you have written in the right-hand column (in juxtaposition to a root sentence in the left-hand column) ends up being the subject of a new, separate discrepancy or juxtaposition (or if the two combined columns do so), you take a fresh blank piece of paper and rewrite that item in the left-hand column of the new page, leaving the right-hand column of that new page blank until you are ready to fill it in.

Rule #3 is that each page has a title. So, after you fold or draw a line down the page lengthwise, you draw a line across the top and put the title in. The title should, of course, identify what that page is for. So, if the page contains a multiple discrepancy list, the top should say something like "Her father was a preacher, AND…". This may be the root sentence which you will also write in the left-hand column, but you should also write it across the top, to identify the page. You shouldn't make up fancy titles. Just use what you have.

Two-column work is excellent for "he is the one who" (ectype) work and there are several different ways to do this work with that. You can write "he is the one who" in the left column and then just use the right column as a list.

Or you can write the root in the left column ("he is the one whose father is a preacher and…") and the juxtaposed phrase in the right column ("he became a law enforcement officer"), adding other behaviors below it (again, just listing them).

Or, you divide the page into two columns only at the top of the page, then do the root on the left, the juxtaposed on the right, and underneath both, writing in the middle of the page, your thoughts, observations, or notes about the combination or what you think are the consequences of the combination. So, he is the one whose father is a preacher… and… he became a law enforcement officer. Then, for example, "His father was a very strict disciplinarian. His religious views were authoritarian." Or, "I met him when we were both in high school before he became a cop," and so on.

These types of notes can lead to subsequent juxtapositions and two-column pages.

You can also use two-column pages to do isotype work. So, on the left side, you would write the entire ectype sentence (not just the root part): "He is the one whose father was a preacher and who went into law enforcement." Then, on the right side, you write the question at the top of the column: "Who is similar to this?"

Later on, you can write all the isotypes (or the amalgam of them — the archetype — in a sentence or paragraph) in the left-hand column and write the consequences or even what you believe is the final destiny of the archetype on the right side.

Why do we bother working this way? Why use up all that paper? Why not just do this work in the straight narrative? Because we *are making space* for things. You will find that you have a lot of blank spaces on various pages in different ways and this will enable your mind to search for what fills that space. But once you have set things up so that each page has its own subject, you will not just be filling blank spaces with random stuff. *It is very important that you get used to making blank spaces and leaving them open until the right material emerges or comes into your ambit.*

So, **Rule #4 is to use the pages to make space for as-yet unidentified and unknown content.** Allow blank spaces.

Sometimes a page will stay largely blank because that is all that belongs there.

USING TWO-COLUMNS TO DO INTEGRATIVE WORK

Two-column work is probably the most important technique (apart from the component skills) in the archetypes approach. When I teach beginning individual private sessions, I will sometimes start with guided two-column work that walks the individual through the entire method. Then I go back and give them the individual exercises. Two-column work, however, cannot be done on your own before doing the component exercises.

When I start beginning private work this way, I ask the individual to think of two different expressions of themselves, two different ways of being that they can identify in themselves. For example, Kate at home and Kate at work. Or Dave with his family and Dave with friends.

Kate at home will be in the left column and I ask the student to come up with a handful of descriptors of what Kate *does* at home, how she acts. (I ask the student to avoid adjectives, just like in character facts.) She lists these in the left column. Then the other column with Kate at work.

Then on a separate page, I may have the student write "She is the one who does XYZ at home and…" in one column and "who does ABC at work" in the other. The person can then find other examples of people doing XYZ or ABC and list those in the appropriate columns.

Then on a separate page, I may have the student write both parts in one column and then find examples of others who engage in similar discrepant combinations (isotypes) in the other column.

I will apply the other techniques at various points during the session in the process of using the two columns. This is an intensive way to learn arkhelogy which in itself, as I've seen, can be misleading. It must be followed with concentration and mastery of each of the individual component exercises. (And then, integrative work must follow component skill work as well.)

LAYERING JUXTAPOSITIONS IN TWO-COLUMN WORK

Not all juxtapositions are necessarily made to a root sentence. Some grow out of multiple juxtapositions. Thus, one student noted that he had had sex with a friend in NYC on the night of 9/11. The initial juxtaposition is (1) sex with friend and (2) 9/11. The root is "having sex with a friend." The juxtaposition is to 9/11.

The individual also had previously discussed his predilection for unavailable women. Thus, one could juxtapose sex with a friend on 9/11 with an unavailable-woman predilection. In this case, "sex with a friend on 9/11" would be joined and moved to the left column, making a new juxtaposition to "attraction to unavailable women" in the right column.

Notice that when we do this kind of "layering," we always retain two columns. We don't expand into three or more columns. And each new juxtaposition is done on a separate page.

If we add another fact, that this individual's mother died when he was five years old, we would put (1) sex with friend on 9/11 and attraction to unavailable women in one column, and (2) mother died at age five in the other.

It is also okay to divide this way: (1) sex with friend on 9/11, and (2) attraction to unavailable women and mother died at age five.

Underneath these headers, you can discuss the meanings or consequences of each, or you can list possible isotypes, etc.

Note that these items are character facts, but we are not simply doing the character facts exercise. We are collecting facts that contribute *meaning* to the root statement or to the entire combination.

In addition to making space, two-column work also often facilitates or causes insights. It shows you what is and what is not a compelled connection or result and enhances your ability to work with the elements of character archetypes.

ANALOGUES, ETC., IN TWO-COLUMN WORK

Another way to use two-column work is to head a column with one complete juxtaposition or incident and use the other column for an analogue.

Juxtapositions of People, Facts, Conditions, Circumstances
Any of these is valid. Two-column work is a way to experiment.

Interpretation of Discrepancies, Juxtapositions and Other Two-Column Work
See discrepancy chapter for discussion on logic and inferences.

PRETENDING

Pretending is a form of juxtaposition. When you pretend something, you are juxtaposing what is real with what is pretend. When you pretend to be somebody else, you are juxtaposing your real self with the person you're pretending to be. Thus, pretending is not just for kids. It is extremely valuable to adults, too.

This fact is the reason why role playing games (RPGs) are so popular (both the computer games and the real life ones).

"PINGING" OR "REVERSE ANALOGUES"

Pinging is a name I came up with to identify a different type of analogue. The basic analogue is where you observe someone experiencing something and you try to find an example in your own life than enables you to feel what you think the observed person felt during his experience.

Pinging is where you observe yourself, make an ectype sentence out of the observed behavior (making "I did X" into "She is the one who did/does X"), then look for isotypes to that. During this process you "objectify" yourself and try to look dispassionately and objectively at your behavior, making it less personal to you by forming it into an ectype sentence and looking for and incorporating isotypes. After this, you then try to "reinvest" your emotions, try to relate to the archetype you've constructed through this process, by the same process as with analogues (trying to find another experience that enables you to feel what you think the archetype might feel).

It's kind of a reverse analogue, since in the basic analogue technique, you are relating to someone other than yourself, whereas in pinging, you are projecting yourself outward, then separating from that projection, and then relating back to it. But it's also a technique that, unlike analogues, uses ectype sentences and isotype work.

I call it pinging after what sonar does by bouncing a signal off the bottom of the ocean (or an object in the water). When the signal comes back, it confirms the presence and location of the other object.

Pinging here means dispossessing yourself of a behavior and then bouncing yourself back to it.

Pinging can be used to solve the problem of how to know what you are identifying with. For example, a student problem:

"In many fairy tales, there is an image of a jealous woman plotting against a young girl and then being discovered and punished. This feels connected to me to why the little girl must die. Not sure which one I identify with. I think the little girl has all kinds of angry and cruel thoughts. She wants everything for herself all the time. (In reality she wants what any little girl wants - love - but the way she is treated she is made to feel like she is a voracious monster who will swallow anything in her path.)"

How can the student find out whether the connection she senses is "correct" or not, or whether her conclusions about the little girl are correct?

Solution:

1. Make an archetype out of her, remove her from you, make her into a "she" separate from you
2. Give her a different name and find an isotype (or combine several isotypes)
3. Then, and only then, reinvest your emotions in her.

Student Question:

"When you say 'reinvest your emotions in her' I'm not sure what you mean. Do you mean to create a separate entity (archetype) and then be like an isotype to it – so the feelings are in relation to the archetype rather than myself?"

My response to student:

It is not "being like an isotype" when you "reinvest your emotions." Isotypes are external, factually similar, but nonetheless different.

You are talking about doing a sort of reverse analogue, where you form the archetype, add in isotype material, and then see if you can relate yourself to it through your own similar but separate experiences.

The analogue is actually still in the same direction as the usual ones. In other words, you still find an experience in your own life which you think enables you to experience what someone else experienced, but in this case, since you are creating the archetype out of yourself, making it separate from yourself by adding isotype material, then going from the archetype back to yourself, and finding an analogue in your own life to relate it back to, it is kind of a reverse process. A ping effect.

LOOKING FROM ANOTHER'S POINT OF VIEW

This exercise can be seen as an extension of the analogue exercise but it is in fact the basis of analogues, rather than the other way around. It is also the foundation or relative of the being-in-the-moment work.

It's pretty simple in premise: you just try to imagine what a situation feels like to another person. But in practice it can be the hardest work. As one student wrote me about doing this work with respect to her father:

> To let in the beginnings of an awareness of what it was to be him is one of the hardest emotional hurdles I've ever encountered. It calls into question a lot of things I have believed and felt all my life. Easier to just make judgments than to imagine what he might have felt crossing the Atlantic with my half-sister, leaving his life and much of his family behind. And just the isolation of being him.

Thus, we first learn analogues before doing the broader, more open-ended work of imagining another person's life.

The simplest way to imagine the life of another is to consider a situation and engage in a dialogue with yourself about it. In the dialogue, you can and should raise all the character facts, discrepancies, juxtapositions, For example, one student emailed me about a comment made by a woman whose father was Jewish and had to leave Europe during WWII, that she was glad her mother was "Christian and Aryan." My friend, who is Jewish, was astonished that a Holocaust survivor could have such a sentiment. I wrote back:

> She'd say that because being Christian and Aryan was something of a protection. This illustrates the incredible confusing, traumatizing, and absolutely disabling nature of the whole Jewish/Aryan Holocaust part of history. That she would be forced to feel grateful that her mother was, as it were, a member of those who ultimately wanted her and her race dead. Her mother was the one who was supposed to love and care for her, but if she was also a member of those who wanted to kill her, how could she absorb that as a young child? Then the mother went off and left her with her father, who could not adequately protect her and took her far away and left her with strangers....

It should be clear from this example that logic and inference are also a large part of imagining another person's life. In fact, in doing this work, one rallies ALL the component skills: character facts, going into the moment, discrepancies, drives, etc. This is thus an integrative exercise.

Nonetheless, the *intention* of this exercise is specific and different from the others. The sole goal here is to see and feel things from the point of view of the other. Sometimes this means seeing things that the person himself does not see or know. In this sense, this exercise is like a form of advocacy. You are advocating for another human being who is not able to advocate or speak for himself.

Seeing from another's point of view leads to other combinations and uses of the component skills and their progeny. See a detailed example in the section on "Isotype Rules & Prototypes" below.

EXTRACTING PRINCIPLES FROM FACTS

When you do archetypes work, during some part of the work, you are extracting principles from facts. This means that you are finding meaning in sets of facts and developing theories about what they mean generally.

The student whose story was mentioned above about her half-sister escaping with her father from Nazi Germany discussed the idea of having to choose between being true to yourself and being able to continue living.

The student said: "This is (obviously) a major theme. And 'continue living' can mean whatever the person considers 'living' (survive — UD), which can encompass who they feel they need to be accepted by, receive "love" from, be recognized by, etc."

When I pointed out to the student that she was extracting principles from facts, she said: "I feel like I am looking at facts across different times and events and finding commonalities in what they 'say' — is that what you mean?"

(I answered yes.)

The student continued: "I feel right now driven to read history and to know what went on then. Like it will explain something about the present. Like when people want to learn about their family history to understand where they come from and maybe why they are the way they are — as though the history of civilization is my family history."

Thus, extracting principles leads to isotypes work, reading history, finding other examples, and so on.

RULE OF CONSTRUCTION: ALWAYS GO BACK TO CHILDHOOD

When working with archetypes, we always look for the earliest version of it, the earliest possible point an incident or pattern of behavior could have occurred. We work forward from that point. If we observe an individual doing something in front of us, we have no way of knowing when that behavior first was manifest. Thus, we extract from the actual incident the key ingredients — in other words, we take it out of the personal and put it in the third person, form an ectype — and then we consider what is the earliest point in that person's life those ingredients *could have* existed.

The earliest point a pattern of behavior could have occurred is the point that contains the meaning of it.

Obviously, the more you know about child development and human behavior, the more skilled you will become at doing this. It requires putting yourself in that time and place and imagining what it would be like for a child in the situation indicated by the ectype. It requires considering general principles of child development, understanding the dynamics of early child/mother/father triangular relationships (or the absence of it or any part of it). It requires juxtaposing the ectype with the appropriate stage of development involved in the ectype (i.e. the earliest point at which it could exist) and considering the consequences.

For example, if you see a father torment or abuse his children, what would be the earliest point at which he could have engaged in such a thing in his own life? Obviously, he could not torment his own children until he had them, so the question is at what point could he have had enough power to torment creatures smaller than and less powerful than him? Would he have been able to do that before he crawled? Before he walked? Before he was in school? An understanding of child development would inform you that children do not develop a conscience until about the age of six. It would also inform you that many children are quite unkind to other children their age as early as 12 or 18 months, but they cannot do so intentionally until they have some sense of conscience. So, at what point could a child intentionally torment someone smaller than him? It would probably be age five or six (as early as three or four, if you only require that he would be acting out rage without understanding it hurt the other). By five or six, the child could torment others *intending* to hurt them.

If by the age of five or six, a boy was already tormenting others, he must have learned that behavior *before* that age. This brings up the dynamics of parental treatment and messages to the child. These are always embodied in very specific situations and behaviors. If a man punishes his children whenever they show any initiative, his parents probably did the same to him at an early age. Thus, present behavior becomes a template to discover its origin. In turn, the origin explains much of the dynamics of the behavior and can lead to the isotype or even an isotype rule (see below).

ISOTYPE RULES (ISO-RULES) & PROTOTYPES

When you have been using isotypes for a long time, you will find certain truths in some sets of isotypes that create a kind of rule for all the examples of that kind. We call these rules *Isotype Rules* or *Iso-Rules*. Each isotype rule applies only to one set of isotypes. Once identified, an isotype rule is something like a psychological or human behavioral truth. Some isotype rules can require a complex process and years to discover.

Once you find a rule for a group of isotypes it will replace the work of finding isotypes individually for that behavior and it can then be separately juxtaposed with appropriate individual examples.

An *iso-rule* also becomes a *proto-rule* or *prototype*: a generic framework for all subsequent things of its kind. A *proto-rule* or *prototype* is a primitive form, structure, type or instance that serves as a model on which later stages are based or judged.

Rules of isotypes, which grow out of specific examples, in turn become prototypes to form part of the basis for archetypes. (An isotype rule is the rule of a set of isotypes — a set of examples that have a similar meaning to an original example. A prototype is simply that rule turned into an independent framework or model. It is independent of any single example.)

Prototypes are not proto-archetypes, however, as they embody only the rule of a batch of isotypes and do not form an entire archetype.

Thus, in something of a reversal of terms, in the archetypes approach proto-rules or prototypes do not precede isotypes; they emerge from them.

Isotype rules and prototypes are the result of highly advanced work. While an archetype, which is something like "the rule of the character," can be discovered sometimes in a matter of minutes (more often in a matter of days, weeks, months, and sometimes longer), prototypes are discoverable only through years of high-level, advanced work in handling ectypes and isotypes (which means, integrative work utilizing *all* the component skills).

Every true written work of art intrinsically contains many isotype rules.

EXAMPLE OF A SEEING FROM ANOTHER'S POINT OF VIEW EXERCISE, THE FORMATION OF AN ISO-RULE & ITS USE AS A PROTOTYPE

Let me walk you through the evolution of an isotype rule and prototype.

Getting Inside

During a session with me, in doing the "seeing from another's point of view" exercise, a student states that the man she is dating (let's call him Mark) confirms to her that "moving forward to the next step (going to the movies, being more sexual, etc.) feels to him like he's signing up to marry me and be together forever. He does not feel ready to have a committed relationship. [In his mind, he] skips from casual sex to marriage and nothing in between."

I ask the student, whom we'll call Katherine, whether this is her description of what she thinks he feels. She responds that "he feels he is not ready to make a commitment to me because 'making a commitment' means giving up all of his freedom and being solely responsible for my happiness." I ask her again whether this is her response to my question as to what he feels. She answers yes.

I then state that I believe that those are Katherine's words, not Mark's. She asks, "How would I know his words?" I tell her that I think she actually does not hear him except through the filter of her cognition. I say that she translates him to herself and to me, probably because she views his thoughts as incoherent. She had earlier described his thinking as somewhat autistic. She confirms that "That's what I meant about autistic."

I tell Katherine that I doubt that Mark's reactions are about "commit-ment." I ask Katherine to again think about what is in his mind. She answers immediately: "Fear."

Although it seems likely that fear is at least in part behind Mark's reluctance to get more deeply involved with Katherine, her response is still not quite inside Mark's mind yet. I pursue my inquiry further, saying "Okay, but what is the thought? Does he think 'I'm afraid'?"

Katherine then immediately responds, speaking in the voice of Mark, as she imagines it: "I'll never be able to do what she wants. I don't want to do what she wants."

An Isotype Rule

At this point, I make a leap and state an isotype rule that Katherine, understandably, has a hard time accepting. I say: "That makes him into a little boy and you into his mother. It disables his adult self so that sex would be incest."

These two sentences grow out of the process of ectype-work combined with the rule of construction (finding the earliest point) and is a preliminary formulation of the iso-rule.

Katherine now reveals that Mark had trouble maintaining an erection the second time they had sex and says that he told her that that "he avoided having sex come up with his wife in the last several years" of his marriage.

But when I continue applying the above conclusion, Katherine remarks that I'm making "a bit of a leap" in her opinion. She admits that she doesn't "want to think he thinks sex is incest because then it would be hopeless to be sexual with him."

Most people react to iso-rules in a similar way. They feel a leap has taken place that they can't follow and/or they don't want to believe the conclusion because it is shocking or offensive to them. Often the iso-rule embodies a conclusion or rule that seems to foreclose any possibility of progress or change. This is one of the odd things about any identified isotype or archetype. And, even more oddly, only once that absoluteness is identified, accepted, and acknowledged, can it change. The odd truth about isotypes and archetypes in life (as opposed to "in stories") is that when they are seen and articulated, they disappear. (This of course often leads the identifier/observer to the unfortunate conclusion that s/he was wrong about it.)

In any event, iso-rules contain a principle the source of which is often obscured to recipients or listeners, since they (iso-rules) are formed by a high-level, complex process: removing-it-one-step work (ectype work, making it more generic and less personal) — a process which is largely unknown to and unpracticed by most people; the rule of construction (also unknown to most); and isotype formations over long periods of time (also not widely known) with lots of examples.

So, we backtrack and parse it out. If Mark does indeed feel he'll never be able to do what Katherine wants, "his" sentence would be, as Katherine stated it: "I'll never be able to do what Katherine wants; I don't want to do what she wants." We "remove this one step" — "*He'll* never be able to do what *she* wants," etc.

Remember the rule of construction: we always find the earliest instance in which a statement could have meaning. Thus, the earliest time in which the sentence "He'll never be able to do what she wants and does not want to do what she wants," could have meaning would be Mark's early childhood.

I ask Katherine, "Who is HE and who is SHE?" Katherine replies somewhat mechanically, not really answering my question: "He is the one who feels he will never be able to do what she wants and doesn't want to do what she wants."

But Katherine knows that I am asking her to consider who the original "he" and "she" were in Mark's life. Katherine then asks me, "Is the SHE his version of HER (his mother) or is it me — the one in the present day who he is superimposing her onto?"

I say simply: "HE is the little boy; SHE is the mother. Why? Because everything originates in childhood. We always go to the earliest point possible and to the original people and situation(s)." That will always be the relationships between the child and the parents. Where, as here, the present sentiment is about a member of the opposite gender, we go back to the boy's relationship with his mother (or girl's with her father).

In the midst of this discussion, Katherine interjects and tells me that Mark was the first-born and when he was 12 or so his father "had a breakdown." She notes that Mark "was the oldest son and his father became incapacitated emotionally, so [the burden] naturally falls to the oldest son."

Katherine doesn't spell it out, but she meant that Mark was thrust into an adult relationship with his mother when his father had the breakdown. He became the man of the house, as it were. But he was still a boy. Thus, he was likely asked to "Grow up!" and "Be a man!" before he was physically, mentally and emotionally able to fulfill such expectations. This means that he associates expectations of his virility or sexuality with the impossible demands made on him (by his mother) when his father became emotionally unavailable. She may have expected the boy to meet her emotional, or even her physical, needs. Even if there was no actual incest, the demand was made, and he lived it.

I tell Katherine that I believe this situation (of being asked by his mother to do what he felt he was not able to do) happened before his father had a breakdown. I think his father's breakdown may have been in the works long before it actually happened, and I believe that the relationship between Mark and his mother was established long before the breakdown. Again, we always look for the earliest possible point. If we don't find an actual example at the earliest point (which we usually won't since early childhood memories are preverbal and difficult to access), we simply deduce it by asking "When was the earliest point this *could* have existed?"

We are not quite at the point of completely articulating the iso-rule.

I ask Katherine what she imagines Mark's mother is demanding he do. (I put this in the present tense because the demand is always present, although the first instances were in the past.) I say: "She could be demanding he clean up his room. She could be demanding he do the dishes. She could be demanding he wash his hands...."

Katherine interrupts me and says, "It is something that she needs to survive." I ask why. Katherine replies: "Because it has a life and death quality to it. He needs her. She is his mother. He needs her love; he wants her love, and his getting that is in jeopardy, because she needs something in order to be able to survive and he must supply it but he can't."

Notice that Katherine is applying universal drives here (drive to survive).

I delve more: "He needs something from her little boy. What could it be? What does she want and need that she asks this innocent little boy to do?"

Katherine observes that "it's some kind of exclusive connection."

Katherine and I then offer various possible thoughts the mother might have: "Be my one and only darling little boy. Do this for me, darling. Mommy likes it when you do that.... Mommy loves you — mommy needs you — mommy wants you...."

This is going momentarily inside the mother's mind.

I remark that the boy *cannot* do what the mother wants him to do because she is asking him to do something — it doesn't really matter exactly what — that he is not yet capable of doing. When a parent demands something of a child that an adult could do but the child cannot yet do, she is asking him to be an adult. This could be something as innocuous as expecting him to understand her adult needs and be there for her in some way. Here, Mark's mother was asking him to be an adult man. I ask Katherine, "What is the primary thing that adult males can do that male children cannot?"

The answer is to obtain an erection, produce sperm, have sex, procreate, etc. Thus, Mark's mother is (surely unconsciously) asking Mark to engage in a sexual act.

Katherine asks me, "Does everyone agree that the primary thing an adult can do that a child cannot is sex and adult love?" I say to Katherine, "Well, you tell me — go through it yourself — what can adults do that children cannot? List all the things."

Without further inquiry, however, Katherine concludes it is true, "primary" being the key word, she says.

Katherine then reframes the principle — the isotype rule: "ALL demands to a child to do what he cannot will be a demand to do the primary thing adults can do that children cannot."

But then Katherine says, "I'm not sure how you got to that principle though — I mean, I see how it is true, but not sure how you got there from the work we did just before it.It seemed like something you knew independently that you could apply it."

Katherine was right, of course. The iso-rule results from making templates out of real-life examples, out of creating ectypes, extracting principles from facts, and working with isotypes. While you can tentatively arrive at an iso-rule through singular ectype/isotype work, it is more likely that you will discover them, as I noted above, through extensive work at the isotype/archetypal level, while applying the component skills and rules of construction (everything originates at the earliest possible point, universal drives always exist in every person in every situation, you must imagine what the other feels and go into the moment, etc.).

From Iso-Rule to Prototype

The discovery of an iso-rule (a rule of human behavior in a certain set of circumstances) now becomes a tool for further use in the archetypes method. If all demands to a child to do what he cannot are a demand to engage in sex, what does this mean about Mark? We juxtapose the iso-rule to the facts of Mark's life.

Like ectypes and isotypes themselves, an iso-rule may be hard to keep in the forefront of your mind. This is where meditative or ruminative work comes in and it is another instance where you can use two-column work. (This is also where trance states can be useful.)

To keep an isotype rule in the front of your mind so you can keep referring back to and applying it, you have to write it down on a piece of paper and put it where you can look at it often. (When you are engaged in doing further isotype work, you will need to look at it quite often, every 15 to 30 seconds or so.)

The rule we discovered is: "ALL demands to a child to do what he cannot will be a demand to do the primary thing adults can do that children cannot."

To parse this rule out a bit: Wherever an individual feels another person is demanding he do what he cannot, it is about (equivalent to) a parent asking a child to be an adult. This involves everything that adults do that children cannot, but most of all, the primary thing an adult can do that a child cannot do is engage in sexual intercourse. Thus, the demand on a child to do what he cannot do always involves incest or molestation, even if latent or indirect, whether intentional or not. In other words, *to the child*, the meaning of the demand *is* that the child engage in a sexual act with the parent making the impossible demand. The child will not consciously know this and the parent may not intend it, but this meaning will always be intrinsic.

Once an iso-rule is articulated, it can (and should) be juxtaposed with specific examples, such as Mark's situation and background.

Hereafter, one may make a few logical inferences from the isotype rule applied to the particular facts: "When Mark feels you are asking him to do something he can't, it is ABOUT the time in his childhood where it was demanded of him by his mother that he do what he couldn't do, so in fact you are catapulting him back to his boyhood and making an impossible demand on him."

Of course, as Katherine notes, she is not in fact doing anything but because Mark genuinely does have feelings of love for Katherine, it triggers his reaction. Why? Because while Mark was angry at his mother for asking him to do what was impossible for him, he also loved her and needed her and knew she loved him. This is a very toxic mix which locks the boy/man into an unhappy binding of the love with the impossible demand.

So Katherine always finds herself in the position of having to ask Mark to consider even the smallest of her needs or wants, because from the moment Mark felt love for her, he has always been in retreat.

You can see from this in-depth discussion how powerful and revealing this work can be. I recommend you attempt this work only after mastering the full archetypes approach. Best would be to work through this in a private or group session with me.

TECHNIQUES FOR PRECIPITATING EMOTIONS AND ACTIONS IN OTHERS

Every playwright knows that conflict reveals things about people. This is true in real life, too. But whereas drama is conflict, in real everyday life most well-bred people will avoid conflict like the plague. It is not considered nice or polite to create conflict, to challenge others' views, talk about topics of potential disagreement or deep personal issues, or to see beyond the mere social niceties. (Indeed, in the United States, it is considered impolite to talk about politics in most social situations. Europeans are a bit more at ease with political discussions.)

For writers who have developed a high level of awareness of the causes of human decisions and behaviors, it can be maddening to see people engage in this kind of absolute avoidance. We get to the point where we *know* what's going on but nobody will admit it, everybody hides it. We are often inclined to chuck the rules of etiquette and catch "liars" red-handed. We can't stand the falsities, the lies, the masks. We want the truth. We want, at least, to *speak* the truth!

The archetypes approach does not rely on people telling us the truth about themselves. In fact, it rests on the premise that there are secret lives and invisible worlds going on all the time that we can discover without anyone spelling them out for us.

However, it is nonetheless important to writers to have people speak their real words. Rather than saying "How are you? I'm fine, thanks," writers want to hear the inner dialogues people have. We want the *words*. We want to know exactly what paths people take in their minds.

Equally as important for the writer is to see people fulfilling in real life the silent dances they do in their heads. And, in fact, usually writers become healers because they understand better than most what fulfillment is for any given individual they encounter.

There are some techniques writers can use to precipitate hidden emotions and latent actions in others, without invading privacy or creating disastrous consequences. The techniques are not only helpful to the writer but to others, because they promote recognition, understanding, and acknowledgment of others.

Technique One: Natural Consequences

When a person denies s/he's doing or intends something this is, in itself, something a writer can write about, but if we are to fully understand and portray the person (e.g., the archetype), we need to know the inner thoughts, too. The technique is to simply speak our opinion and then let the consequences happen. We don't have to be right but we do have to see what happens.

Sometimes it helps to speak the conclusion the person is making (without admitting it), particularly when the result would be absurd. This works well where the individual sets up impossibilities. So, instead of arguing that they are wrong because their conclusion would be impossible, we simply state that the conclusion must be that "It can't work" or the like.

People want to be seen as logical but they often aren't. But it is in the illogic that the truths about them can be found. So, a colleague of mine says that the FBI should not ever monitor people. Although I'm a strong civil libertarian, I try to get him to admit that the FBI's mission is legitimate: to monitor foreign persons in order to protect our country from terrorism, sabotage, etc. No, he says, the FBI's mission is not legitimate and he's alarmed that I would ever suggest it is, since I am the one who has written so much about how the government is abusing its foreign intelligence surveillance powers. So, I simply make the conclusions his position implies: if the FBI's mission is never legitimate then that means that they should not even monitor people where there is probable cause of criminal activity? Finally, my colleague becomes irritated enough at being confronted with his own illogic that he blurts out that the FBI has the right to monitor others but not him. This fact about him is revealing and could illustrate a core belief. This is somebody, in other words, who believes that rules should not apply to him. Rather than arguing with his beliefs, I simply let them play out until he had to state their logical conclusion.

Technique Two: Bearing Witness

Bearing witness usually applies to risky, dangerous, or threatening situations. The technique not only provides you with a way of keeping yourself relatively safe but enables you to watch what is going on. The situation thus does not become buried by your fears or embarrassments. Embarrassing, humiliating or frightening situations are not ones we like to experience, so they are not likely to be ones we have experienced enough to write about. I am not suggesting here that a writer seek out such situations but where appropriate, bearing witness can help the writer to deal with a difficult situation while enabling it to play out sufficiently to garner an understanding of it.

It has amazed me since I learned this technique how effective it is in outing bad people and preventing wrongdoing, but it is also useful as another way of enabling yourself to see.

To use this technique you must watch without looking directly at the person's eyes. If, for example, a creepy man is harassing a young woman on a bus or subway, even if there is nothing I can do to prevent the visual or verbal harassment, I can bear witness. I place my line of sight directly between the man and the woman so that I create a kind of "witness barrier" through which the man must move whatever action he takes. I keep my eyes directly in the line of sight between them so that I can see every move he makes and every response of hers. Usually, this makes the man very uncomfortable and he eventually stops harassing her.

Most amazingly, if I look into his eyes, he will step up his harassment. Any eye contact is interpreted by him as a challenge or disapproval which he obviously has already decided to ignore or counter. Sometimes eye contact is even seen by such a person as an additional come-on. So, I keep my eyes below his, in the area to the immediate right or left of his chest. This is a tactic used in martial arts. If you watch the chest, you can perceive movement before it is made. The person watched can feel this.

Bearing witness is such a powerful technique that you must be very careful how you use it. Wrong-doers will do wrong as long as they can get away with it. If you are unprotected and you become a witness to a crime or bad act, you can become a target yourself. Wrong-doers don't like to be caught, because usually they know they're doing wrong. This is why you must never make eye contact with a wrong-doer, if you can help it.

If you must make eye contact, look from the eyes immediately down to the chest, and down towards the groin, AS YOU LOOK AWAY INDIFFERENTLY. But afterwards, keep your eyes fixed on something that enables you to see the harasser's every movement. Make no response or expression or movements yourself.

You can also bear witness in a similar way to pain, suffering, or other emotions that people are often embarrassed or humiliated about. If the sufferer senses you are quietly watching without staring or judging, s/he will sometimes out of the blue literally tell you what the cause is. This also goes for bearing witness to joy, pleasure, and other positive states and emotions. I've obtained unexpected and startling revelations this way from utter strangers many times. Sometimes even wrong-doers will tell you why they are doing what they're doing.

Technique Three: Speaking the Archetype

This is a very advanced technique that can only be done when you get really good at unearthing key archetypes in people. For example, taking our example above, if Katherine said to Mark: "You feel I am asking you to do what you can't and don't want to do" at just the right moment, Mark would be likely to feel a great sense of relief at being understood and might say in his own words what he's experiencing.

Of course, this is another technique you must be careful with. Generally, I do not use the pronoun "you" when I speak to a person about himself. Especially if you are really close to home in your observations, it can feel very threatening. What you can do is to say "It seems to me (and please tell me if I'm wrong) that you might feel...." Or you can say "Yes, sometimes people feel that they're being asked by others to do what they can't do." Either of these statements is a door opener for the person to give you his or her own words.

But if you go around doing this without having a very keen understanding (that is, without having applied all the techniques this book teaches!), you are likely only to make enemies.

Technique Four: Accepting & Voicing the Inevitable

Sometimes people get stuck like broken records in a kind of unhealthy mantra of complaints. Friends don't like to see their friends suffer, so they try to convince them things aren't so bad, but the complainers refuse to hear a word of optimism. In such cases, what is really going on? Does the complainer simply want to complain? That's what it may seem like. Does he really want everything to be so bad? Does he want disaster, death, illness, or whatever else he constantly forebodes? Sometimes people have to go through things. Sometimes they cannot be stopped from the wrong choices they are walking towards. But more interestingly, sometimes (not always) the mere acknowledgment by someone of the approaching doom is enough to stop it from coming (or the person from going towards it).

Thus, a friend of mine was suicidal, but she rebuffed all her friends' attempts to show her she had their support. No matter what anyone did, no matter how kind or sympathetic or helpful people were to her, nothing mattered to her, it was all a waste, all in vain.

After months of this, I told her that she was using people and that I would not allow her to use me like she used everyone else: to put herself down and define everything as hopeless. I told her that if nothing anybody offered made any difference to her, there indeed was no hope because she had foreclosed any possibility of it. I told her I would not stay around to see the end of that.

This was, on my part, an acknowledgment of the real possibility that my friend was capable of taking her life, that it was very serious. I was not trying to convince her that things she felt were bad or hopeless were good. I acknowledged that things were indeed bad and hopeless and could have terrible consequences for her. I also relinquished power I did not in fact possess over her or the situation, and handed it squarely back into her hands.

The key to the success of these techniques can be summed up as discretion and care, but in fact, it is something that the entire archetypes approach promotes: a kind of stillness in receiving what life can offer, an acceptance of what is inevitable, a continual relinquishment of power where it is not authorized by those it affects and the courage to accept all the powers one possesses where one *is* authorized to use them, and (like the Serenity Prayer) the wisdom to know the difference.

SECTION FIVE

Theoretical Epilogue:
Metaphysics of Archetype Work

This section is for people who are interested in a more philosophical, metaphysical, psycho-historical, or just a more scholarly discussion about some of the topics in this book. It offers various sources for the ideas without delving into any specific religious or spiritual views or doctrines. It finds sources within psychology, geometry, anthropology, Native American practices, theater, drawing, advertising, hypnotism, and esoteric practices. These are certainly not meant to be exclusive; they are merely illustrative of the range and diversity of sources for the principles and ideas used in this book.

CHAPTER SIXTEEN

ARCHETYPES

The events of our lives happen in a sequence in time, but in their significance to ourselves, they find their own order ... the continuous thread of revelation.

— Eudora Welty[15]

For the human spirit caught within a spinning universe in an ever confusing flow of events, circumstances and inner turmoil, to seek truth has always been to seek the invariable, whether it is called Ideas, Forms, Archetypes, Numbers or Gods.

— Robert Lawlor, *Sacred Geometry*[16]

Archetypes are a central component of the Method: the concept of archetypes, the skill of *arkheloging*, or working "at the archetypal level," and the archetypes exercise that teaches the skill.

According to *A Critical Dictionary of Psychoanalysis*, an archetype is a "Jungian term for the contents of the collective unconscious, i.e. for innate ideas or the tendency to organize experience in innately predetermined patterns."[17] Carl G. Jung, one of Sigmund Freud's students who broke off from Freud and formulated his own ideas, wrote in his book *The Archetypes and the Collective Unconscious* that "[t]he term 'archetype' occurs as early as Philo Judeaus, with reference to the *Imago Dei* (God image) in man."[18] Jung quotes Saint Irenaeus: "The creator of the world did not fashion these things directly from himself but copied them from archetypes outside himself."[19] Jung notes that the term archetype "is helpful, because it tells us that so far as collective unconscious contents are concerned we are dealing with archaic or — I would say — primordial types, that is, with universal images that have existed since the remotest times."[20]

Some of the basic archetypal patterns, according to Jung, are: the Shadow, the Anima/Animus (the gender-opposite completion of oneself), the Syzygy (Divine Couple), the Child, the Mother, the Father, the Self, the Mana (spiritual power), and others. Christopher Vogler, in *The Writer's Journey*, compiled a list of archetypes for the purpose of what he defines as the "hero's journey." It is as follows: the Hero, the Mentor (or Wise Old Man or Woman), the Threshold Guardian, the Herald, the Shapeshifter, the Shadow, and the Trickster. Vogler draws on the work of Joseph Campbell who in turn drew on the work of Jung.

But it is not exactly in the Jungian/Voglerian sense that I use the term archetype. In the archetypes approach, the work on finding character archetypes does not begin with labeling people as falling into this or that archetype. Vogler's work, which I much admire, approaches the story from the opposite end of the archetypes approach. As emphasized throughout this book, archetype work is a global skill comprised of numerous component skills. As we've discussed throughout this book, archetypes work requires integrating all these skills.

According to Robert Lawlor in his book *Sacred Geometry*, the "archetypal level is that of the *principle* or *power-activity*."[21] At another point, Lawlor refers to it as an "action-principle."[22] Affirming Lawlor's definition, Dr. C. George Boeree, a professor of psychology at Shippensburg University, Pennsylvania, writes that archetype "has no form of its own, but it acts as an 'organizing principle' on the things we see or do."[23]

Lawlor notes that geometric diagrams "can be contemplated as still moments revealing a continuous, timeless, universal action generally hidden from our sensory perception."[24] He continues: "The archetypal is concerned with universal processes or dynamic patterns which can be considered independently of any structure or material form."[25]

He says that "[a]ncient cultures symbolized these pure, eternal processes as gods, that is, powers or lines of action through which Spirit is concretized into energy and matter." Thus, "the archetypes or gods represent dynamic functions forming links between the higher worlds of constant interaction and process and the actual world of particularized objects."[26]

Archetypes, under the Platonic model, "cannot be perceived by the senses," but only "by reason alone."[27] Lawlor provides a useful example to understand what an archetype is:

> A revolving sphere presents us with the notion of an axis. We think of this axis as an ideal or imaginary line through the sphere. It has no objective existence, yet we cannot help but be convinced of its reality; and to determine anything about the sphere, such as its inclination or its speed of rotation we must refer to this imaginary axis.[28]

Drawing together these definitions and descriptions, the question is how can we find the "action principle" or "power-activity" of a character. By "character" I mean simply: having to do with a human being. Notice I do not use the phrase "character traits." If we began either with Jungian/Campbellian archetypes or with character traits, or for that matter, a character sketch or "back-story," we would be predefining the character. Instead, I propose that we observe and learn from people. This means that we must figure out a way to find an action principle or power-activity embodied in each person we observe.[29] This work is what I call *arkhelogy*: "working at the archetypal level" or "doing archetype work."

The process of finding the action-principle/power-activity, or archetype, of a character is, of course, what this whole archetypes approach is about. The primary work that begins this process is the act of separating, of distinguishing two things within the same person. This is, as Lawlor says, "one of the most basic processes of intelligence in that it symbolizes the comparison between two things."[30]

Archetype work is the culmination of all the other underlying, incremental characterization skills contained in this book. It is a kind of binding of two extremes in several ways.[31] It relies on a fundamental discrepancy or set of discrepancies within a person, joined with knowledge gained from juxtaposing this discrepancy-set with an "isotype," or something "having a similar structure or appearance but being of different ancestry."[32] Thus, the archetype begins with a discrepancy-set (which is framed in a "discrepancy sentence," which will be discussed in the chapter on discrepancies), a binding of two extremes, which discrepancy-set is then compared to other similar discrepancy-sets (e.g., isotypes). When one finds another discrepancy-set which is not in any way related in its origins to the first one but nonetheless contains a similar set-meaning, one is engaged in isotyping.

There are a few steps in-between this bare outline, but this is the general approach. All the other component skills dissolve into the discrepancy-archetype-isotype work.

CHAPTER SEVENTEEN

THE STILL POINT:
BEING IN THE MOMENT

[A] vibrating string... moves above and below an abstract node or inexpressible still point.
— Robert Lawlor, *Sacred Geometry*[33]

And if I forgot, could you make me remember
The piece of myself that I left winding by
It's on the top current of love's final breeze
There at the still point,
That's where I'll be.
— Jonatha Brooke, "At the Still Point"[34]

Moment-to-moment investigation requires an open awareness of the unique existence of each moment.
— Ned Manderino, *All About Method Acting*[35]

An important component skill of Arkhelogy is "being in the moment." In theater and film work, and in meditative practices, *being in the moment* is simply "being aware of what precisely is occurring in the moment." It is sometimes referred to as "living in the now."[36]

These definitions, however, are deceptively simple, because even though there are few people who have no clue what the terms mean, and most people can sit quietly and direct their attention to the immediate moment they're in, at least for a moment (!), in all the years of my teaching, out of perhaps thousands of students, maybe one or two actually succeeded in attaining the state of suspended time and semi-trance which is the goal of the exercise.

To be sure, the *being in the moment* exercise is meant primarily to teach the concept and raise the practitioner's awareness of the mechanism itself, while there are other practices that work better at bringing a person into the intended state. It is important, nonetheless, to define the process and the steps a practitioner can expect to experience, as well as the event and the faculty themselves, separately from the intentional practice.

As just mentioned, *being in the moment* is both an event and a faculty. An event because it *happens* to you, and a innate faculty because it is a perceptive ability we all inherently possess. Further, *being in the moment* is fundamentally bound to archetype work, while remaining a separate component skill and function.

There are three stages to the *being in the moment* exercise I teach: (1) focusing; (2) hovering; and (3) suspending time/trance. When I speak about the faculty of *being in the moment*, I mean to include all three of these stages; the last stage, suspending time/trance, which Lawlor calls *poise of mind*, intrinsically includes the first two stages.

The faculty is one not largely valued in our present-day culture, but it is nonetheless a common heritage of great significance to creative work (or any work of the higher mind). Robert Lawlor writes that "there is... a consciousness which is capable of temporarily arresting, both conceptually and perceptually, segments of the universal continuum. This objective consciousness might be seen as a reduced velocity of the universal consciousness, and has as its instrument the cerebral cortex of man."[37] At another point, Lawlor refers to the "poise of mind" which "much of post-Einsteinian physics seems to have... as its basis."[38]

Felicitas D. Goodman, former Associate Professor of Anthropology at Denison University and the author of several books on altered states of consciousness, states that "the ability to go into trance is genetically transmitted."[39] However, she adds that while the ability is part of our genetic endowment, "it needs to be triggered in some way in order to be available for ritual purposes."[40] About the state of possession, she notes that it "constitutes a manipulation of brain processes that can be learned."[41]

The great French novelist, Marcel Proust, wrote in detail about this poise of mind, the ability to temporarily arrest time, in his novel *The Past*

Recaptured, which was the last volume in his work *Remembrance of Things Past*. Proust wrote about

> a marvelous expedient of nature which had caused a sensation ... to be
> mirrored at one and the same time in the past, so that my imagination
> was permitted to savor it, and in the present, where the actual shock
> to my senses ... had added to the dreams of the imagination the
> concept of "existence" which they usually lack, and through this
> subterfuge had made it possible for my being to secure, to isolate, to
> immobilize — for a moment brief as a flash of lightning — what
> normally it never apprehends: a fragment of time in the pure state.[42]

Proust described not only the circumstances of the event itself that
enabled him to suspend the moment, but "an extra-temporal being" in
himself that did the work. "A minute freed from the order of time has re-
created in us, to feel it, the man freed from the order of time."[43] While
Proust attributed the cause of this happening to "the miracle of an analogy," here we are concerned primarily with the action of "temporarily
arresting... moments," or what may be more casually called "being in the
moment."

The renowned Hollywood acting teacher, Eric Morris, wrote in his
book *Acting from the Ultimate Consciousness*: "The more open and available
the actor is to conscious stimuli, the more accessible he becomes to the
flow of unconscious impulses and signals."[44] Goodman provides a helpful
metaphor for understanding "how the ordinary state of consciousness and
the altered ones relate to each other":

> We might think of the ordinary state of perception as a building that
> is our home for most of our waking hours. It surrounds us, protects
> us, but also confines us. This solid building does not even seem to have
> any windows, so that the illusion arises that there is nothing beyond
> its walls. That is not the case, however. We regularly escape when we
> dream, to what we might think of as another building next door,
> which is equally ours. It contains a number of separate rooms, of
> which that of our dreams is only one. The door to the dream room is
> sleep: we cannot dream unless we sleep. There are also rooms of day-
> dreaming, the hypnotic state, the various meditative states, ecstasy, and

many other hitherto unidentified changes of consciousness, each one with its own door of the physically changes necessary to enter it. There may be some resistance when we want to get into the second building, its front door may be heavy, but once inside, it is relatively easy to pass from room to room.[45]

Morris gives some useful instructions to actors interested in heightening their awareness. These instructions focus on any given moment the person is in. He writes:

At first, you must consciously decide to "pick up" on the things around you. Asking questions is a great technique. You might also look at an object and encourage your eyes — like a radar scanner — to dance all over it. Encourage yourself to respond with feelings for the object you are scanning. While resting your hand on it, explore its texture. Learn to sense the presence of things behind you. Dissect single sounds, and identify parts of those sounds. Becomes aware of temperature and changes in the direction of the wind. Become increasingly aware of energies — the energy in a room or the energy of another person.[46]

Wa'Na'Nee'Che' (Dennis Renault) and Timothy Freke give similar guidance in their book on *Native American Spirituality*, directed towards understanding the language of nature:

Is there something around you that seems to pull your attention towards it? It may be an animal or plant, a tree or a stone. Concentrate on this "being" as a living spirit. Open your senses fully and embrace its nature. Relate to it in ways more intimate than words: feel it, listen to it, taste it, smell it. Consciously send out your love to it, honouring it as an expression of the Creator.

Suspend the doubts of your rational mind for a moment and allow this living being — this animal or plant, tree or stone — to talk to you. But don't expect this other being to speak in English. It will speak its own language which you must translate. Close your eyes and "listen" to what this being is saying to your sense of touch and smell. Let colours and pictures come into your mind. Allow the spirit of this being to enter into your imagination. Use the power of your intuition to understand and appreciate this communication.

When you feel it is time to move on, give thanks to this spirit-being, to the spirit of this place and to the "Great Spirit." Affirm *mitakuye oyasin* — "we are all related."[47]

These are descriptions of *"initiatory system[s]* for transforming consciousness and energy," which exist in innumerable esoteric practices, from simple meditation to those closely tied to particular religious or metaphysical beliefs.[48] Initiatory systems open the door to the focusing, hovering, and suspended time/trance states. A practitioner of visitations to the faery realm notes that one prepares for the "Underworld" experience through "a period of silence and stillness," a dedication and attunement to Sacred Space, involving being aware of the Seven Directions (North, East, South, West, Above, Below, Within), and visualization of the journey.

This visualization includes a) visualizing a means of entry; b) passing within; c) traveling through the Underworld; d) encountering specific places and people; e) returning through the Underworld; f) exiting, usually by the same means as the entry; and g) concluding and closing the visualization to return to regular outer awareness.[49]

Goodman describes such initiatory practices as trance inductions:

In order for the switch from the ordinary perceptual state to the ecstatic one to take place, people first of all have to prepare physically. They fast, take a ritual bath, or purify themselves in a sweat lodge. At the ritual itself, the expectation that something extraordinary is about to happen is a powerful conditioning factor. But mainly, people need to concentrate.... Concentration is aided by the festive air and by whatever sensory cues may be customary in the particular religious community — music, drumming, singing, the fragrance of incense or of crushed aromatic herbs, flickering candles, or bright lights. However, concentration alone will not do it. Only very knowledgeable practitioners can change their perceptual state without any external help. Such help is termed an induction strategy, most of the time involving stimulation, an excitation directed at the nervous system, a certain "driving" provided by rhythmic activity.

However, the practice of *being in the moment* is not exclusively about sensory or perceptual awareness. Being in the moment, on the most basic level, is simply about *being*. But in order to arrive at the *still point* at which one is able to *temporarily arrest segments of the universal continuum*, something more must occur. The mental/emotional state that exists in the act of arresting the movement of time is the same as that of a trance state. That *poise of mind* is the same as the "both/and" logic of trance thinking: where two diametric opposites can exist side by side simultaneously, where the binding of two extremes occurs. This is where the *being in the moment* work moves from focusing to hovering into arresting segments of the universal continuum.

Lawlor writes:

[T]he moment itself of transformation, from one state to another, from one quality of being to another, from one form or level of consciousness to another, is always a leap, a jump, an incomprehensible velocity, as it were, outside of time, as when one cell divides into two. If we approach life or evolution with only the sequential intelligence, only the rational, measuring facility, the reality of genesis will always elude us. This transformative moment is all that really exists; the phenomenal worlds are a transitory reflection. They are the past and future of this one ever-present eternity, the only possibly eternity without duration which is the present moment.[51]

Wa'Na'Nee'Che' and Freke write:

Ultimately, the great Native American medicine teachers, like all great mystics, point us beyond symbols and visions, to the deep understanding that is latent in silence and stillness. This is experienced unconsciously by us all in the total rest of deep sleep — the stillness that lies behind both the seen world and the unseen world.[52]

According to these authors, Native Americans "did not understand linear time as the modern world does," their "languages do not have past and future tenses, but portray a perennial 'now'," the "future is seen as existing now, as an idea in the mind," and myths "are not stories from the past, but exist eternally outside of time."[53] In the Lakota language, there is no noun for the ultimate creative power. The word *Wakan Tanka* "portrays something in movement, perhaps better translated as the 'Great Mysterious.'"[54]

CHAPTER EIGHTEEN

UNIVERSES OF DISCOURSE: CONSCIOUS vs. SUBCONSCIOUS

As I described earlier, the *universes of discourse* exercise is about the interaction of the conscious and subconscious minds.[55] The exercise teaches the basic "rules" of interaction between those minds. The UoD movies teach how the dual mind works, but they do not teach how to approach establishing and promoting connections between one's conscious and subconscious minds, which is a primary goal of doing archetypes. Those connections can be begun through an understanding of *trance* in writing work.

Betty Edwards notes that many artists say that "drawing puts them into a somewhat altered state of consciousness."[56] James Hughes wrote in *Altered States: Creativity Under the Influence*: "To bring something — an idea, an object — into external reality out of 'nowhere' is associated with a whole range of 'abnormal' states of consciousness, from daydreaming and fantasy to trances and drug-induced hallucinations."[57]

The altered state is a semi-conscious state that draws on the subconscious. Wilson Bryant Key wrote in his classic book, *Subliminal Seduction*, that "mythology, folklore, and music… are the unconscious of the storyteller, composer, or musician speaking to the unconscious of the audience, society, or culture."[58]

This state can be attained by all human beings. Hughes notes that trance is "part of everyone's evolutionary equipment, a means of producing original solutions to problems, a basic ability."[59] Anthropologist Felicitas D. Goodman agrees. She writes that "humans apparently utilize … trance for ritual purposes the world over, which suggests that it is part of our genetic endowment."[60]

Trance is an important part of the interaction of the conscious and subconscious. According to Stephen G. Gilligan, PhD, the author of *Therapeutic Trances: The Cooperation Principles in Ericksonian Hypnotherapy*: "Trance is an experience in which a person surrenders to his or her deeper experiential self, allowing unconscious processes to express themselves in a therapeutic fashion."[61]

Trance is part of what happens in *being-in-the-moment* work, and in fact, trance is a necessary state when one is "doing archetypes." Numerous authors agree that trance "constitutes a manipulation of brain processes that can be learned."[62]

CHAPTER NINETEEN

TRANCE: THE LOGIC OF ART

In the previous few chapters, I have discussed trance in connection with archetypes, "being in the moment," and universes of discourse. But trance also needs to be considered separately, albeit briefly, of its own accord since it is so much misunderstood and confused with other things, believable and unbelievable.

When one tries to imagine what a tranced person might be like, for some people the old Svengali movies come to mind, where hypnotized subjects wander around like zombies, committing acts at the hypnotist's command. These images of what tranced persons are supposed to be like causes some people to conclude that neither trance nor hypnosis exist at all. Other more recent popular movies like *Conspiracy Theory* or either version of *The Manchurian Candidate*, which are about mind-controlled assassins, while entertaining, make many people more skeptical.

It is important to understand that there are many forms of trance. Deep hypnosis, where someone has no memory of what transpires during the trance, is unusual and not helpful to artists. But, as I discussed earlier, altered states of consciousness are often identified with artistic work, including writing. The question is: exactly what kind of altered state are we talking about? What exactly *is* trance? Is trance necessary for genuine writing to occur? And is it really trance we're talking about, or is it something else — a certain kind of "high" not related to trance, or just a state of heightened conscious awareness? And what does trance have to do with writing and archetypes work?

Trance is actually something that is happening to us in varying degrees all the time. If you have ever witnessed sleight-of-hand, you will find it easier to understand trance. The conscious mind weaves "reality" together into something coherent and consistent. Incongruities are frequently sifted out and forgotten. Thus, when I once handed my daughter's French tutor a $20 bill and simultaneously introduced her to a friend of mine, what she remembered later was the introduction and not the payment.

This is, in fact, a well-known scam technique called bait-and-switch. It relies on distraction, which is essentially the introduction of two discrete (and often contradictory) pieces of information at once or in rapid sequence *such that only one requires immediate conscious response*. The subconscious sees all, but the conscious mind can only handle that to which it can respond within acceptable parameters.

One doesn't generally view being momentarily distracted as a trance, but the principle and the mechanism of trance are the same in both cases. What the conscious mind cannot process engages the subconscious, or, in other words, causes trance. Is subconscious activity therefore identical to trance activity? No, not in itself. Trance occurs when the active functioning of the conscious mind is at least partially and momentarily suspended.

Highway hypnosis is trance. You're driving but part of your mind is somewhere else. Daydreaming is trance. Staring off over the ocean for an hour, thinking it is just a few minutes, is trance. Forgetting where you put something is trance. The fact is, we function on many different levels at once. We are not always either fully conscious or completely unconscious, even when tranced. Trance states are actually normal parts of everyday experience, although few are aware of it.

Working at the archetypal level causes trancing, and archetype work cannot be carried out without entering into a trance. This result is a function of the continual and varying types of juxtapositions one must perform in this work — from various character facts, to various moments, to discrepancies, to analogues, to isotypes. The greater the incongruities in these juxtapositions, the more useful they are, and the more likely they are to produce trance.

The Logic of Art

Trance can be induced by disorientation. Similarly, when under trance, one is more easily able to accept simultaneous opposing realities. This is called "both/and" logic. We can accept, for example, both that a public leader sees himself as a savior and that he is deeply insecure. We can accept that somebody who threatened us with physical harm or death might also love us.

There are obviously good reasons why we don't operate in the both/and mode on a daily basis. We probably would not survive long. But that mode is essential to artistic work and to writing. It requires a kind of brain-stretching, which is really the basis of all the work in this book and of arkhelogy itself. Our brains can do more than we normally recognize. Trance is one part of what arkhelogy enables us to experience.

CONCLUSION

I hope you have enjoyed reading about the wonderful world of arkhelogy and learning about this incredible process, the seeds for which are already contained within you.

There are many terrible things going on in the world today: hunger, war, poverty, terrorism, global warming, destruction of rain forests, and so on. The causes of these things are to be found within human beings. While corporations and nation states make global decisions, these entities are run by individual people and people banding together into "compatible" groups to achieve goals that are not always for the betterment of mankind.

Yet there is awesome beauty in the world. Every human being has tremendous powers within him or her to create beauty and truth in the world. The difference between the devastation we are creating and the beauty we could create is what the archetypes approach is really about. We are all flawed people. We make mistakes, we do things wrong, we hurt others, we harm the environment, we feel greed and pursue it regardless of consequences, we want power, we want money, we want safety, or we want revenge and justice. All of these things are what make the human world what it is. Whether or not we see it and write about it honestly and truthfully, it continues to exist in all its shades and hues.

But if more of us were able to speak our silent truths to the world, more of us would feel loved and recognized, and fewer of us would seek revenge or greed or needless and illegitimate power. True power comes from only two sources: oneself and consent of others. Humans have long been frustrated by their relative helplessness against the forces of nature and against the power of other humans or the brute force of predator animals. We have wanted to control it all: control our fellow humans, control animals, control the earth and climate. It is a misplaced desire. On the one hand, we must recognize that we only have the power over ourselves or power which others have consented to give us (and which they can always take away). On the other hand, we often do not realize how much power we really do have, if we only work with the forces we see as lined up against us. It is not really those forces that are the problem: it is our own unwillingness to let ourselves be tools of something beyond our small human lives.

One does not have to believe in God, Allah, Jahweh, or the Great Spirit to know that we humans simply do not control the fate of the world or the universe, and that if we are to use our powers wisely and well, we must use them in concert with forces greater than ourselves. No, not just forces of the wealthy and powerful. For those persons, too, will one day be swallowed up by things beyond their control. Only the powers that control the making of the universe — powers we will never have in our individual selves, but powers we can tap into and funnel into our work — are worth seeking. And to tap into those powers as writers, we must learn to work with the archetypal elements hidden within each of us.

Because writers who do their "own writing" tap into forces greater than themselves, they must ultimately be the ones to lead the world forward to a peaceful and accomplished future for everyone.

Because writers write about the human lot and elevate the understanding of others about each other, they must lead. Every little life deeply and truthfully loved and revealed brings the world forward to a real Brave New World. And, finally, because archetypes when fully spoken and revealed attain their fulfillment in that moment, even the worst of humans will be able to live in peace, knowing that someone saw and witnessed their life and made something useful and beautiful of it. And maybe, maybe, others will want to follow the writer into the world of Self-expression, with a capital S, as we define it in this book.

It is in the secret lives and invisible worlds that all the real actions take place and here in this book, you have the map to those obscure places. Good luck and may the wind be at your back.

ENDNOTES

[1]The term arkhelogy is adapted from the obsolete word: *archelogy*, which during the 17th and 18th centuries meant "the study of principles." The spelling has been modified to avoid confusion with the modern word: archeology, to which it is not related. The word forms are: *arkhelogy* — the skill of doing archetypes, working at the archetypal level, the practice of doing archetypes; *arkhelogist* — someone who practices working at the archetypal level; *arkheloge* — to engage in arkhelogy; *arkheloging* — actively engaging in arkhelogy.

The Greek root, *arch(e)-* (or *archi-*) means primary, chief, highest, most important. *Logy* (from *logos*) means knowledge (science), study, word. The etymology of both words is rife with abundant, powerful meanings. *Logos* was the word used in the Greek version of the Bible, translated in English to mean "the word of God" or simply "the Word." Some have interpreted this to mean that the Word itself (speech) is what embodies God or the primary principles of the Universe. ("In the beginning was the Word and the Word was God.")

Pronunciation is as follows: *arkhelogy* (pronounced *ar-KĔL-ogee* or *ark-heh-LOH-gee*); *arkhelogist* (*ar-KĔL-ogist ar-keh-LOH-gist*); *arkheloging* (*ar-keh-LŎH-ging*); "to *arkheloge*" (*ar-keh-LOZH*).

[2]Marcel Proust, *The Past Recaptured*, translated by Andreas Mayor (New York: Vintage, 1971), 133.

[3]Robert Lawlor, *Sacred Geometry: Philosophy & Practice* (Thames & Hudson, 1989), 24.

[4]Lawlor, 31.

[5]Proust, 159.

[6]Copyright 1991 Wet Sprocket Songs (Sony Music Entertainment, Inc.)

[7]Proust, *The Captive* (Vintage, 1971), 347-8.

[8]Elizabeth Barrett Browning, *Aurora Leigh and Other Poems*, (New York: Penguin, 1955) 5:223-8. Spelling modernized.

[9]Proust, *The Past Recaptured*, 140.

[10]Proust, 139.

[11]This book cannot be and is not intended to be a treatise on the complex inner workings of the mind. For purposes of the archetypes approach, sufficient evidence of these workings is found in a few central works upon which I rely and which I discuss towards the end of the book. I reach no further into the subject than that which is needed to clarify certain aspects of this approach.

[12]The term *nos-amianthy* (pronounced *NOS-AH-mé-anthee*) is adapted from Greek word *gignôskô* — to perceive, discern, to know by reflection or observation, to distinguish, recognize, learn to know (from *gnôs* — to know, knowledge), and *a-mianth* — (i) pure, uncorrupted; (ii) a stone which can be separated into threads and spun but cannot be consumed by fire.

In our lexicon, *nos-amianthy* means both "the skill of finding UDs" and "engaging in the use of the skill and practice of finding UDs" or just "the practice of finding UDs." *Noaamianthist* is someone who engages in the practice of finding UDs, particularly someone who uses the skill well. The infinitive verb would be *noaamianthe*: to find UDs.

[13]Quoted in Ruggero J. Aldisert, Logic for Lawyers: A Guide to Clear Legal Thinking (Clark Boardman Co., 1990), xi.

[14]Note that while this example is based on real persons, names and some facts have been changed to protect the privacy of those involved. Furthermore, any conclusions drawn here are merely illustrative and do not intend to offer actual opinions about any real persons.

[15]*Quoted in* Julia Cameron, *The Artist's Way: A Spiritual Path to Higher Creativity* (Jeremy P. Tarcher/Putnam, 1992), 11.

[16]Lawlor, 10.

[17]Charles Rycroft, *A Critical Dictionary of Psychoanalysis* (Penguin, 1972), 9.

[18]Carl G. Jung, *The Archetypes and the Collective Unconscious* (Collected Works of C.G. Jung, Vol. 9, Part 1) (Princeton University Press; 2nd edition, 1981), 4. Philo Judaeus (ca. 30 B.C. — 45 A.D.) was an Alexandrian Jewish philosopher known for his attempts to reconcile religious faith and philosophical reason.

[19]St. Ireneaus (ca. 130-202 A.D.) was a bishop of Lugdunum of Gaul, which is now Lyons, France. He is recognized as a saint by both the Eastern Orthodox Church and the Catholic Church and his writings were formative in the early development of Christian theology. *See* http://encyclopedia.thefreedictionary.com/Irenaeus.

[20]Jung, 4-5.

[21]Jung, 6. (Emphasis in original.)

[22]Jung, 24.

[23]Dr. C. George Boeree, *Personality Theories*, Carl Jung (1875-1961), www.ship.edu/~cgboeree/jung.html.

[24]Lawlor, 6.

[25]Lawlor, 6, 8.

[26]Lawlor, 8.

[27]Lawlor, 9.

[28]Lawlor, 10-11.

[29]Notice that I say "an" action-principle, not "the" action-principle. Human beings can carry any number of archetypes in their beings and behaviors. An archetype does not define a human being, but it can define a character.

[30]Lawlor, 44.

[31]Archetype work is similar to the contemplative geometric principle of "mediation" which arises out of the Platonic concept of "essential knowledge." Essential knowledge, according to Lawlor, "is not a simple accumulation of factual or even conceptual data pertaining to objects or phenomena, but rather consists of an awareness of the metaphysical constructs through which the mind is able to gain its comprehension." Lawlor elaborates that "[t]he laws which govern the creation of things are the same laws which allow for their comprehension, and essential knowledge is an understanding of these laws." Such knowledge can be gained

through the study of "mediation," which is "the binding of two extremes by a single mean term." Lawlor, 80.

[32] *The American Heritage Dictionary.* The mathematical definition is also of interest: "a one-to-one correspondence between the elements of two sets such that the result of an operation on elements of one set corresponds to the result of the analogous operation on their images in the other set."

[33] Lawlor, 42.

[34] Jonatha Brooke, "At the Still Point"

[35] Ned Manderino, *All About Method Acting* (Manderino Books, 1985), 21.

[36] Manderino (both quotes).

[37] Lawlor, 24.

[38] Lawlor, 21.

[39] Felicitas D. Goodman, *How About Demons? Possession and Exorcism in the Modern World* (Indiana University Press, 1988), 10.

[40] Goodman, 10.

[41] Goodman, 21.

[42] Proust, *The Past Recaptured*, 133-34. In the original publication of Proust's novel, *Remembrance of Things Past*, there were seven separate volumes. *The Past Recaptured* was the seventh.

[43] Proust, 134.

[44] Eric Morris, *Acting from the Ultimate Consciousness* (Ermor Enterprises, 1988), 21.

[45] Goodman, 31.

[46] Morris, 27. *See also* Manderino, 81-82 and S. Loraine Hull, Strasberg's *Method* (As Taught by Lorrie Hull): *A Practical Guide for Actors, Teachers and Directors*, Chapters 4 and 5 (Ox Bow Publishing, 1985) for a detailed description of sensory memory work and affective memory retrieval through sensory memory. Sensory memory, which is the primary component of Lee Strasberg's "method acting," addresses only the sensory part of *being in the moment*. Strasberg's affective (or emotional) memory work ties emotions into sensory memory. Marcel Proust's insights are often cited as the basis for sensory memory work. In my opinion, this is a misreading of Proust.

[47] Wa'Na'Nee'Che' (Dennis Renault) & Timothy Freke, *Thorsons Principles of Native American Spirituality* (Thorsons, 1996), 49-50. Wa'Na'Nee'Che' is a Native American teacher and civil rights attorney. Freke is the author of a number of books on world spirituality. For more on Native American spirituality, *see* Peggy V. Beck., et al., *The Sacred: Ways of Knowledge, Sources of Life* (Navajo Community College Press, 1992).

[48] R.J. Stewart, *Earth Light: The Ancient Path to Transformation — Rediscovering the Wisdom of Celtic and Faery Lore* (Mercury Publishing, 1998), 4.

[49] Stewart, 41-43. It is noteworthy that Stewart's visualization sequence resembles the Hero's Journey enumerated by Vogler: 1) the Ordinary World; 2) Call to Adventure; (3) reluctant or refuse Call; (4) encouraged by Mentor; (5) cross the First Threshold and enter Special World;

(6) encounter Tests, Allies, and Enemies; (7) approach Inmost Cave, crossing second threshold; (8) endure the Ordeal; (9) take possession of their Reward; (10) pursued on the Road Back to Ordinary World; (11) cross third threshold, experience a Resurrection; (12) return with the Elixir. Vogler, 26.

[50] Goodman, 11.

[51] Lawlor, 31.

[52] Wa'Na'Nee'Che' and Freke, 87-88.

[53] Wa'Na'Nee'Che' and Freke, 31-32.

[54] Wa'Na'Nee'Che' and Freke, 30.

[55] My understanding of conscious and subconscious processes is wholly my own. I do not have a degree in psychology and do not pretend to give psychological advice to my students. My conclusions are based on years of experience *with the archetypes approach*, which is premised upon my views of the dual mind. The works I refer to in this chapter are those which I have found provide cornerstones of my views.

[56] Betty Edwards, *Drawing on the Right Side of the Brain* (St. Martin's Press, 1989), 4.

[57] James Hughes, *Altered States: Creativity Under the Influence* (Watson-Guptill Publications, 1999), 7.

[58] Wilson Bryan Key, *Subliminal Seduction: Ad Media's Manipulation of a Not So Innocent America* (Signet, 1972), 12.

[59] Hughes, 12

[60] Goodman, 10.

[61] Stephen G. Gilligan, Ph.D., *Therapeutic Trances: The Cooperation Principles in Ericksonian Hypnotherapy* (Brunner/Mazel, A member of the Taylor & Francis Group, 1987), 172. Gilligan, of course, focused on the therapeutic uses of trance. Here we are focused on its use for writing.

[62] Goodman, 21. Goodman is discussing "possession," which is a kind of trance.

ABOUT THE AUTHOR

Jennifer is best known for her political/legal commentaries found abundantly on the internet at sites such as *http://writ.findlaw.com*, *www.counterpunch.org*, *www.tompaine.com*, and *www.truthout.org*. She has also done reporting for *www.rawstory.com*. Her book, *The Twilight of Democracy: The Bush Plan for America* (Common Courage Press, 2004), discusses principles of democracy, the rule of law, and the U.S. Constitution in the context of the Bush Administration. Jennifer has also published law review articles on the civil liberties implications of provisions of the U.S. antiterrorism laws, on detention and torture from Vietnam to Abu Ghraib, and on the presidential electoral tie of 1801 between Thomas Jefferson and Aaron Burr.

However, Jennifer was in the arts long before she obtained a law degree and began her career as a journalist and book author. She trained with Toni Donley at the Bennett Conservatory, Croton-on-Hudson, New York from age 9 through 18 and spent her summers during those years doing Shakespeare in the Croton Shakespeare Festival. By age 15, Jennifer was also writing prolifically: short stories, plays, poems, etc.

She starred in many roles over the years in community theater, operettas and musicals. At age 16, she played Juliet in Shakespeare *Romeo & Juliet*. At 17, she played Gianetta in Gilbert & Sullivan's *The Gondoliers*, and at 18, Philia in the New York State Community Theater production of *A Funny Thing Happened on the Way to the Forum*. She also studied with Eve Collyer and Sande Shurin in New York and worked in master classes with Mark Lenard and Jack Hoffsis.

Jennifer has recorded two CDs of her own music: *Sand Songs* (1978) and *Black Hole* (1998, Puzzle Element Music). The latter is a collection of songs about and for trauma survivors and is available on *www.cdbaby.com*. She is presently working on a novel about the Aaron Burr conspiracy.

She taught early versions of the archetypes approach under her own business (The Writer's Place) from 1983-1993 and continued to teach and develop the course during her tenure as an adjunct faculty at the New School University in Manhattan (1993-2003).

Jennifer's websites are *www.jvbline.org* and *www.puzzle-element.org*. She can be contacted at *jvbxyz@earthlink.net*.

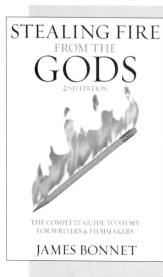

THE WRITER'S JOURNEY

2ND EDITION
MYTHIC STRUCTURE FOR WRITERS

CHRISTOPHER VOGLER

BEST SELLER
OVER 160,000 COPIES SOLD!

See why this book has become an international best seller and a true classic. *The Writer's Journey* explores the powerful relationship between mythology and storytelling in a clear, concise style that's made it required reading for movie executives, screenwriters, playwrights, scholars, and fans of pop culture all over the world.

Both fiction and nonfiction writers will discover a set of useful myth-inspired storytelling paradigms (i.e., "The Hero's Journey") and step-by-step guidelines to plot and character development. Based on the work of Joseph Campbell, *The Writer's Journey* is a must for all writers interested in further developing their craft.

The updated and revised second edition provides new insights and observations from Vogler's ongoing work on mythology's influence on stories, movies, and man himself.

"This book is like having the smartest person in the story meeting come home with you and whisper what to do in your ear as you write a screenplay. Insight for insight, step for step, Chris Vogler takes us through the process of connecting theme to story and making a script come alive."
> – *Lynda Obst, Producer,* Sleepless in Seattle, How to Lose a Guy in 10 Days
> *Author,* Hello, He Lied

"This is a book about the stories we write, and perhaps more importantly, the stories we live. It is the most influential work I have yet encountered on the art, nature, and the very purpose of storytelling."
> – *Bruce Joel Rubin, Screenwriter*
> Stuart Little 2, Deep Impact, Ghost, Jacob's Ladder

CHRISTOPHER VOGLER, a top Hollywood story consultant and development executive, has worked on such high-grossing feature films as *The Lion King, The Thin Red Line, Fight Club,* and *Beauty and the Beast.* He conducts writing workshops around the globe.
artist, screenwriter, producer, and director.

$24.95 · 325 PAGES · ORDER NUMBER 98RLS · ISBN: 0941188701

THE HOLLYWOOD STANDARD

THE COMPLETE & AUTHORITATIVE GUIDE TO SCRIPT FORMAT AND STYLE

CHRISTOPHER RILEY

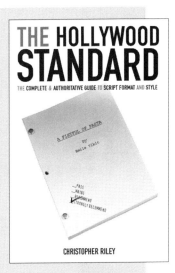

Finally, there's a script format guide that is accurate, complete, and easy to use, written by Hollywood's foremost authority on industry standard script formats. Riley's guide is filled with clear, concise, complete instructions and hundreds of examples to take the guesswork out of a multitude of formatting questions that perplex screenwriters, waste their time, and steal their confidence. You'll learn how to get into and out of a POV shot, how to set up a telephone intercut, what to capitalize and why, how to control pacing with format, and more.

"The Hollywood Standard *is not only indispensable, it's practical, readable, and fun to use.*"
— Dean Batali, *Writer-Producer,* That '70s Show; *Writer,* Buffy the Vampire Slayer

"Buy this book before you write another word! It's required reading for any screenwriter who wants to be taken seriously by Hollywood."
— Elizabeth Stephen, President, Mandalay Television Pictures;
Executive Vice President Motion Picture Production, Mandalay Pictures

"Riley has succeeded in an extremely difficult task: He has produced a guide to screenplay formatting which is both entertaining to read and exceptionally thorough. Riley's clear style, authoritative voice, and well-written examples make this book far more enjoyable than any formatting guide has a right to be. This is the best guide to script formatting ever, and it is an indispensable tool for every writer working in Hollywood."
— Wout Thielemans, Screentalk Magazine

"It doesn't matter how great your screenplay is if it looks all wrong. The Hollywood Standard *is probably the most critical book any screenwriter who is serious about being taken seriously can own. For any writer who truly understands the power of making a good first impression, this comprehensive guide to format and style is priceless.*"
— Marie Jones, www.absolutewrite.com

CHRISTOPHER RILEY, based in Los Angeles, developed Warner Brothers Studios script software and serves as the ultimate arbiter of script format for the entertainment industry.

$18.95 · 208 PAGES · ORDER # 31RLS · ISBN: 1932907017

SELLING YOUR STORY IN 60 SECONDS

THE GUARANTEED WAY TO GET YOUR SCREENPLAY OR NOVEL READ

MICHAEL HAUGE

Best-selling author Michael Hauge reveals:

- How to Design, Practice and Present the 60-Second Pitch
- The Cardinal Rule of Pitching
- The 10 Key Components of a Commercial Story
- The 8 Steps to a Powerful Pitch
- Targeting Your Buyers
- Securing Opportunities to Pitch
- Pitching Templates
- And much more, including "The Best Pitch I Ever Heard," an exclusive collection from major film executives

"Michael Hauge's principles and methods are so well argued that the mysteries of effective screenwriting can be understood — even by directors."
> – Phillip Noyce, Director, Patriot Games, Clear and Present Danger, The Quiet American, Rabbit Proof Fence

"... one of the few authentically good teachers out there. Every time I revisit my notes, I learn something new or reinforce something that I need to remember."
> – Jeff Arch, Screenwriter, Sleepless in Seattle, Iron Will

"Michael Hauge's method is magic — but unlike most magicians, he shows you how the trick is done."
> – William Link, Screenwriter & Co-Creator, Columbo; Murder, She Wrote

"By following the formula we learned in Michael Hauge's seminar, we got an agent, optioned our script, and now have a three picture deal at Disney."
> – Paul Hoppe and David Henry, Screenwriters

MICHAEL HAUGE, is the author of *Writing Screenplays That Sell*, now in its 30th printing, and has presented his seminars and lectures to more than 30,000 writers and filmmakers. He has coached hundreds of screenwriters and producers on their screenplays and pitches, and has consulted on projects for Warner Brothers, Disney, New Line, CBS, Lifetime, Julia Roberts, Jennifer Lopez, Kirsten Dunst, and Morgan Freeman.

$12.95 · 150 PAGES · ORDER NUMBER 64RLS · ISBN: 1932907203

MYTH AND THE MOVIES

DISCOVERING THE MYTHIC STRUCTURE OF 50 UNFORGETTABLE FILMS

STUART VOYTILLA

FOREWORD BY CHRISTOPHER VOGLER
AUTHOR OF *THE WRITER'S JOURNEY*

BEST SELLER
OVER 20,000 COPIES SOLD!

An illuminating companion piece to *The Writer's Journey*, *Myth and the Movies* applies the mythic structure Vogler developed to 50 well-loved U.S. and foreign films. This comprehensive book offers a greater understanding of why some films continue to touch and connect with audiences generation after generation.

Movies discussed include *The Godfather, Some Like It Hot, Citizen Kane, Halloween, Jaws, Annie Hall, Chinatown, The Fugitive, Sleepless in Seattle, The Graduate, Dances with Wolves, Beauty and the Beast, Platoon,* and *Die Hard.*

"Stuart Voytilla's Myth and the Movies *is a remarkable achievement: an ambitious, thought-provoking, and cogent analysis of the mythic underpinnings of fifty great movies. It should prove a valuable resource for film teachers, students, critics, and especially screenwriters themselves, whose challenge, as Voytilla so clearly understands, is to constantly reinvent a mythology for our times."*
　　　　　- Ted Tally, Academy Award®Screenwriter, *Silence of the Lambs*

*"*Myth and the Movies *is a must for every writer who wants to tell better stories. Voytilla guides his readers to a richer and deeper understanding not only of mythic structure, but also of the movies we love."*
　　　　　- Christopher Wehner, Web editor
　　　　　　The Screenwriters Utopia and *Creative Screenwriting*

"I've script consulted for ten years and I've studied every genre thoroughly. I thought I knew all their nuances - until I read Voytilla's book. This ones goes on my Recommended Reading List. A fascinating analysis of the Hero's Myth for all genres."
　　　　　- Lou Grantt, *Hollywood Scriptwriter* Magazine

STUART VOYTILLA is a screenwriter, literary consultant, teacher, and author of *Writing the Comedy Film.*

$26.95 · 300 PAGES · ORDER NUMBER 39RLS · ISBN: 0941188663

MICHAEL WIESE PRODUCTIONS

Since 1981, Michael Wiese Productions has been dedicated to providing both novice and seasoned filmmakers with vital information on all aspects of filmmaking. We have published nearly 100 books, used in over 600 film schools and countless universities, and by hundreds of thousands of filmmakers worldwide.

Our authors are successful industry professionals who spend innumerable hours writing about the hard stuff: budgeting, financing, directing, marketing, and distribution. They believe that if they share their knowledge and experience with others, more high quality films will be produced.

And that has been our mission, now complemented through our new web-based resources. We invite all readers to visit www.mwp.com to receive free tipsheets and sample chapters, participate in forum discussions, obtain product discounts — and even get the opportunity to receive free books, project consulting, and other services offered by our company.

Our goal is, quite simply, to help you reach your goals. That's why we give our readers the most complete portal for filmmaking knowledge available — in the most convenient manner.

We truly hope that our books and web-based resources will empower you to create enduring films that will last for generations to come.

Let us hear from you at anytime.

Sincerely,

Michael Wiese

Publisher, Filmmaker

www.mwp.com

FILM & VIDEO BOOKS

Cinematic Storytelling: *The 100 Most Powerful Film Conventions Every Filmmaker Must Know* / Jennifer Van Sijll / $24.95

Complete DVD Book, The: *Designing, Producing, and Marketing Your Independent Film on DVD* / Chris Gore and Paul J. Salamoff / $26.95

Complete Independent Movie Marketing Handbook, The: *Promote, Distribute & Sell Your Film or Video* / Mark Steven Bosko / $39.95

Could It Be a Movie?: *How to Get Your Ideas Out of Your Head and Up on the Screen* / Christina Hamlett / $26.95

Creating Characters: *Let Them Whisper Their Secrets* Marisa D'Vari / $26.95

Crime Writer's Reference Guide, The: *1001 Tips for Writing the Perfect Crime* Martin Roth / $20.95

Cut by Cut: *Editing Your Film or Video* Gael Chandler / $35.95

Digital Filmmaking 101, 2nd Edition: *An Essential Guide to Producing Low-Budget Movies* / Dale Newton and John Gaspard / $26.95

Digital Moviemaking, 2nd Edition: *All the Skills, Techniques, and Moxie You'll Need to Turn Your Passion into a Career* / Scott Billups / $26.95

Directing Actors: *Creating Memorable Performances for Film and Television* Judith Weston / $26.95

Directing Feature Films: *The Creative Collaboration Between Directors, Writers, and Actors* / Mark Travis / $26.95

Eye is Quicker, The: *Film Editing; Making a Good Film Better* Richard D. Pepperman / $27.95

Fast, Cheap & Under Control: *Lessons Learned from the Greatest Low-Budget Movies of All Time* / John Gaspard / $26.95

Film & Video Budgets, 4th Updated Edition Deke Simon and Michael Wiese / $26.95

Film Directing: Cinematic Motion, 2nd Edition Steven D. Katz / $27.95

Film Directing: Shot by Shot, *Visualizing from Concept to Screen* Steven D. Katz / $27.95

Film Director's Intuition, The: *Script Analysis and Rehearsal Techniques* Judith Weston / $26.95

Film Production Management 101: *The Ultimate Guide for Film and Television Production Management and Coordination* / Deborah S. Patz / $39.95

Filmmaking for Teens: *Pulling Off Your Shorts* Troy Lanier and Clay Nichols / $18.95

First Time Director: *How to Make Your Breakthrough Movie* Gil Bettman / $27.95

From Word to Image: *Storyboarding and the Filmmaking Process* Marcie Begleiter / $26.95

Hitting Your Mark, 2nd Edition: *Making a Life - and a Living - as a Film Director* Steve Carlson / $22.95

Hollywood Standard, The: *The Complete and Authoritative Guide to Script Format and Style* / Christopher Riley / $18.95

I Could've Written a Better Movie Than That!: *How to Make Six Figures as a Script Consultant even if You're not a Screenwriter* / Derek Rydall / $26.95

Independent Film Distribution: *How to Make a Successful End Run Around the Big Guys* / Phil Hall / $26.95

Independent Film and Videomakers Guide - 2nd Edition, The: *Expanded and Updated* / Michael Wiese / $29.95

Inner Drives: *How to Write and Create Characters Using the Eight Classic Centers of Motivation* / Pamela Jaye Smith / $26.95

I'll Be in My Trailer!: *The Creative Wars Between Directors & Actors* John Badham and Craig Modderno / $26.95

Moral Premise, The: *Harnessing Virtue & Vice for Box Office Success* Stanley D. Williams, Ph.D. / $24.95

Myth and the Movies: *Discovering the Mythic Structure of 50 Unforgetta Films* / Stuart Voytilla / $26.95

On the Edge of a Dream: *Magic and Madness in Bali* Michael Wiese / $16.95

Perfect Pitch, The: *How to Sell Yourself and Your Movie Idea to Hollywoo* Ken Rotcop / $16.95

Power of Film, The Howard Suber / $27.95

Psychology for Screenwriters: *Building Conflict in your Script* William Indick, Ph.D. / $26.95

Save the Cat!: *The Last Book on Screenwriting You'll Ever Need* Blake Snyder / $19.95

Screenwriting 101: *The Essential Craft of Feature Film Writing* Neill D. Hicks / $16.95

Screenwriting for Teens: *The 100 Principles of Screenwriting Every Bud Writer Must Know* / Christina Hamlett / $18.95

Script-Selling Game, The: *A Hollywood Insider's Look at Getting Your Scri Sold and Produced* / Kathie Fong Yoneda / $16.95

Selling Your Story in 60 Seconds: *The Guaranteed Way to get Your Scree or Novel Read* / Michael Hauge / $12.95

Setting Up Your Scenes: *The Inner Workings of Great Films* Richard D. Pepperman / $24.95

Setting Up Your Shots: *Great Camera Moves Every Filmmaker Should Kn* Jeremy Vineyard / $19.95

Shaking the Money Tree, 2nd Edition: *The Art of Getting Grants and Donations for Film and Video Projects* / Morrie Warshawski / $26.95

Sound Design: *The Expressive Power of Music, Voice, and Sound Effects in Cinema* / David Sonnenschein / $19.95

Stealing Fire From the Gods, 2nd Edition: *The Complete Guide to Story Writers & Filmmakers* / James Bonnet / $26.95

Storyboarding 101: *A Crash Course in Professional Storyboarding* James Fraioli / $19.95

Ultimate Filmmaker's Guide to Short Films, The: *Making It Big in Shorts* Kim Adelman / $16.95

Working Director, The: *How to Arrive, Thrive & Survive in the Director's Ch* Charles Wilkinson / $22.95

Writer's Journey, - 2nd Edition, The: *Mythic Structure for Writers* Christopher Vogler / $24.95

Writer's Partner, The: *1001 Breakthrough Ideas to Stimulate Your Imagin* Martin Roth / $24.95

Writing the Action Adventure: *The Moment of Truth* Neill D. Hicks / $14.95

Writing the Comedy Film: *Make 'Em Laugh* Stuart Voytilla and Scott Petri / $14.95

Writing the Killer Treatment: *Selling Your Story Without a Script* Michael Halperin / $14.95

Writing the Second Act: *Building Conflict and Tension in Your Film Script* Michael Halperin / $19.95

Writing the Thriller Film: *The Terror Within* Neill D. Hicks / $14.95

Writing the TV Drama Series: *How to Succeed as a Professional Writer in* Pamela Douglas / $24.95

DVD & VIDEOS

Field of Fish: *VHS Video* Directed by Steve Tanner and Michael Wiese, Written by Annamaria Murphy / $9

Hardware Wars: *DVD* / Written and Directed by Ernie Fosselius / $14.95

Sacred Sites of the Dalai Lamas - DVD, The: *A Pilgrimage to Oracle Lake* A Documentary by Michael Wiese / $22.95